CAMBRIDGE GREEK AND LATIN CLASSICS
IMPERIAL LIBRARY

GENERAL EDITORS

E. J. KENNEY
Emeritus Kennedy Professor of Latin, University of Cambridge

AND

P. E. EASTERLING
Regius Professor of Greek, University of Cambridge

D1232296

AUGUSTINE

CONFESSIONS

BOOKS I–IV

EDITED BY

GILLIAN CLARK

*Senior Lecturer in Classics
in the University of Liverpool*

*See p.5 for meaning of title
(double ll).*

 **CAMBRIDGE**
UNIVERSITY PRESS

Published by the Press Syndicate of the University of Cambridge
The Pitt Building, Trumpington Street, Cambridge CB2 IRP
40 West 20th Street, New York, NY 10011-4211, USA
10 Stamford Road, Oakleigh, Melbourne 3166, Australia

First published 1995

Printed in Great Britain at the University Press, Cambridge

A catalogue record for this book is available from the British Library

Library of Congress cataloguing in publication data

Augustine, Saint, Bishop of Hippo.
[Confessiones. Liber 1–4]
Confessions. Books I–IV/Augustine; edited by Gillian Clark.
p.   cm. – (Cambridge Greek and Latin classics.
Imperial library)
Includes bibliographical references and indexes.
ISBN 0 521 49734 5 (hbk.). – ISBN 0 521 49763 9 (pbk.)
1. Augustine, Saint, Bishop of Hippo.   2. Christian saints –
Algeria – Hippo (Extinct city) – Biography.   3. Hippo (Extinct city) –
Biography.   I. Clark, Gillian.   II. Title.   III. Series.
BR65.A6   1995
242–dc20   95-3118 CIP

ISBN 0 521 49734 5 hardback
ISBN 0 521 49763 9 paperback

CONTENTS

PREFACE

The thirteen books of the *Confessions* form an interconnected whole, but it was not possible to include all of them in a volume of this size, and neither the series editors nor the volume editor wanted to cut 'selections' from Augustine's complex texture. The easy option is to go for autobiography at the expense of theology, but that makes nonsense of what Augustine was trying to do. He was well aware that some of his readers were a *curiosum genus ad cognoscendam uitam alienam, desidiosum ad corrigendam suam* (10.3.3), curious about other people's lives but disinclined to do something about their own, and he did his best to turn them around. This volume begins where Augustine meant readers to begin, and ends where he ended book 4. It thus includes what he wanted us to think about in relation to his childhood, his student days and the beginning of his teaching career. The editors hope that readers will find it impossible to stop there.

The commentary is intended for students like my own: unfamiliar with 'late' Latin, late antiquity and Christian theology, and belonging to a generation which has grown up without absorbing the words of the Bible or, perhaps, of any other great literary text, but ready to respond to all of these. I have therefore concentrated on explaining theological and philosophical questions, and on calling to mind some of the reading from Scripture and classical culture which formed Augustine's mind and informed the remarkable Latin of the *Confessions*. Many English translations are readily available, and instead of providing yet another, I have assumed that readers have the excellent annotated translation by Henry Chadwick. The bibliography is, deliberately, modest: so far as possible, it is both recent and usable by students.

This book was commissioned in 1990, but other commitments made it impossible for me to begin sustained work before Easter 1993. In this I was doubly fortunate. Henry Chadwick's annotated translation came out in 1991, James O'Donnell's text and commentary in 1992, and using these books has been one of the many delights of working on the *Confessions*. I have sometimes taken a different route, and even, greatly daring, a different line, but Augustine may have the last word on that:

'It means what I say.' 'No, it means what I say.' I think there is more true piety in saying 'why not both, if both are true, or a third or a fourth interpretation or whatever other truth anyone has ever found in these words?' (12.31.42)

Very many people have found truth in Augustine's words, and one could go on happily working for ever. Ideally, a commentary on any part of the *Confessions* would be written in relation to all the earlier and later works of Augustine, and with the help of many interpreters. But, as everyone working on him says, it is impossible to read everything, or to acknowledge all the insights of other scholars. My debt to Jim O'Donnell's understanding of Augustine, both as theologian and as writer of Latin, is apparent throughout this book. Henry Chadwick and Robert Markus, with characteristic benevolence, read the commentary in draft and improved it from their immense experience of Augustine; Ted Kenney, most alert and perceptive of editors, prompted several additions and reassessments. I am of course responsible for errors which remain. Gerald Bonner and Gerard O'Daly kindly sent me some recent and illuminating work. Pat Easterling and Pauline Hire gave sympathetic editorial support, and Averil Cameron, as always, gave support or stimulus according to need. Thanks are also due to members of the Department of Classics and Ancient History in the University of Liverpool: Anne Beckerlegge, who chose to read book 1 of the *Confessions* in her final year as an undergraduate, and my colleagues, who even in the hard-pressed 1990s benignly endured 'Augustine says ...'

This book is dedicated to two of Augustine's fellow-teachers and fellow-members of the universal Church: my parents, John and Edith Metford.

November 1994   E. G. C.

ABBREVIATIONS AND REFERENCES

C.   Henry Chadwick, *Saint Augustine, Confessions: translated with an introduction and notes.* Oxford 1991. (Pbk 1992.)

G–M   (ed.) John Gibb and William Montgomery, *The Confessions of Augustine.* Cambridge 1908.

O'D.   James J. O'Donnell, *Augustine: Confessions.* Introduction, text and commentary. 3 vols. Oxford 1992.

V.   (ed.) L. Verheijen OSA, *Sancti Augustini Confessionum libri XIII.* Corpus Christianorum, series Latina 27. Turnhout 1981.

AV   Authorised (or King James') Version of the Bible.

CCL   *Corpus Christianorum, series Latina.* Turnhout 1953–

CSEL *Corpus Scriptorum Ecclesiasticorum Latinorum.* Vienna 1866–

OLD   (ed.) P. G. W. Glare, *Oxford Latin Dictionary.* Oxford 1982.

PL   *Patrologiae cursus completus, series Latina.* ed. J.-P. Migne. Paris 1844–64.

PLRE (ed.) A. H. M. Jones, J. R. Martindale, J. Morris, *Prosopography of the Later Roman Empire.* 3 vols. Cambridge 1971–92.

TLL   *Thesaurus Linguae Latinae.* Munich 1900–

VL   *Vetus Latina.* (ed.) Monks of Beuron, *Die Reste der altlateinischen Bibel.* Beuron 1949–

Works by Augustine

For ease of reading, these are referred to in the commentary by an English title. This list gives the English title used, the probable year(s) of writing, the standard Latin title (for variations, see the *Augustinus-Lexikon* 1.1–2 (1986) xxvi–xli), and the volume number in the three major series, *PL, CSEL, CCL. PL* includes all the works of Augustine except for some letters and sermons which were discovered after Migne's edition. The other two series do not yet include all Augustine's works. Information on these and other works by Augustine, with bibliography, is available in the survey by A. Trapè in (ed.) A. di Bernardino, *Patrology* vol. IV (English translation by P. Solari OSB). Westminster, Maryland 1986.

Against the Academics (386) *Contra academicos PL* 32, *CSEL* 63, *CCL* 29

Against Faustus (397–8) *Contra Faustum Manichaeum PL* 42, *CSEL* 25.1

Against Julian (421–2) *Contra Iulianum PL* 44, *CSEL* 85

City of God (412–26) *De ciuitate Dei PL* 41, *CSEL* 40, *CCL* 47–8

Confessions (397–?401) *Confessionum libri tredecim PL* 32, *CSEL* 33, *CCL* 27

Letters (from 386) *Epistulae PL* 33, *CSEL* 34, 44, 57–8, 88

Literal Interpretation of Genesis (401–14) *De Genesi ad litteram PL* 34, *CSEL* 28.1

Manichaean Morals (387–9) *De moribus ecclesiae catholicae et de moribus Manichaeorum PL* 32

Notes on Job (397–400) *Adnotationes in Iob PL* 34, *CSEL* 28.2

On the Beautiful and Fitting (381?) *De pulchro et apto*. Lost.

On Catechising the Untrained (399) *De catechizandis rudibus PL* 40, *CCL* 46

On Christian Teaching (397–426) *De doctrina Christiana PL* 34, *CSEL* 80, *CCL* 32

On Free Choice (388–94) *De libero arbitrio PL* 32, *CSEL* 74, *CCL* 29

On the Good of Marriage (401) *De bono coniugali PL* 40, *CSEL* 41

On the Gospel of John (begun 406) *In euangelium Ioannis tractatus CXXIV, PL* 35, *CCL* 36

On the Happy Life (386) *De beata uita PL* 32, *CSEL* 63, *CCL* 29

On Heresies (428) *De haeresibus, ad Quoduultdeum PL* 42, *CCL* 46

On the Psalms (from ?392) *Enarrationes in Psalmos PL* 36–7, *CCL* 38–40

On the Quantity of the Soul (387) *De quantitate animae PL* 32, *CSEL* 89

On the Soul and its Origin (419) *De anima et eius origine PL* 44, *CSEL* 60 (with title *De natura et origine animae*)

On the Teacher (388–90) *De magistro PL* 32, *CSEL* 77, *CCL* 29

On the Trinity (400–20) *De Trinitate PL* 42, *CCL* 50

On the Two Souls (391–2) *De duabus animabus contra Manichaeos PL* 42, *CSEL* 25

On the Usefulness of Believing (391–2) *De utilitate credendi PL* 42, *CSEL* 25

Retractations (426–7) *Retractationes PL* 32, *CSEL* 36, *CCL* 57

To Simplicianus (389–96) *De diuersis quaestionibus ad Simplicianum PL* 40, *CCL* 44

Unfinished Book on the Literal Interpretation of Genesis (393–426) *De Genesi ad litteram liber imperfectus PL* 35, *CSEL* 28.1

Possidius, *Life of Augustine Vita sancti Augustini PL* 32

INTRODUCTION

1. The *Confessions* in Augustine's life

(a) *Life history*

When Augustine began work on the *Confessions*, in the final years of the fourth century, he was in his early forties and had not long been bishop of Hippo Regius, a prosperous seaport (now Annaba in Algeria) on the north African coast. A decade before, in 386, he had given up a promising career as a teacher and practitioner of public speaking and the prospect of a good marriage. He resigned the chair of rhetoric at the imperial capital Milan, was baptised by bishop Ambrose of Milan, and returned in 388 to his family home at Thagaste (Souk Ahras in Algeria) to lead a life of prayer and study with a group of friends. A few years later, in 391, A. visited a friend at Hippo. His reputation as an orator and an ascetic went before him: the congregation of the church at Hippo insisted on his ordination as priest. He became their bishop in 396, and continued until his death in 430.

The *C.* are the main source of information on A.'s life, but they are not his life story. A detailed biography has to supplement the *C.* from other writings, because A. did not set out to write a narrative autobiography. (See further, for A.'s life, Bonner in the *Augustinus-Lexikon* s.v. *Augustinus* (*uita*).) He is concerned with his relationship to God and his awareness of that relationship as his life progressed, and he says very little about its historical and local setting (this is vividly evoked in Brown (1967) and briefly described in G. Clark (1993) 5–32). The narrative sequence ends in book 9 as he waits for a passage back to Africa from Italy. Book 10 in part reflects on the spiritual hazards of being a bishop, but gives no account of what he does: it is much more concerned to analyse what memory is and what A. has been doing in remembering his past life. Books 11–13 express his current understanding of human life in relation to God, by reflection on time, creation, and the opening verses of the book of Genesis, the beginning of Scripture which describes the beginning of the world.

There survives a short biography by A.'s friend and admirer

Possidius, a member of the community A. established at Hippo, who became bishop of Calama. It gives interesting details of A.'s life as a bishop, but Possidius too relies on the *C.* for A.'s earlier career. A. was the son of Patricius, a not very rich (*admodum tenuis*, 2.3.5) landowner of Thagaste in north Africa, and of Monnica, who was, unlike her husband, a committed Christian. Some fifth-century writers, and some early MSS of his works, give his name as Aurelius Augustinus, but there is no evidence that people called him Aurelius. A. was perhaps the eldest of his family: he describes (2.3.6) Patricius rejoicing in the prospect of grandchildren after observing at the baths that A. had reached puberty. There were at least two other children, a son and a daughter. The daughter, who later became head of a community of nuns, is not mentioned in the *C.*, but the son appears, without explanation, at Monnica's deathbed (9.11.27). Perhaps it was this son, Navigius, who inherited the financial responsibilities of Patricius.

According to Possidius (*Life of Augustine* 1), Patricius belonged to the 'curial' class: that is, he was a member of the local *curia* or council, and shared responsibility for subsidising local needs and for ensuring that taxes were collected. *Curiales* were liable for any shortfall in taxes. Teachers holding public appointments, as A. did at Carthage and Milan, were often exempt from these obligations (Kaster (1988) 224–6), on the grounds that they were already making a contribution to civic well-being. But when A. returned to Thagaste to live as a 'servant of God', he was liable for civic *munera* so long as he retained his property. He says (*Letter* 126.7) that he gave his inheritance to the Church at Thagaste (probably when he was ordained), but fourth-century legislation insisted that if a *curialis*, out of Christian commitment, gave up his property, someone else must take on his responsibilities. (See further Lepelley (1981) 177–8.) So Navigius may have resembled the 'good brother' in the story of the Prodigal Son (see on 1.18.28) which is so important for A., sharing the duties at home while the Prodigal wandered, and finally inheriting the estate. But A.'s family, with the exception of his mother and (briefly, see on 2.3.5) his father, is not present in the *C.*

A.'s parents made an unusual investment in his education. They sent him to primary school in his home town, then to a *grammaticus*, a teacher of literature (see on 1.12.19), in the larger town of Madauros.

When he was sixteen, they could not immediately afford the fees for higher education, even with the help of the richer landowner Romanianus who took an interest in the family (6.14.24), and A. had a year at home before going on to Carthage (in 370) for an advanced training in rhetoric and techniques of argument.

At Carthage, A. discovered philosophy by reading Cicero's (now lost) *Hortensius* (3.4.7), and also became an adherent of Manichaeism (see below, §3*a*). He found a partner who was not a suitable wife (see on 4.2.2), but to whom he remained faithful for thirteen years. Their only child, his son Adeodatus, was born in the first year of their relationship: he implies (4.2.2) that they had not intended to have any children. His training was expected to make him a lawyer (3.3.6), probably (like his friend Alypius, 6.10.16) serving as adviser to a governor, but in fact he became a teacher of rhetoric. He taught first, in 373–4, as a *grammaticus* in his home town Thagaste (see on 4.4.7), where he had no public appointment and depended on fees, presumably from parents who did not want to send their sons away to Madauros. Then, in 374, he moved to a salaried post at Carthage (6.7.11). There he was probably paid by the town council at a rate fixed by imperial legislation (see on 1.16.26), but would also expect fees and presents from his pupils.

From Carthage, the provincial capital, A. went (in 383) to Rome, where his Manichaean contacts helped him to find students and made his name known to Symmachus, the prefect of the city (5.12.22–3). Symmachus was himself a man of letters, and by a law of 370 was responsible as prefect for the conduct of students in the city; he had also been the (unpopular) proconsul of Africa in 373–4. When the town council of Milan asked him to recommend a candidate for the chair of rhetoric, Symmachus may have been pleased to find one who was obviously talented but was not an orthodox Christian. He was engaged in a power-struggle with Ambrose, bishop of Milan, on the survival of Roman traditional worship, and had no wish to strengthen Ambrose's hand.

The chair at Milan was not necessarily a route to power, but there were instances of *grammatici* (Kaster (1988) 130–1) who had achieved a reasonably high status in public service. A. had a better chance than many, because Milan was one of the imperial capitals in the west. Rome, in the late fourth century, was a place of tradition and influence, but Milan was on an important east–west military route. A.'s duties included panegyrics, formal speeches in praise of the emperor and other leading statesmen (6.6.9). Monnica, widowed while A. was a student at Carthage, had followed him to Italy, and negotiated a betrothal to a girl of good family who was not yet old enough to marry (6.13.23). The status which A. had already achieved, in his early thirties, was a remarkable example of the workings of patronage and talent.

But, in 386, he gave it all up. Books 6–8 of the *C.* trace the progress of his decision to renounce his job and the prospect of marriage in favour of a celibate life devoted to wisdom, and his realisation that wisdom was to be found in Christianity. Book 6 describes his conflicts about success, his forced separation from his partner when his marriage was arranged, and the problem of addiction – to sex in his case, to watching 'the games' (see on 1.10.16) in the case of his friend Alypius. Book 7 shows how he rejected both Manichaeism and astrology, how he was influenced by Platonist philosophy (see below, §3*b*), and how it too was inadequate because it relied too much on human reason. In book 8 he hears how the great orator Marius Victorinus made a public commitment to Christianity, and how some members of the imperial civil service resigned their posts to join a community of monks; a decisive moment of conversion, in the garden of his house at Milan, leaves him free to lead a celibate life. In book 9 he resigns his chair, is baptised, and decides to return to Africa. The last event to be described is the death of Monnica at Ostia, in 387, while they wait for a passage home.

(*b*) *Date and purpose*

The dating of the *C.* depends on A.'s survey of his own works, the *Retractations* (perhaps better the *Revisions*), written at the end of his life when he reread, and commented on, everything he had written. To judge by the sequence of works discussed in the *Retractations*, he started the *C.* in 397, when he was forty-three: ten years after he had renounced his worldly career, six years after his enforced ordination as priest and two after his consecration as bishop. It is not clear whether he also finished them in that year. Some scholars argue for a delay before he wrote book 10, which is concerned with memory and also with the temptations which affected A. at the time of writing, and perhaps a further delay before the addition of books 11–13, which are concerned with the problem of time and with A.'s current understanding of the creation narrative in Genesis 1–3. These arguments, and the counter-argument that A. wrote the *C.* as one continuous work, depend on theories about the overall structure and purpose of the *C.*, not on any further biographical data.

Confessio means 'acknowledgement'. Christians used it both for the confession of sins and for the acknowledgement of faith in God: a *confessor* is someone honoured for having declared his or her faith at the risk of martyrdom, even though he or she did not in fact die a martyr. Acknowledgement of faith in God becomes praise of God's greatness and goodness, even in the basic acknowledgement 'Jesus is Lord'. A.'s *Confessiones*, as the opening paragraph makes clear, are a declaration of faith and praise by someone who is conscious of sin and who seeks to know God. But why did he write them at this time in his life, in the midst of intensive theological, pastoral and administrative work?

One possibility is that A. wrote the *C.* as apologia. He defended his own past life, acknowledging the distance he had put between himself and God, but also recognising the presence of God in his life even when A. seemed to be trapped in error and sin. His mother's influence was evidence for a Christian upbringing, and her weeping for his sins (3.11.19, 4.4.7) maintained a Christian presence in his Manichaean years. His horror at past sins which many Christians would regard as minor (see on 1.7.11, 2.4.9), and his concern for his present spiritual state in book 10, pre-empted charges that he was not fit to be ordained, and marked him as a Christian of the highest spiritual standards. His exposition of Scripture in books 11–13 demonstrated the focus of his life as a bishop (11.2.2), the abilities he brought to it, and his commitment to finding a Christian solution for the problems which had helped to keep him from God: that is, an authoritative text which might seem either too easy or too obscure, and philosophical difficulties about God in relation to the world. He needed such a defence because he had come under attack, in his first years as a bishop, from those who remembered his Manichaean past. The rival Donatist church, which claimed to be the true church in Africa, was powerful in Hippo, and the Donatist Petilianus accused him of being still a secret Manichaean. A Manichaean, Secundinus, accused him of leaving the sect only because he was afraid of persecution (see on 4.1.1), not because he had shown that its beliefs were false. He had been baptised not in Africa but in Italy, and there had been no request for letters of commendation from his home church. He had been ordained priest without a proper enquiry into his fitness. When his bishop, Valerius, sought agreement that A. should be consecrated as his successor, the senior bishop of the region, Megalius of Calama, wrote a letter expressing shock; he later withdrew his charges and apologised, but the letter was still being used against A. years later, in 411, by the Donatists. A.'s consecration as bishop during the lifetime of his predecessor was, as he later realised (Possidius, *Life of Augustine* 8), a breach of the rules agreed at the council of Nicaea in 325. His awareness of a mocking, hostile readership for the *C.* (1.6.7), and his hopes for some charitable readers (5.10.20, 10.3.3–4.5), reflect these difficulties.

Moreover, there was a possibility of making himself known – or of clearing his name – among influential Christians outside Africa. His friend Alypius, in 395, wrote to Paulinus of Nola, sending some of A.'s anti-Manichaean writings. Paulinus, a Spanish aristocrat, had sold his family property and retired to live in chastity with his wife at Nola in Campania (see below, §3c), but he kept in touch with other ascetic aristocrats in France, Spain, Italy and the Holy Land (see E. A. Clark (1992) for these networks). Like A. and Alypius, he had been baptised by Ambrose; but A. and his friends had not, apparently, become part of the ascetic connection before they left Italy. Paulinus (*Letter* 24) replied with friendliness, but asked to know more about this new correspondent. A. took over, offering an account of Alypius on the grounds that Alypius was far too modest (*Letter* 27), and perhaps also decided to give an account of himself and what the Lord had done for him.

Such an account could serve several purposes. In addition to presenting A. as he wished to be known, it confirmed others in their commitment to a Christian life, especially if they too had renounced worldly success and family life, and it might persuade some who had not yet made the commitment. A. recommended, as a method for teaching (catechising) those who had no knowledge of Christianity, starting from what God had done in one particular human life (*On*

Catechising the Untrained 5). Having established that God does reach out to help people, the catechist can move on to expound basic Christian teaching. The *C.* can be read, as Courcelle (1950) 21–6 suggested, in this light. It gives a very full, though still incomplete, account of God's action in a human life (cf. 3.12.21 and 9.8.17, *multa praetereo*), followed by the beginnings of an exposition which, as A. acknowledges (12.6.6), cannot possibly fit into a manageable book. Looking back, in the *Retractations* (2.6), A. commented that the *C.* had in fact helped people to lift their hearts and minds to God.

One further possibility is that writing the *C.* was, for A., an act of therapy, an attempt to work out how he came to be where he was and what he must now do. He had abandoned his career and the prospect of marriage in favour of peaceful study in a small community of friends. Then he had been forced into the life of a priest and had soon become a bishop, responsible for preaching and administration and the well-being of his people, and confronted once again with the temptations of success and with the harshness of other people's judgements. He had also reached a new understanding of his utter dependence on God. In the course of writing a commentary on Paul's Letter to the Romans (in 394/5), and answering questions from Simplicianus (who succeeded Ambrose as bishop of Milan) in 396, he came to be convinced that it is only God's free gift, not human free choice, which makes it possible to escape from sin (see on 2.7.15). In *Retractations* 2.1, commenting on his *To Simplicianus*, he cites what Paul says in 1 Corinthians 4: 7, 'Who singles you out? What do you have that you did not receive? And if you received it, why do you boast as if you had not received it?' The *C.* can be read as an illustration of what A. had received. His life is determined by what he experiences as chance encounters, his own mistakes, and the silence of God. There is no answer to his endless questions about what he is and why his life took the course it did, except in his understanding of what the Bible says about God's creation and redemption of the world.

In 397 A. was physically ill, 'unable to walk or stand still or sit down for the pain and swelling of sores and piles' (*Letter* 38.1; perhaps cf. *C.* 3.1.1). He may also have been suffering from writer's block. Several unfinished projects were abandoned, or completed only later in life (O'D. I xlii n.69): a 'literal exposition' of Genesis,

commentaries on Paul, an attack on Manichaeism, and *On Christian
Teaching* which deals with the proper use of rhetoric. His preaching,
to judge by audience reactions, was a great success, but that too
made him uneasy. 'The enemy of our real happiness is on the attack,
scattering everywhere the snares of "Bravo! bravo!"' (10.36.59). A.
knew that he should not be thinking whether he had just preached a
brilliant sermon, but whether he had managed to teach the people in
his congregation: his own experience as a teacher made him doubt
that there was any obvious connection between what the teacher
said and what the student learned (*On the Teacher* 38–44). He thanks
God (9.4.7) because in 386 'you rescued my tongue from where you
had already rescued my heart', that is, from the job of a professional
speaker. But he still had to find a preaching style which would work
for his congregation in a cosmopolitan but provincial town. He had
been teaching rhetoric students in the provincial capital, Carthage,
and then the cultural capital, Rome, and had gone on to speak
before sophisticated audiences in the political capital, Milan. His
rhetorical training was associated, for him, with conveying what he
should have known, or did know, was not true. He now had to find a
persuasive voice for what he believed to be true and of ultimate importance.

2. Genre and style

The *C.* is a one-sided conversation with God, who speaks to A. only
in the words of Scripture which come to his mind: in that sense it is
an extended prayer, overheard by A.'s readers. A. was expected, as a
bishop, to extemporise prayer, and had heard Ambrose of Milan use
a form of prayer which interwove biblical quotation and rhetorical
invocation of God (Verheijen (1949) 80–1). But the *C.* does not consistently use a formal prayer-style, and A. only sometimes reminds
his readers of themselves as, so to speak, a congregation, as active
and reactive listeners to the confession of a living human being, not
as eager consumers of sensational literature (see further Miles (1992)
on A.'s provocation of the reader). A. speaks to God sometimes in
direct invocation, and sometimes in reflection addressed to God. He
speaks as a Christian who is trained in classical culture, that is, in
literature, philosophy and rhetoric. Christian preachers had to be

aware that their congregations included people of little or no education. When A. makes in sermons points that he also makes in the *C.*, he does it quite differently, explaining Scripture slowly and in detail, repeating himself when he sees that his audience is puzzled, and using lively illustrations and word-plays which can be easily appreciated. But in the *C.*, he assumes that his human audience shares his culture and can move with him from Scripture to philosophical analysis to high classical rhetoric, even within one sentence.

A. said of the *C.* 'book 1 to book 10 is about me' (*Retractations* 2.6), and that is a more helpful starting-point than any discussion of genre. The *C.* is about the relationship to God of a man formed by intense reading, who is trained to persuade by words and who expects his own readers to be moved and changed by what they read, just as Cicero's *Hortensius* 'changed my emotional state' (*mutauit adfectum meum*, 3.4.7). What he says about himself depends on what a cultured Christian reader wants to know and on what A. finds theologically important in human nature (see below, §3*c*, and G. Clark (1993) 33–53), and the way he says it depends on what he is. It is difficult to make any general comment on the style of the *C.*, because there are so many voices present in A.'s own voice: the reader needs to hear the Bible (including the unstated contexts, see e.g. 2.3.6), Plotinus (see below, §3*b*), Virgil and Cicero speaking in and to A. The studies of Balmus (1930), Finaert (1939), Verheijen (1949), and Mohrmann (1958), all contribute to the analysis of A.'s style in the *C.*, which they agree in finding unique within the immense range of his writings. A. cannot be classified as a 'late Latin' writer because he was trained to write and speak classical Latin for professional purposes; but his grammar and syntax are influenced both by the Latin Bible and by Latin as it was commonly spoken, and are often disconcerting for classically trained readers (see below *b*). There are patient documentations of A.'s uses of language, many inspired by Roy Deferrari at the Catholic University of America in the 1920s: this approach is seen in Hrdlicka (1931) and in the introduction to Campbell and McGuire (1931). In recent years, machine-readable texts have made it very much easier to trace A.'s use of particular words, and there is now a Concordance to the *C.* There are also wide-ranging studies of the cultural context and of the rhetoric which A.'s audience might expect and enjoy. The classic work of

Marrou (1938) presented A. as a manifestation of late antique cultural decline; its dramatic *Retractatio* (1949) argued for vigour and originality in place of decadence. Kaster (1988) defends the culture of teachers of literature, Roberts (1989) discusses the preferred techniques of late Latin poetry, and Cameron (1991) discusses Christian uses of rhetoric. Finally, there is an inexhaustible supply (annually surveyed in the *Revue des Etudes Augustiniennes*) of readings which suggest overall structures and patterns of imagery in the *C*. There are always more connections and patterns to be found, both because A. himself was so sharply aware of the associations of words and images, and because his habit of antithesis – balanced comparison and contrast – coexists with his passion for metaphor, that is, describing one thing in terms of a seemingly unrelated other.

(a) *The Latin Bible*

The level of tension between Christianity and the classics varied in different contexts (see further Kaster (1988) 70–95). It could be felt immediately in the choice of language. 'Christian Latin' is not a separate kind of Latin, but it is recognisable by its distinctive theological vocabulary (often, like Cicero's philosophical vocabulary, adopted or translated from Greek), and by its quotations from the Bible. The speech-patterns of the Latin Bible were formed by translation from Greek, either from the Greek New Testament or from the Septuagint, the Greek version of the Hebrew Old Testament. The translations were made by people who lacked high literary culture, and who thought it important to keep close to the Bible text. Their effect was very different from the classical Latin which A., and other educated persons, had been trained to use in public speech and formal writing. A. remarks in *On Christian Teaching* (2.14.21) that, by contrast, people brought up on Scripture are puzzled by classical Latin idiom. This is not surprising, because the classics of the fourth-century school curriculum – Terence, Sallust, Virgil and Cicero – were 400 or 500 years old, whereas the Scriptures were translated into 'vulgar' Latin, that is, the Latin which was commonly spoken. (See further Coleman (1987), and Herman (1991), on spoken and written Latin in the late empire.) A. was not alone in finding the Old Latin Bible inferior to the classics (3.5.9), and that is why Pope Damasus, in the

380s, started Jerome on what was in effect a New Latin Bible, which became the Vulgate or Common Bible (see Sparks (1970) on this project). Jerome's translations were much more accurate, provoking the usual cries of protest from people who liked what they were used to, or, more seriously, thought that the Septuagint in particular was divinely inspired for the use of the whole Church. He used the Hebrew text of the Old Testament, on which he did serious critical work, and preserved its characteristic speech rhythms, but with greater elegance and clarity (see further Kamesar (1993) for Jerome's scholarship).

Hebrew-influenced narrative style sets clauses in parallel (the technical term is parataxis), joining them by 'and', which often occurs as the first word in a sentence; it also tends to place the main verb early in the sentence (Verheijen (1949)). These patterns also occur in the Old Latin translations of the Greek New Testament, perhaps, as Coleman (1987) suggests, because they were familiar in spoken Latin as well as in *koinē* Greek. By contrast, classical Latin prefers to subordinate clauses to a main clause (hypotaxis) and to postpone the main verb. The opening sentence of 1.6.9 provides a simple example: *et ecce infantia mea olim mortua est et ego uiuo* (not, for instance, *mortua olim infantia mea uiuo*). Hebrew poetry (chiefly the Psalms) provided A. with vivid, often physical, metaphors (see on 1.5.5), and with distinctive rhythms which derive from its technique of parallelism: a verse will make a point, then restate it in slightly different terms. For instance, in the psalm which A. could not use (see on 4.4.9) to relieve his grief for his dead friend there is a refrain

> quare tristis es, anima mea?
> et quare conturbas me?

In the equally distinctive rhythms of the Book of Common Prayer (1662), this becomes

> Why art thou so full of heaviness, O my soul,
> and why art thou so disquieted within me?

The Psalms are very often heard in the *C.* They are the obvious model for an address to God, and A. knew them better than any other part of the Bible. He was deeply moved by them at the time when he was waiting for baptism (9.4.8–11), he used them in the daily worship of his community of clergy at Hippo, and he preached on them regularly. His sermons *On the Psalms*, some of which had been written down when he started work on the *C.*, often help to show what text he read (see below, §4*b*) and how he interpreted it. Although the Psalms predominate in the *C.*, A. draws on the whole of the Bible. When he was ordained in 391 he had asked for a few months' leave for intensive study of the Bible, and after six years of preaching, discussion and writing, he knew it so well that phrases and verses came at once to mind, and one allusion prompted another (as in the sequence at the end of 1.5.6). They are interwoven in the text of the *C.*, evoked by a word A. has used or an idea he wants to present rather than deployed in support of an argument (as they often are in A.'s sermons). In books 1–4, there are very few paragraphs which do not make use of the Bible, and never more than two together.

(*b*) *The classics*

A.'s use of the classics in the *C.* expresses the problem which confronted him: he denounces the educational system which had formed his mind and which continues to inform the *C.* All four classic authors appear in the first two books. Terence (see on 1.16.25–6) supplies an example of literature which corrupts the young: while supposedly improving their vocabulary and style, they absorb bad morality exemplified by false gods. Sallust's Catiline suggests the glamour of anti-social behaviour by young men and helps to analyse their motivation (see on 2.4.9, 2.5.11). Virgil is a more constant presence. The schoolboy A. loves Virgil's fictitious narrative, weeps for the illicit love of the non-existent Dido, and wins a prize for a speech conveying the unrighteous wrath of the false goddess Juno (see on 1.13.20–2, 1.17.27). Probably, though not explicitly, Virgil supplied A. with images of his own life, tossed on a stormy sea with his companions, seeking to understand the commands of a distant father, and diverted by erotic love from his true purpose of his life (see Bennett (1988) for A.'s transformations of Virgil). But though A. sometimes incorporates Virgilian tags (e.g. 1.13.22), he cannot merge Virgil's hexameters into a prose text as easily as he can integrate phrases from the Psalms. It is Cicero who is the pervasive classical influence, both on passages of high rhetoric and on the philosophical analysis for which he had often supplied the material (see further Hagendahl (1967) 486–553).

When A. finds the Latin Bible unsatisfactory (3.5.9), it is by comparison with *Tulliana dignitas*, Ciceronian dignity, expressed in the *Hortensius* which had inspired him with a love of wisdom. Cicero's style was characteristically ample: *copiosus* and *ornatus*, used by A. at 1.18.28, were favourite terms of praise. He liked pairs of synonyms, and used an elaborate structure of subordinate clauses, displacing the main verb to the end of a long sentence. He had strong preferences about *clausulae*, that is, the rhythmical patterns formed at the end of a sentence and, to a lesser extent, at breaks within the sentence. The Latin Bible, as A. comments in *On Christian Teaching* 4.20.41, rarely has clausulae; and this is also true of the *C.*, except in its more Ciceronian moments (e.g. 2.5.11; see further Verheijen (1949) 124–33).

Rhythm is one of the most distinctive features of an author's style, but the prose rhythms of the *C.* are difficult to analyse. In classical Latin, prose rhythms were quantitative: that is, they depended on short and long syllables. In the early Middle Ages, quantitative rhythms had been replaced by the *cursus*, a system which depends on accent – that is, where the stress falls in the word – not on quantity. A. lived in a time of transition between quantitative and accentual patterns, and uses both systems in his immense output of work. He notes (*On Christian Teaching* 4.10.24) that Africans had trouble distinguishing quantity, and it is possible (Marrou (1938) 80–1) that, for him, metrical (quantitative) clausulae required more conscious thought than accentual clausulae. But his contemporary Jerome, who came from north Italy, similarly uses a mix of classical prose-rhythms, *cursus*, and no particular rhythm. (See further Scourfield (1993) 233–42 on Jerome, and Oberhelman (1988) for the analysis of prose rhythm.)

(c) Rhetorical technique

As student, teacher and public speaker A. was trained to be intensely aware of the choice of words, their arrangement within a sentence and the impact it would make upon the listener. In the *C.*, he presents rhetoric as deceptive, a *linguosa ars* (see on 1.9.14) which persuades people to believe lies, and which is imposed on the young so that they will maintain a corrupt social system. Some readers, agreeing with this judgement of rhetoric, regard the *C.* as a 'rhetorical work' which aims to impress rather than to tell the truth about A. They might find a plain style more acceptable, but should take to heart A.'s comment (5.6.11) 'I am aware of another kind of people who distrust even the truth and will not accept it, if it is presented in a rich and elegant style'. Rhetoric, which is the art of speaking so as to please and persuade an audience, can be used to make the truth convincing and to influence people for their good.

When he wrote the last book of *On Christian Teaching* (4.7.11–12), after long experience of preaching, A. was dismissive about rhetorical skill: anyone could pick up the essentials, he said, just as well from the Bible as from the classics. His analysis of the essentials focusses, conventionally, on the 'limbs' of a sentence (Latin *membra* translating Greek *cola*), that is, its main separable units, and their arrangement in the overall structure that Greeks called a *periodos*, a period (there was no consistent Latin translation for this term). Writers on rhetoric varied in what exactly they counted as a colon (see further Habinek (1985) 21–41). Some groupings of cola made a particular impact, especially *isocola* which had approximately the same length and rhythm, and the *tricolon*, a group of three cola. The 'rising *tricolon*', in which the second colon is longer than the first and the third than the second, was and remains a favourite: it can be heard in almost any prepared speech at a political conference. There are fine examples in 1.6.9 and 1.7.12.

The effect of a group of cola can be enhanced by rhetorical marking: for instance, each colon can end with a similar sound-pattern (*homoioteleuton*); a colon can pick up a phrase or a word from the preceding colon (*anaphora*); or the cola, or words within the cola, can be organised for contrast (antithesis). This last is A.'s favourite technique, if 'technique' is the right word: antithesis is so frequent in all his writing that it seems rather to be the way he thinks. Antithesis is often combined with word-plays which exploit groups of related words or double meanings of words, for instance, the contrast between a feeling of misery and a condition which really deserves pity, both of which can be called *miseria* (see on 1.5.5).

3. Philosophy and theology

A.'s very great intelligence and rhetorical skill may obscure the fact that Thagaste, Madauros and Carthage had given him a good but limited education, reflected in his intense response to a small number of books. He had friends who shared his interests, but it was not until he reached Milan that he heard Christian preaching, and encountered philosophical discussion, of the level he needed. At Carthage he had been deeply impressed by Cicero's *Hortensius*, an exhortation to philosophy – which means, literally, the love of wisdom (see on 3.4.7). To judge from the fragments which survive (mostly in quotation by A.: see Hagendahl (1967) 81–94) it was 'protreptic': not technical philosophy, but writing designed to inspire enthusiasm for the intellectual and moral hard work which philosophy demanded. Present-day philosophers may hope to change people's opinions on specific ethical problems, but Greek and Roman philosophers thought they had failed if their students did not live in accordance with their teaching. A philosopher, they said, is concerned to understand the nature of the universe and the purpose of human life within it. It is impossible to do this if one is constantly distracted by irrelevant desires – for luxuries, for retaliation against an insult, for sex, for political gains. Cicero wrote the *Hortensius* when he was about sixty, at what seemed to be the end of a very distinguished career. A. read it at eighteen, with a career to make. He was ambitious and had a strong sexual drive (like the father he did his best to disown, see on 2.3.5); he also felt the attraction of austerity, self-discipline and a life of study. The tension remained with him until, at the age of thirty-two, he experienced conversion. Meanwhile, he tried to understand what he was in relation to God. In books 1–4, he remembers what it was like in earlier stages of his life, when he was a nominally Christian child and young adolescent, then for nine years a Manichaean with a passion for philosophy. But he also judges his past self in terms of what he later understood, so the Platonism of his years in Milan and the Christian commitment of his years in Africa are important in his account of his earlier beliefs.

(a) Manichaeism

A. encountered Manichaean teaching soon after the impact of the *Hortensius*, and remained an adherent for nine years. His subsequent attacks on Manichaeism are a major source of information, but of course they are polemic against the system, not exposition of it. In the *C.* he is concerned with the effect of Manichaeism on his own relationship with God. Instead of explaining what he believed as a Manichaean and why, he denounces the aspects of his belief which, in the light of Platonist philosophy and the preaching of Ambrose, he had come to see as its major confusions. But it is now possible to give a general account of western Manichaeism which does not depend chiefly on Christian polemic (see Lieu (1985) for recent developments). Several Manichaean texts have been discovered this century: the Coptic texts from Medinet Medi in the Fayyum include a book of psalms, and the Greek 'Mani codex', a tiny papyrus volume, is an anthology on the birth and early life of Mani.

Mani, born in 216 in southern Mesopotamia, was brought up in an ascetic Judaeo-Christian sect which he left in his mid-twenties. He believed himself to be the Paraclete, the 'Advocate' who, as Jesus promised to his followers (John 14: 26), would lead them into all truth. Revelations from his 'divine twin' taught him the doctrines and the organisation of Manichaeism, and instructed him to travel and preach. His teaching spread eastward and westward, adapting to existing religious beliefs and practices: some of the most important Manichaean texts, written in various Central Asian languages, were found at Turfan in China. In the Roman empire, Manichaeism was regarded by Christians as heretical and by the state as a dangerous import from the rival power, Persia (Iran). In Persia there was religious toleration until the death of Shapur I (*c.* 272), but under his successor Zoroastrianism became the most influential religion, and Mani was imprisoned and died after torture. His death was commemorated in the festival of the Bēma, which western Manichaeans celebrated rather than Easter.

Mani's claim to a new revelation was not a new phenomenon in the west. Jesus had told his followers (John 16: 12–13) 'I still have many things to tell you, but you cannot handle them now. But when the spirit of truth comes, he will lead you into all truth.' He had said that the Paraclete was 'the spirit of truth which the world cannot receive, because it neither sees nor knows it; but you know it, because it remains with you and is in you' (John 14: 17). Several religious leaders had convinced their followers that they had the truth, the *gnosis* (knowledge), which most people could not see. The 'knowledge' took the form of a deeper understanding of what is really happening in human lives. Gnostics believed that the physical world is of no value: it is the temporary, illusory stage for a struggle of spiritual powers, and all that matters is the release of the divine spirit within us from the contamination of the material body and its return to its true home. They produced complex mythologies of angels and demons to explain the workings of the universe. They refused to accept the affirmation of Genesis that God made the world, 'and God saw all the things that God had made, and they were very good' (Genesis 1: 31). Consequently, they also refused to accept the Incarnation, the union of God and human in a human body, and taught that Christ was a divine spirit in the appearance of a human body, and that his death on the cross was an appearance of death.

Gnosticism recurs through the history of Christianity, but Gnostic sects tended to fragment. Mani combined impressive teaching, reinforced by hymns and splendidly produced books, with effective organisation. He taught that Good and Evil are equal powers, and both have always existed. Each has a kingdom, Good the kingdom of Light and Evil the kingdom of Darkness. Darkness invaded Light, and fragments of light are still entrapped in the darkness; this world was created in order to free them. Jesus of Light, who is pure spirit, shows humans how the light may be freed, and the Suffering Jesus is the Light which is entrapped in this world. The human soul is a fragment of Light which has fallen from its home, the kingdom of heaven, and is trapped in the body. It can escape by disciplining the body and with the help of saving powers.

There were two kinds of Manichaeans, the Elect Saints and the Hearers. The Elect, who formed the nucleus of a Manichaean 'cell', were committed to a missionary life of poverty and celibacy. They were strict vegetarians, drank no wine, and were forbidden even to harvest or prepare food, because Mani had a revelation that it is a kind of murder to damage plants by harvesting. The sect survived because the Hearers incurred the sin of preparing food, and were released from sin by the prayers of the Elect who ate it: Mani taught that fragments of the divine which were trapped in plants could be released when ingested by the pure body of the Elect. The Hearers were also allowed a wife or concubine, but were taught to avoid procreation because it entraps more divine spirits in matter. Manichaean cells, like Christian churches, were kept in touch with one another by a hierarchy analogous to the Christian clergy, so when A. left Carthage for Rome he was able to stay with another Hearer and meet some of the Elect (5.10.18–19).

Manichaeism offered A. a way to accommodate his conflicts: he could pursue his career, and retain his partner, while purging his sins through his service to the pure Elect (4.1.1); and he could blame those sins on his lower, alien nature, which like the material world had been made by the power of evil, but which his true self would eventually shed (5.10.18). Manichaeism also responded to his need, instilled by his childhood, for the name of Christ, and his initial distaste for the Christian scriptures (3.4.8–6.10). He could regard the Bible as a crude and contaminated attempt at the truth, whereas the Manichaean scriptures offered both the name of Christ and what seemed to be a profound understanding of the universe and of human life (3.6.10).

(b) Platonism

After he became a Manichaean, A. continued to read philosophy, but was hampered by having a small range of books and by not knowing much Greek. He disliked Greek at school, and notes in the *Retractations* some mistakes he made in his early works through ignorance of Greek. In later life he became much better at it, and could check Latin translations against a Greek original (as in *Against Julian* 1.5.18), but in his twenties he would have found it hard work to read a Greek philosophical or theological text (see on 1.14.23).

When A. was about twenty (4.16.28), he read Aristotle's *Categories*, a basic text of logical analysis which was available in Latin translation. He found it very clear, but he says it was a further obstacle to his thought about God, whom he imagined in Aristotelian categories as a subject with attributes, not as greatness itself or beauty itself (see on 4.16.29). He was not, evidently, aware of the Platonist debate on whether the *Categories* was concerned only with human systems of classification, or whether it was applicable to all levels of being. He also read more of Cicero's philosophical works. Some of Cicero's ethical treatises, especially *On Ends* and *Tusculan Disputations*, supply him with the material and the style for ethical analysis in the *C.* (for instance, 2.6.13), though he does not discuss the effect they had on him when he read them (see O'D. ii 388–9 for possible timing). As his commitment to Manichaeism weakened, A. was impressed by Cicero's *Academics* (see O'Daly (1987) 162–71). The 'Academics' were successors of Plato, who had taught at the house he bought near the shrine of the obscure Athenian hero Akademos. Some of them advocated strict agnosticism: as A. put it (5.10.19) 'their opinion was that everything must be doubted, and they declared that nothing of the truth can be understood by a human being'. But, he says, he had not yet understood what they meant, and what this means is that he had read Cicero on the state of philosophical debate 400 years earlier, but had not yet encountered the argument that their apparent scepticism camouflaged an esoteric teaching of the truth which had been expounded by Plato.

At Milan, A. was given 'Platonic books' in a Latin translation by Marius Victorinus (7.9.13, 8.2.3), and, he says, they changed his life. The Platonism A. encountered at Milan, in books and discussion groups and Ambrose's preaching, was 'New Platonism' (Neoplatonism), which set out to explicate Plato in the belief that he had understood the eternal truth and had expounded it in a consistent philosophical system which was passed on by his followers. It required great ingenuity of mind to reconcile Plato's various experiments in thought, Aristotle's critique, and the arguments of their successors, and many debates continued among the New Platonists. Milanese Neoplatonism was very much influenced by the third-century philosopher Plotinus, an impressive ascetic who refused to give formal philosophical lectures, and by his pupil Porphyry, who revised Plotinus' brief written records of his thinking and organised them into groups of nine, the *Enneads* (see O'Meara (1993) on these treatises). The 'Platonic books' may have included writings by

Plotinus and Porphyry: certainly, by the time he wrote the *C.*, A. had read some Plotinus and had been profoundly impressed. Plotinus' style, as well as his arguments, is heard in the *C.*, both in the tenacious strings of questions with which A. pursues a difficult problem (as in 1.3.3–4.4) and in occasional flashes of exhortation (as at 1.18.28).

Plato's philosophy contrasts the uncertain, transitory world we perceive with the senses, and the unchanging reality, grasped by reason, from which the world derives its existence. The dominant Neoplatonist image was of the One, the highest level of being, from which emanates (literally, flows out), or radiates, all else that there is, as if in concentric circles. The circles of being turn back towards the original unity, and thereby define themselves in relation to it, but the outermost circle, the material world, turns away from unity into multiplicity and fragmentation, and finally into nothingness. But even in this material world there is the human mind, which is connected with the centre. A. found in this image a powerful expression of his own choice between focussing on God and dispersing himself among the concerns of the world (see on 2.1.1, 2.3.3, 3.8.16). It also allowed him to challenge the Manichaean account of evil as a substance, an independent and invasive power: instead, evil could be understood as distance from the One which is the source of all being, so that complete alienation from the One is non-existence (2.6.12; 7.12.18). But what A. found most important was that Platonism helped him to think of God as spirit. The Manichaeans attacked what they said was crude Christian anthropomorphism, but themselves taught in terms of very subtle bodies (3.6.10, 5.10.20); this caused A. great difficulties in explaining how God can be present throughout the universe (1.2.2–3.3). He tried (7.1.2) to imagine God permeating the universe like sunlight, but this suggests that some parts of the universe would have more of God than others, 'an elephant's body would have more of you than a sparrow's'. Later (7.5.7) he imagined the universe as a great but finite sponge, saturated by an infinite ocean. The Platonist books made him think in terms of his own thought, the mental power which forms images of everything yet occupies no space (7.1.2), and which can aspire to union with God.

(c) Christianity

Platonism was not the final answer for A. because it relied too much on human reason, and this, he concluded, was pride (see on 1.1.1). Pride, *superbia*, was for him the root of sin: he saw it as a mistaken attempt to take control of one's own life in disregard of God. He thought that human beings consist of body and soul, and 'soul', for him, always included 'mind' (see further O'Daly (1987) 54–60). His own experience convinced him that, just as Manichaeans were wrong to think of the human soul as a fragment of God trapped in the material body (4.16.31), Platonist philosophers were wrong to think of the human mind as reason, which should direct bodily desires and which is capable of union with the thought of God. The human mind, A. found, is changeable and divided (see on 4.15.24), and the human body does not respond to rational control (see on 2.3.3). The death of his unnamed friend at Thagaste (4.4.9) left A. 'a great puzzle', *magna quaestio*, to himself: intelligent as he was, he could not understand his own emotions or escape from the self he experienced as a burden and a conflict. Later, when he read the Platonic books, he found (7.16.22) that he could indeed raise his mind towards God by reflecting on the power by which he made value judgements and thereby had some inner knowledge of goodness and truth. He could find God by introspection, not by going 'outside' (that is, attending to the external world). But he could not sustain his awareness of God, because the demands of his body dragged him down. He had long since felt an inner need or deprivation, *egestas*, but had not yet realised that it was a need to love God. He was still dominated by the 'threefold desire' (see on 1.10.16) for physical pleasure, the satisfaction of curiosity, and status, and although he was unhappy, he saw no escape.

Platonism imagined the unchanging love of God permeating the universe, but did not think in terms of initiatives by God to help humanity, because any such initiative would mean that God was not unchanging and therefore was not perfectly good (see on 1.4.4, 3.2.3). Change must be either for the better or for the worse: if God created the universe, was God before the creation less good than God after the creation, and how can God be less than the greatest possible good? If God responds to human distress, or punishes human wrongdoing, then God is vulnerable, and how can there be anything which has the power to affect God? (See on 4.5.10.) So the Platonist books (7.9.13) did not offer Christ as mediator between God and humanity. A. acknowledges (7.19.25) that at this time he thought of Christ only as a man of exceptional wisdom, not as the reconciliation of divine and human (see on 4.12.19). But Ambrose's preaching had allowed him to hear the Christian scriptures as meaningful, and he found that the letters of Paul offered him everything that Platonism did and also the hope that God would help him (7.21.27). A. now accepted that he did wrong by his own choice (7.3.5), not because his true self was trapped in an alien nature, as the Manichaeans taught, or because of the stars (7.6.8–10): what he needed was not deliverance from an alien self, but healing of a damaged self. He found himself still in a state of conflict, wanting to commit his life to prayer and philosophy, but quite unable to do it until God broke the compulsions which held him to his past life. This was grace, a free gift by God without which he would have continued in wrongdoing (see on 2.7.15).

CONVERSION A.'s 'conversion', the decisive moment in a garden at Milan (8.12.29) when he was enabled to change his life, was one stage in a long process. It was decisive in that A. had acknowledged his total dependence on God's help (in the words he often uses, God resists the proud but gives grace to the humble: see on 1.1.1), and in that he had been liberated from the need for success in his career and for sexual satisfaction. It was not a forgone conclusion that he would resign his chair and live in celibacy, but he and his friends did not think that full Christian commitment could be combined with the demands of marriage and a profession (8.6.15). This opinion was widespread in the late fourth century. It was controversial, both because faithful married Christians who fulfilled their social duties did not see why they should be regarded as second class, and because any disparagement of marriage and childbearing sounded like a Manichaean attempt to devalue God's creation. (See further Hunter (1993) on this debate, and see on 2.2.3 for the question whether procreation was part of God's original plan, or damage limitation after the Fall.) But Ambrose was one of the leading theorists of virginity and continence as the physical analogue of commitment to God, and his preaching met A.'s personal need. A. shared the general belief of Greek and Roman philosophers that the only proper use of sex is for procreation within marriage, and that any other use is indulgence. He had realised that sex was, for him, not just an indulgence but an addiction: he could not do without it even though it prevented him from achieving what he wanted most, namely the ascent of his mind from physical concerns to be united with God (7.17.23). Celibacy was liberation, just as his resignation of his chair was a release from ambition and from the waste of his intellect on falsehood.

4. Text and commentary

(a) The text

There is one very early MS of the *C.*, nine from the ninth century, and 300 to 400 mediaeval MSS, some of which have not yet been catalogued. The earliest is the Sessorianus (S, now in Rome), which may even be late fifth century, but is more likely to be sixth century (Gorman (1983) 114 n.2). Earliest is not best, because the Sessorianus was written in a hurry: words are left out, wrongly repeated, or replaced by similar words. One of the ninth-century MSS (O, now in Paris) has a particularly clear and careful text. Where S and O disagree, other MSS can be used in assessing differences. There is also a sixth-century anthology, edited by Eugippius, which includes passages from books 10 and 12 of the *C.* The history of the text is analysed by Gorman (1983) and discussed by O'D. 1 lvi–xi, and the manuscripts and printed editions are described in detail in V.'s introduction. V. also has a full apparatus criticus, taken over from M. Skutella's edition of 1934.

The first printed text appeared between 1465 and 1470 at Strasbourg; it was followed in 1508, at Basle, by the complete works of Augustine edited by J. Amerbach. When the Benedictines of Saint-Maur edited the complete works of Augustine, the *C.* appeared in their first volume (1679). This Maurist edition, based on the ninth-century MSS available in France, appears with only minor alterations in volume XXXII of J.-P. Migne, *Patrologia Latina* (1845). The *CSEL* edition (1896) was prepared by P. Knöll, who preferred to follow S as the oldest MS, but did not always have a correct report of its readings. His text was used by Gibb and Montgomery (Cambridge 1908), who provided notes for readers trained in theology, Greek and Hebrew. M. Skutella, for the Teubner edition (1934, revised 1969), collated the ninth-century MSS and relied less heavily on S; V., for *CCL*, uses Skutella's collation but often differs from him. O'D. prints a re-examined text which differs both from Skutella and from Verheijen, and which discusses textual problems in the commentary rather than listing them in an *apparatus criticus*. His commentary, the most valuable yet, is particularly rich on questions of theology and of A.'s use of language.

(b) *This volume*

This volume offers a plain text and a commentary. There is no facing translation because so many good translations are available: readers are assumed to have the annotated translation by Henry Chadwick (1991). There is no apparatus criticus because there are few textual problems which seriously affect the reader's interpretation, and these are best discussed in the commentary. Almost always, in the *C.*, the problem is not reconstructing what A. wrote, but interpreting it. Punctuation aims at clarity for the reader, again with discussion in the commentary when needed. We do not know how the earliest texts of the *C.* were punctuated: perhaps, like a fifth-century MS of the *City of God* (Parkes (1992) 276–7), they did not divide words, but marked the beginning of new chapters with a larger letter and, within chapters, left a space before a new topic.

Biblical allusions, and even the (relatively few) direct biblical quotations, are noted in the commentary, not marked in the text by italic or spaced type or quotation marks. One reason is that these markings are devices of printed texts, and it is important to remember that A.'s first readers did not have such distinctions made for them, but were expected to hear the change of style (see further Parkes (1992) 9–19). Another reason is that, as V. explains (lxxix–x), A. rarely quotes outright, but much more often incorporates words and phrases from the Bible into his own prose. It is difficult to decide exactly what to distinguish, the more so because A. used 'Old Latin' versions of the Bible, which were gradually displaced by the Vulgate (see §2a above). Important work has been done to reconstruct the *Vetus Latina* and the text A. used (Beuron 1949– , La Bonnardière 1960–), but we often do not know exactly what A. read in his Bible, and even if we did, he probably relied on memory and did not always (or often) check his references (there is a detailed account in O'D. 1 lxx–lxxi). Chadwick's translation handles the problem neatly by the use of single quotation marks with references for distinct phrases, and references alone for general allusion and reminiscence: this allows the reader to judge the amount of biblical material in any section. In this volume, no one English version of the Bible is used consistently: sometimes it is important to call to mind the wording of the Authorised Version, sometimes clarity (even at the cost of clumsiness) matters more.

One complication arises from A.'s extensive use of the Psalms, because the numbering of psalms differs in the Greek text, which the Old Latin versions used, from the Hebrew text which is used in most English translations. In the Bible as A. read it, Psalms 9 and 10 formed one psalm numbered 9, and the numbering continues one less than in the Hebrew text until Psalm 148, which in the Hebrew text forms one psalm with its predecessor. (Psalms 114 and 115 in the Greek numbering were also combined, but Psalm 116 was divided, so the number-sequence is scarcely affected.) In this volume, as in Chadwick's translation, the Psalms are numbered as they were in A.'s text. Readers looking them up in the Vulgate will find that the number is the same; readers looking them up in almost all English versions will need to add one from Psalm 10 to Psalm 148.

References to the *C.* are conventionally given in three figures: book, chapter, paragraph, e.g. 1.20.31. Paragraphs are not sub-sections of chapters, but run throughout a book. The division into books goes back to A. himself: the books of the *C.* vary in length (for instance, 1 is twice the length of 2) but signal beginnings and endings. The division into chapters goes back to Amerbach's printed text (1506), and the division into paragraphs goes back to the edition by the Benedictines of Saint-Maur (1679). These are sensible (and sensitive) divisions of the text, but readers should remember that they do not necessarily indicate breaks in A.'s thought.

AVGVSTINI CONFESSIONVM
LIBRI I–IV

LIBER PRIMVS

1. Magnus es, domine, et laudabilis ualde: magna uirtus tua **1**
et sapientiae tuae non est numerus. et laudare te uult homo,
aliqua portio creaturae tuae, et homo circumferens mortal-
itatem suam, circumferens testimonium peccati sui et testimonium quia superbis resistis: et tamen laudare te uult homo,
aliqua portio creaturae tuae. tu excitas, ut laudare te delectet,
quia fecisti nos ad te et inquietum est cor nostrum, donec requiescat in te. da mihi, domine, scire et intellegere, utrum sit
prius inuocare te an laudare te et scire te prius sit an inuocare
te. sed quis te inuocat nesciens te? aliud enim pro alio potest
inuocare nesciens. an potius inuocaris, ut sciaris? quomodo
autem inuocabunt, in quem non crediderunt? aut quomodo
credent sine praedicante? et laudabunt dominum qui requi-
runt eum. quaerentes enim inueniunt eum et inuenientes laudabunt eum. quaeram te, domine, inuocans te et inuocem te
credens in te: praedicatus enim es nobis. inuocat te, domine,
fides mea, quam dedisti mihi, quam inspirasti mihi per humanitatem filii tui, per ministerium praedicatoris tui.

2. Et quomodo inuocabo deum meum, deum et dominum **2**
meum, quoniam utique in me ipsum eum uocabo, cum inuocabo eum? et quis locus est in me, quo ueniat in me deus meus,
quo deus ueniat in me, deus, qui fecit caelum et terram? itane,
domine deus meus, est quidquam in me, quod capiat te? an
uero caelum et terra, quae fecisti et in quibus me fecisti, capiunt te? an quia sine te non esset quidquid est, fit ut quidquid
est capiat te? quoniam itaque et ego sum, quid peto, ut uenias
in me, qui non essem, nisi esses in me? non enim ego iam inferi, et tamen etiam ibi es, nam etsi descendero in infernum,
ades. non ergo essem, deus meus, non omnino essem, nisi esses
in me. an potius non essem nisi essem in te, ex quo omnia, per
quem omnia, in quo omnia? etiam sic, domine, etiam sic. quo
te inuoco, cum in te sim? aut unde uenias in me? quo enim

recedam extra caelum et terram, ut inde in me ueniat deus
meus, qui dixit: caelum et terram ego impleo?

3   3. Capiunt ergone te caelum et terra, quoniam tu imples
ea? an imples et restat, quoniam non te capiunt? et quo refun-
dis quidquid impleto caelo et terra restat ex te? an non opus
habes ut quoquam continearis, qui contines omnia, quoniam
quae imples continendo imples? non enim uasa, quae te plena
sunt, stabilem te faciunt, quia etsi frangantur non effunderis.
et cum effunderis super nos, non tu iaces sed erigis nos, nec tu
dissiparis sed conligis nos. sed quae imples omnia, te toto imples omnia. an quia non possunt te totum capere omnia, partem tui capiunt et eandem partem simul omnia capiunt? an
singulas singula et maiores maiora, minores minora capiunt?
ergo est aliqua pars tua maior, aliqua minor? an ubique totus
es et res nulla te totum capit?

4   4. Quid es ergo, deus meus? quid, rogo, nisi dominus deus?
quis enim dominus praeter dominum? aut quis deus praeter
deum nostrum? summe, optime, potentissime, omnipotentissime, misericordissime et iustissime, secretissime et praesentissime, pulcherrime et fortissime, stabilis et incomprehensibilis,
immutabilis mutans omnia, numquam nouus, numquam ue-
tus, innouans omnia et in uetustatem perducens superbos
et nesciunt; semper agens, semper quietus, conligens et non
egens, portans et implens et protegens, creans et nutriens et
perficiens, quaerens cum nihil desit tibi. amas nec aestuas, zelas et securus es, paenitet te et non doles, irasceris et tranquil-
lus es, opera mutas nec mutas consilium; recipis quod inuenis
et numquam amisisti; numquam inops et gaudes lucris, numquam auarus et usuras exigis, supererogatur tibi, ut debeas, et
quis habet quidquam non tuum? reddis debita nulli debens,
donas debita nihil perdens. et quid diximus, deus meus, uita
mea, dulcedo mea sancta, aut quid dicit aliquis, cum de te
dicit? et uae tacentibus de te, quoniam loquaces muti sunt.

5   5. Quis mihi dabit adquiescere in te? quis dabit mihi, ut uenias in cor meum et inebries illud, ut obliuiscar mala mea et

unum bonum meum amplectar, te? quid mihi es? miserere, ut
loquar. quid tibi sum ipse, ut amari te iubeas a me et, nisi faciam, irascaris mihi et mineris ingentes miserias? paruane ipsa
est, si non amem te? ei mihi! dic mihi per miserationes tuas,
domine deus meus, quid sis mihi. dic animae meae: salus tua
ego sum. sic dic, ut audiam. ecce aures cordis mei ante te, domine; aperi eas et dic animae meae: salus tua ego sum. curram
post uocem hanc et apprehendam te. noli abscondere a me
faciem tuam: moriar, ne moriar, ut eam uideam.

6. angusta est domus animae meae quo uenias ad eam:
dilatetur abs te. ruinosa est: refice eam. habet quae offendant
oculos tuos: fateor et scio. sed quis mundabit eam? aut cui
alteri praeter te clamabo: ab occultis meis munda me, domine,
et ab alienis parce seruo tuo? credo, propter quod et loquor.
domine, tu scis. nonne tibi prolocutus sum aduersum me delicta mea, deus meus, et tu dimisisti impietatem cordis mei?
non iudicio contendo tecum, qui ueritas es; et ego nolo fallere
me ipsum, ne mentiatur iniquitas mea sibi. non ergo iudicio
contendo tecum, quia, si iniquitates obseruaueris, domine,
domine, quis sustinebit?

7. Sed tamen sine me loqui apud misericordiam tuam, me **6**
terram et cinerem sine tamen loqui, quoniam ecce misericordia tua est, non homo, inrisor meus, cui loquor. et tu fortasse inrides me, sed conuersus misereberis mei. quid enim
est quod uolo dicere, domine, nisi quia nescio unde uenerim
huc, in istam dico uitam mortalem an mortem uitalem? nescio. et susceperunt me consolationes miserationum tuarum,
sicut audiui a parentibus carnis meae, ex quo et in qua me
formasti in tempore; non enim ego memini. exceperunt ergo
me consolationes lactis humani, nec mater mea uel nutrices
meae sibi ubera implebant, sed tu mihi per eas dabas alimentum infantiae secundum institutionem tuam et diuitias usque
ad fundum rerum dispositas. tu etiam mihi dabas nolle amplius quam dabas, et nutrientibus me dare mihi uelle quod eis
dabas: dare enim mihi per ordinatum affectum uolebant quo

abundabant ex te. nam bonum erat eis bonum meum ex eis,
quod ex eis non, sed per eas erat: ex te quippe bona omnia,
deus, et ex deo meo salus mihi uniuersa. quod animaduerti
postmodum, clamante te mihi per haec ipsa, quae tribuis intus
et foris. nam tunc sugere noram et adquiescere delectationibus, flere autem offensiones carnis meae, nihil amplius.

8. post et ridere coepi, dormiens primo, deinde uigilans.
hoc enim de me mihi indicatum est et credidi, quoniam sic uidemus alios infantes; nam ista mea non memini. et ecce paulatim sentiebam ubi essem, et uoluntates meas uolebam ostendere eis per quos implerentur, et non poteram, quia illae intus
erant, foris autem illi, nec ullo suo sensu ualebant introire in
animam meam. itaque iactabam membra et uoces, signa similia uoluntatibus meis, pauca quae poteram, qualia poteram:
non enim erant ueresimilia. et cum mihi non obtemperabatur
uel non intellecto uel ne obesset, indignabar non subditis maioribus et liberis non seruientibus et me de illis flendo uindica-
bam. tales esse infantes didici quos discere potui, et me talem
fuisse magis mihi ipsi indicauerunt nescientes quam scientes
nutritores mei.

9. et ecce infantia mea olim mortua est et ego uiuo. tu autem, domine, qui et semper uiuis et nihil moritur in te, quoniam ante primordia saeculorum et ante omne quod uel ante
dici potest, tu es et deus es dominusque omnium quae creasti,
et apud te rerum omnium instabilium stant causae, et rerum
omnium mutabilium immutabiles manent origines, et omnium
inrationalium et temporalium sempiternae uiuunt rationes,
dic mihi supplici tuo, deus, et misericors misero tuo dic mihi,
utrum alicui iam aetati meae mortuae successerit infantia
mea. an illa est, quam egi intra uiscera matris meae? nam et de
illa mihi nonnihil indicatum est et praegnantes ipse uidi femi-
nas. quid ante hanc etiam, dulcedo mea, deus meus? fuine
alicubi aut aliquis? nam quis mihi dicat ista, non habeo; nec
pater nec mater potuerunt nec aliorum experimentum nec

memoria mea. an inrides me ista quaerentem teque de hoc
quod noui laudari a me iubes et confiteri me tibi?

10. confiteor tibi, domine caeli et terrae, laudem dicens
tibi de primordiis et infantia mea, quae non memini. et dedisti
ea homini ex aliis de se conicere et auctoritatibus etiam mu-
liercularum multa de se credere. eram enim et uiuebam etiam
tunc, et signa, quibus sensa mea nota aliis facerem, iam in fine
infantiae quaerebam. unde hoc tale animal nisi abs te, domine? an quisquam se faciendi erit artifex? aut ulla uena tra-
hitur aliunde, qua esse et uiuere currat in nos, praeterquam
quod tu facis nos, domine, cui esse et uiuere non aliud atque
aliud, quia summe esse ac summe uiuere idipsum est? summus
enim es et non mutaris, neque peragitur in te hodiernus dies,
et tamen in te peragitur, quia in te sunt et ista omnia: non
enim haberent uias transeundi, nisi contineres ea. et quoniam
anni tui non deficiunt, anni tui hodiernus dies. et quam multi
iam dies nostri et patrum nostrorum per hodiernum tuum
transierunt et ex illo acceperunt modos et utcumque extiterunt, et transibunt adhuc alii et accipient et utcumque existent.
tu autem idem ipse es et omnia crastina atque ultra omniaque
hesterna et retro hodie facies, hodie fecisti. quid ad me, si quis
non intellegat? gaudeat et ipse dicens: quid est hoc? gaudeat
etiam sic, et amet non inueniendo inuenire potius quam
inueniendo non inuenire te.

11. Exaudi, deus. uae peccatis hominum! et homo dicit haec,   7
et misereris eius, quoniam tu fecisti eum et peccatum non fecisti in eo. quis me commemorat peccatum infantiae meae,
quoniam nemo mundus a peccato coram te, nec infans cuius
est unius diei uita super terram? quis me commemorat? an quilibet tantillus nunc paruulus, in quo uideo quod non memini
de me? quid ergo tunc peccabam? an quia uberibus inhiabam
plorans? nam si nunc faciam, non quidem uberibus, sed escae
congruenti annis meis ita inhians, deridebor atque reprehen-
dar iustissime. tunc ergo reprehendenda faciebam, sed quia

reprehendentem intellegere non poteram, nec mos reprehen-
di me nec ratio sinebat, nam extirpamus et eicimus ista cre-
scentes. nec uidi quemquam scientem, cum aliquid purgat,
bona proicere. an pro tempore etiam illa bona erant, flendo
petere etiam quod noxie daretur, indignari acriter non subiectis hominibus liberis et maioribus hisque, a quibus genitus
est, multisque praeterea prudentioribus non ad nutum uoluntatis obtemperantibus feriendo nocere niti quantum potest,
quia non oboeditur imperiis, quibus perniciose oboediretur?
ita imbecillitas membrorum infantilium innocens est, non animus infantium. uidi ego et expertus sum zelantem paruulum:
nondum loquebatur et intuebatur pallidus amaro aspectu
conlactaneum suum. quis hoc ignorat? expiare se dicunt ista
matres atque nutrices nescio quibus remediis. nisi uero et
ista innocentia est, in fonte lactis ubertim manante atque ab-
undante opis egentissimum et illo adhuc uno alimento uitam
ducentem consortem non pati. sed blande tolerantur haec,
non quia nulla uel parua, sed quia aetatis accessu peritura
sunt. quod licet probes, cum ferri aequo animo eadem ipsa
non possunt, quando in aliquo annosiore deprehenduntur.

12. tu itaque, domine deus meus, qui dedisti uitam infanti
et corpus, quod ita, ut uidemus, instruxisti sensibus, compe-
gisti membris, figura decorasti proque eius uniuersitate atque
incolumitate omnes conatus animantis insinuasti, iubes me
laudare te in istis et confiteri tibi et psallere nomini tuo, altissime, quia deus es omnipotens et bonus, etiamsi sola ista
fecisses, quae nemo alius potest facere nisi tu, une, a quo
est omnis modus, formosissime, qui formas omnia et lege tua
ordinas omnia. hanc ergo aetatem, domine, quam me uixisse
non memini, de qua aliis credidi et quam me egisse ex aliis in-
fantibus conieci, quamquam ista multum fida coniectura sit,
piget me adnumerare huic uitae meae quam uiuo in hoc saeculo. quantum enim attinet ad obliuionis meae tenebras, par
illi est quam uixi in matris utero. quod si et in iniquitate conceptus sum et in peccatis mater mea me in utero aluit, ubi, oro

te, deus meus, ubi, domine, ego, seruus tuus, ubi aut quando
innocens fui? sed ecce omitto illud tempus: et quid mihi iam
cum eo est, cuius nulla uestigia recolo?

13. Nonne ab infantia huc pergens ueni in pueritiam? uel **8**
potius ipsa in me uenit et successit infantiae? nec discessit illa:
quo enim abiit? et tamen iam non erat. non enim eram infans
qui non farer, sed iam puer loquens eram. et memini hoc, et
unde loqui didiceram post aduerti. non enim docebant me
maiores homines praebentes mihi uerba certo aliquo ordine
doctrinae, sicut paulo post litteras, sed ego ipse mente, quam
dedisti mihi, deus meus, cum gemitibus et uocibus uariis et
uariis membrorum motibus edere uellem sensa cordis mei, ut
uoluntati pareretur, nec ualerem quae uolebam omnia nec
quibus uolebam omnibus, prensabam memoria. cum ipsi ap-
pellabant rem aliquam et cum secundum eam uocem corpus ad
aliquid mouebant, uidebam, et tenebam hoc ab eis uocari rem
illam, quod sonabant cum eam uellent ostendere. hoc autem
eos uelle ex motu corporis aperiebatur tamquam uerbis natu-
ralibus omnium gentium, quae fiunt uultu et nutu oculorum ceterorumque membrorum actu et sonitu uocis indicante
affectionem animi in petendis, habendis, reiciendis fugiendis-
ue rebus. ita uerba in uariis sententiis locis suis posita et cre-
bro audita quarum rerum signa essent paulatim conligebam
measque iam uoluntates edomito in eis signis ore per haec
enuntiabam. sic cum his, inter quos eram, uoluntatum enun-
tiandarum signa communicaui, et uitae humanae procellosam
societatem altius ingressus sum, pendens ex parentum auctori-
tate nutuque maiorum hominum.

14. Deus, deus meus, quas ibi miserias expertus sum et ludi- **9**
ficationes, quandoquidem recte mihi uiuere puero id proponebatur, obtemperare monentibus ut in hoc saeculo florerem et
excellerem linguosis artibus ad honorem hominum et falsas
diuitias famulantibus. inde in scholam datus sum ut discerem
litteras, in quibus quid utilitatis esset ignorabam miser. et
tamen, si segnis in discendo essem, uapulabam. laudabatur

enim hoc a maioribus, et multi ante nos uitam istam agentes
praestruxerant aerumnosas uias, per quas transire cogebamur
multiplicato labore et dolore filiis Adam. inuenimus autem,
domine, homines rogantes te et didicimus ab eis, sentientes
te, ut poteramus, esse magnum aliquem, qui posses etiam non
apparens sensibus nostris exaudire nos et subuenire nobis.
nam puer coepi rogare te, auxilium et refugium meum, et in
tuam inuocationem rumpebam nodos linguae meae et roga-
bam te paruus non paruo affectu, ne in schola uapularem. et
cum me non exaudiebas, quod non erat ad insipientiam mihi,
ridebantur a maioribus hominibus usque ab ipsis parentibus,
qui mihi accidere mali nihil uolebant, plagae meae, magnum
tunc et graue malum meum.

15. estne quisquam, domine, tam magnus animus, prae-
grandi affectu tibi cohaerens, estne, inquam, quisquam – facit
enim hoc quaedam etiam stoliditas: est ergo – qui tibi pie
cohaerendo ita sit affectus granditer, ut eculeos et ungulas
atque huiuscemodi uaria tormenta, pro quibus effugiendis tibi
per uniuersas terras cum timore magno supplicatur, ita parui
aestimet, diligens eos qui haec acerbissime formidant, quemadmodum parentes nostri ridebant tormenta quibus pueri a
magistris affligebamur? non enim aut minus ea metuebamus
aut minus te de his euadendis deprecabamur, et peccabamus
tamen minus scribendo aut legendo aut cogitando de litteris,
quam exigebatur a nobis. non enim deerat, domine, memoria
uel ingenium, quae nos habere uoluisti pro illa aetate satis, sed
delectabat ludere et uindicabatur in nos ab eis qui talia utique
agebant. sed maiorum nugae negotia uocantur, puerorum autem talia cum sint, puniuntur a maioribus, et nemo miseratur
pueros uel illos uel utrosque. nisi uero approbat quisquam
bonus rerum arbiter uapulasse me, quia ludebam pila puer
et eo ludo impediebar quominus celeriter discerem litteras,
quibus maior deformius luderem. aut aliud faciebat idem ipse
a quo uapulabam, qui si in aliqua quaestiuncula a condoctore

suo uictus esset, magis bile atque inuidia torqueretur quam
ego, cum in certamine pilae a conlusore meo superabar?

16. Et tamen peccabam, domine deus, ordinator et creator 10
rerum omnium naturalium, peccatorum autem tantum ordinator, domine deus meus, peccabam faciendo contra praecepta parentum et magistrorum illorum. poteram enim postea
bene uti litteris, quas uolebant ut discerem quocumque animo
illi mei. non enim meliora eligens inoboediens eram, sed
amore ludendi, amans in certaminibus superbas uictorias et
scalpi aures meas falsis fabellis, quo prurirent ardentius, eadem curiositate magis magisque per oculos emicante in spectacula, ludos maiorum; quos tamen qui edunt, ea dignitate
praediti excellunt, ut hoc paene omnes optent paruulis suis,
quos tamen caedi libenter patiuntur, si spectaculis talibus im-
pediantur ab studio quo eos ad talia edenda cupiunt per-
uenire. uide ista, domine, misericorditer, et libera nos iam
inuocantes te, libera etiam eos qui nondum te inuocant, ut
inuocent te et liberes eos.

17. Audieram enim ego adhuc puer de uita aeterna pro- 11
missa nobis per humilitatem domini dei nostri descendentis ad
superbiam nostram, et signabar iam signo crucis eius et condiebar eius sale iam inde ab utero matris meae, quae multum
sperauit in te. uidisti, domine, cum adhuc puer essem et quo-
dam die pressu stomachi repente aestuarem paene moriturus,
uidisti, deus meus, quoniam custos meus iam eras, quo motu
animi et qua fide baptismum Christi tui, dei et domini mei,
flagitaui a pietate matris meae et matris omnium nostrum,
ecclesiae tuae. et conturbata mater carnis meae, quoniam et
sempiternam salutem meam carius parturiebat corde casto in
fide tua, iam curaret festinabunda ut sacramentis salutari-
bus initiarer et abluerer, te, domine Iesu, confitens in remis-
sionem peccatorum, nisi statim recreatus essem. dilata est
itaque mundatio mea, quasi necesse esset ut adhuc sordidarer,
si uiuerem, quia uidelicet post lauacrum illud maior et

periculosior in sordibus delictorum reatus foret. ita iam credebam et illa et omnis domus, nisi pater solus, qui tamen non
euicit in me ius maternae pietatis, quominus in Christum crederem, sicut ille nondum crediderat. nam illa satagebat ut tu
mihi pater esses, deus meus, potius quam ille, et in hoc ad-
iuuabas eam, ut superaret uirum, cui melior seruiebat, quia et
in hoc tibi utique id iubenti seruiebat.

18. rogo te, deus meus, uellem scire, si tu etiam uelles, quo
consilio dilatus sum ne tunc baptizarer, utrum bono meo mihi
quasi laxata sint lora peccandi. an non laxata sunt? unde ergo
etiam nunc de aliis atque aliis sonat undique in auribus nostris: 'sine illum, faciat; nondum enim baptizatus est.' et tamen
in salute corporis non dicimus: 'sine uulneretur amplius; nondum enim sanatus est.' quanto ergo melius et cito sanarer et id
ageretur mecum meorum meaque diligentia, ut recepta salus
animae meae tuta esset tutela tua, qui dedisses eam. melius
uero. sed quot et quanti fluctus impendere temptationum post
pueritiam uidebantur, nouerat eos iam illa mater et terram
per eos, unde postea formarer, quam ipsam iam effigiem committere uolebat.

12   19. In ipsa tamen pueritia, de qua mihi minus quam de
adulescentia metuebatur, non amabam litteras et me in eas
urgeri oderam, et urgebar tamen et bene mihi fiebat, nec faciebam ego bene: non enim discerem, nisi cogerer; nemo autem
inuitus bene facit, etiamsi bonum est quod facit. nec qui me
urgebant, bene faciebant, sed bene mihi fiebat abs te, deus
meus. illi enim non intuebantur quo referrem quod me discere
cogebant, praeterquam ad satiandas insatiabiles cupiditates
copiosae inopiae et ignominiosae gloriae. tu uero, cui numerati sunt capilli nostri, errore omnium qui mihi instabant ut
discerem utebaris ad utilitatem meam, meo autem qui discere
nolebam utebaris ad poenam meam, qua plecti non eram
indignus, tantillus puer et tantus peccator. ita de non bene
facientibus tu bene faciebas mihi et de peccante me ipso iuste

retribuebas mihi. iussisti enim et sic est, ut poena sua sibi sit
omnis inordinatus animus.

20. Quid autem erat causae, cur Graecas litteras oderam, **13**
quibus puerulus imbuebar, ne nunc quidem mihi satis explo-
ratum est. adamaueram enim Latinas, non quas primi magistri, sed quas docent qui grammatici uocantur. nam illas
primas, ubi legere et scribere et numerare discitur, non minus
onerosas poenalesque habebam quam omnes Graecas. unde
tamen et hoc nisi de peccato et uanitate uitae, qua caro eram
et spiritus ambulans et non reuertens? nam utique meliores,
quia certiores, erant primae illae litterae, quibus fiebat in me
et factum est et habeo illud ut et legam, si quid scriptum inue-
nio, et scribam ipse, si quid uolo, quam illae quibus tenere cogebar Aeneae nescio cuius errores oblitus errorum meorum et
plorare Didonem mortuam, quia se occidit ab amore, cum interea me ipsum in his a te morientem, deus, uita mea, siccis
oculis ferrem miserrimus.

21. quid enim miserius misero non miserante se ipsum
et flente Didonis mortem, quae fiebat amando Aenean, non
flente autem mortem suam, quae fiebat non amando te, deus,
lumen cordis mei et panis oris intus animae meae et uirtus
maritans mentem meam et sinum cogitationis meae? non te
amabam, et fornicabar abs te, et fornicanti sonabat undique:
'euge, euge.' amicitia enim mundi huius fornicatio est abs te et
'euge, euge' dicitur, ut pudeat, si non ita homo sit. et haec non
flebam, et flebam Didonem extinctam ferroque extrema secutam, sequens ipse extrema condita tua relicto te et terra iens in
terram. et si prohiberer ea legere, dolerem, quia non legerem
quod dolerem. talis dementia honestiores et uberiores litterae
putantur quam illae quibus legere et scribere didici.

22. sed nunc in anima mea clamet deus meus, et ueritas tua
dicat mihi: non est ita, non est ita: melior est prorsus doctrina
illa prior. nam ecce paratior sum obliuisci errores Aeneae atque omnia eius modi quam scribere et legere. at enim uela

pendent liminibus grammaticarum scholarum, sed non illa
magis honorem secreti quam tegimentum erroris significant.
non clament aduersus me quos iam non timeo, dum confiteor
tibi quae uult anima mea, deus meus, et adquiesco in repre-
hensione malarum uiarum mearum, ut diligam bonas uias
tuas, non clament aduersus me uenditores grammaticae uel
emptores, quia, si proponam eis interrogans, utrum uerum
sit quod Aenean aliquando Carthaginem uenisse poeta dicit,
indoctiores nescire se respondebunt, doctiores autem etiam
negabunt uerum esse. at si quaeram, quibus litteris scribatur
Aeneae nomen, omnes mihi qui haec didicerunt uerum re-
spondent secundum id pactum et placitum quo inter se homines ista signa firmarunt. item si quaeram quid horum maiore
uitae huius incommodo quisque obliuiscatur, legere et scribere an poetica illa figmenta, quis non uideat quid respon-
surus sit qui non est penitus oblitus sui? peccabam ergo puer
cum illa inania istis utilioribus amore praeponebam, uel potius
ista oderam, illa amabam. iam uero unum et unum duo, duo
et duo quattuor, odiosa cantio mihi erat, et dulcissimum spectaculum uanitatis equus ligneus plenus armatis et Troiae in-
cendium atque ipsius umbra Creusae.

14　　23. Cur ergo Graecam etiam grammaticam oderam talia
cantantem? nam et Homerus peritus texere tales fabellas et
dulcissime uanus est, mihi tamen amarus erat puero. credo
etiam Graecis pueris Vergilius ita sit, cum eum sic discere co-
guntur ut ego illum. uidelicet difficultas, difficultas omnino
ediscendae linguae peregrinae, quasi felle aspergebat omnes
suauitates Graecas fabulosarum narrationum. nulla enim
uerba illa noueram et saeuis terroribus ac poenis ut nossem
instabatur mihi uehementer. nam et Latina aliquando infans
utique nulla noueram et tamen aduertendo didici sine ullo
metu atque cruciatu, inter etiam blandimenta nutricum et
ioca adridentium et laetitias adludentium. didici uero illa sine
poenali onere urgentium, cum me urgeret cor meum ad pa-
rienda concepta sua, et qua non esset, nisi aliqua uerba didi-

cissem non a docentibus sed a loquentibus, in quorum et ego
auribus parturiebam quidquid sentiebam. hinc satis elucet
maiorem habere uim ad discenda ista liberam curiositatem
quam meticulosam necessitatem. sed illius fluxum haec restringit legibus tuis, deus, legibus tuis a magistrorum ferulis
usque ad temptationes martyrum, ualentibus legibus tuis mi-
scere salubres amaritudines reuocantes nos ad te a iucunditate
pestifera, qua recessimus a te.

24. Exaudi, domine, deprecationem meam, ne deficiat ani- **15**
ma mea sub disciplina tua neque deficiam in confitendo tibi
miserationes tuas, quibus eruisti me ab omnibus uiis meis
pessimis, ut dulcescas mihi super omnes seductiones quas
sequebar, et amem te ualidissime, et amplexer manum tuam
totis praecordiis meis, et eruas me ab omni temptatione usque in finem. ecce enim tu, domine, rex meus et deus meus,
tibi seruiat quidquid utile puer didici, tibi seruiat quod
loquor et scribo et lego et numero, quoniam cum uana discerem, tu disciplinam dabas mihi, et in eis uanis peccata delectationum mearum dimisisti mihi. didici enim in eis multa
uerba utilia; sed et in rebus non uanis disci possunt, et ea uia
tuta est, in qua pueri ambularent.

25. Sed uae tibi, flumen moris humani! quis resistet tibi? **16**
quamdiu non siccaberis? quousque uolues Euae filios in mare
magnum et formidulosum, quod uix transeunt qui lignum
conscenderint? nonne ego in te legi et tonantem Iouem et
adulterantem? et utique non posset haec duo, sed actum est, ut
haberet auctoritatem ad imitandum uerum adulterium lenocinante falso tonitru. quis autem paenulatorum magistrorum
audit aure sobria ex eodem puluere hominem clamantem
et dicentem: 'fingebat haec Homerus et humana ad deos
transferebat; diuina mallem ad nos'? sed uerius dicitur quod
fingebat haec quidem ille, sed hominibus flagitiosis diuina
tribuendo, ne flagitia flagitia putarentur et ut quisquis ea
fecisset, non homines perditos, sed caelestes deos uideretur
imitatus.

26. et tamen, o flumen tartareum, iactantur in te fili hominum cum mercedibus, ut haec discant, et magna res agitur
cum hoc agitur publice in foro, in conspectu legum supra
mercedem salaria decernentium, et saxa tua percutis et sonas
dicens: 'hinc uerba discuntur, hinc adquiritur eloquentia rebus persuadendis sententiisque explicandis maxime necessaria.' ita uero non cognosceremus uerba haec, imbrem et
aureum et gremium et fucum et templa caeli et alia uerba
quae in eo loco scripta sunt, nisi Terentius induceret nequam
adulescentem proponentem sibi Iouem ad exemplum stupri,
dum spectat tabulam quandam pictam in pariete ubi inerat
pictura haec, Iouem quo pacto Danaae misisse aiunt in gremium quondam imbrem aureum, fucum factum mulieri? et
uide, quemadmodum se concitat ad libidinem quasi caelesti
magisterio:

'at quem deum (inquit), qui templa caeli summo sonitu
    concutit!
ego homuncio id non facerem? ego illud uero feci ac libens.'

non omnino per hanc turpitudinem uerba ista commodius
discuntur, sed per haec uerba turpitudo ista confidentius per-
petratur. non accuso uerba quasi uasa electa atque pretiosa,
sed uinum erroris, quod in eis nobis propinabatur ab ebriis
doctoribus, et nisi biberemus, caedebamur nec appellare ad
aliquem iudicem sobrium licebat. et tamen ego, deus meus,
in cuius conspectu iam secura est recordatio mea, libenter
haec didici et eis delectabar miser et ob hoc bonae spei puer
appellabar.

17 27. Sine me, deus meus, dicere aliquid et de ingenio meo,
munere tuo, in quibus a me deliramentis atterebatur. proponebatur enim mihi negotium animae meae satis inquietum
praemio laudis et dedecoris uel plagarum metu, ut dicerem
uerba Iunonis irascentis et dolentis quod non posset Italia
Teucrorum auertere regem, quae numquam Iunonem dixisse
audieram. sed figmentorum poeticorum uestigia errantes
sequi cogebamur et tale aliquid dicere solutis uerbis, quale

poeta dixisset uersibus: et ille dicebat laudabilius, in quo pro
dignitate adumbratae personae irae ac doloris similior affectus eminebat uerbis sententias congruenter uestientibus. ut
quid mihi illud, o uera uita, deus meus, quod mihi recitanti
acclamabatur prae multis coaetaneis et conlectoribus meis?
nonne ecce illa omnia fumus et uentus? itane aliud non erat,
ubi exerceretur ingenium et lingua mea? laudes tuae, domine,
laudes tuae per scripturas tuas suspenderent palmitem cordis mei, et non raperetur per inania nugarum turpis praeda
uolatilibus. non enim uno modo sacrificatur transgressoribus
angelis.

28. Quid autem mirum, quod in uanitates ita ferebar et a **18**
te, deus meus, ibam foras, quando mihi imitandi propone-
bantur homines, qui aliqua facta sua non mala, si cum barbarismo aut soloecismo enuntiarent, reprehensi confundebantur,
si autem libidines suas integris et rite consequentibus uerbis
copiose ornateque narrarent, laudati gloriabantur? uides haec,
domine, et taces longanimis et multum misericors et uerax.
numquid semper tacebis? et nunc eruis de hoc immanissimo
profundo quaerentem te animam et sitientem delectationes
tuas, et cuius cor dicit tibi: quaesiui uultum tuum; uultum
tuum, domine, requiram: nam longe a uultu tuo in affectu tenebroso. non enim pedibus aut spatiis locorum itur abs te aut
reditur ad te, aut uero filius ille tuus minor equos uel currus
uel naues quaesiuit aut auolauit pinna uisibili aut moto po-
plite iter egit, ut in longinqua regione uiuens prodige dissi-
paret quod dederas proficiscenti, dulcis pater quia dederas, et
egeno redeunti dulcior: in affectu ergo libidinoso, id enim est
tenebroso atque id est longe a uultu tuo.

29. uide domine deus, et patienter, ut uides, uide quomodo
diligenter obseruent filii hominum pacta litterarum et syllabarum accepta a prioribus locutoribus et a te accepta aeterna
pacta perpetuae salutis neglegant, ut qui illa sonorum uetera
placita teneat aut doceat, si contra disciplinam grammaticam
sine aspiratione primae syllabae hominem dixerit, magis dis-
pliceat hominibus quam si contra tua praecepta hominem

oderit, cum sit homo. quasi uero quemlibet inimicum hominem perniciosius sentiat quam ipsum odium, quo in eum inri-
tatur, aut uastet quisquam persequendo alium grauius quam
cor suum uastat inimicando. et certe non est interior litterarum scientia quam scripta conscientia, id se alteri facere quod
nolit pati. quam tu secretus es, habitans in excelsis in silentio,
deus solus magnus, lege infatigabili spargens poenales caecita-
tes supra inlicitas cupiditates, cum homo eloquentiae famam
quaeritans ante hominem iudicem circumstante hominum
multitudine inimicum suum odio immanissimo insectans uigi-
lantissime cauet, ne per linguae errorem dicat 'inter hominibus' et ne per mentis furorem hominem auferat ex hominibus,
non cauet.

19 30. Horum ego puer morum in limine iacebam miser, et
huius harenae palaestra erat illa, ubi magis timebam barba-
rismum facere quam cauebam, si facerem, non facientibus
inuidere. dico haec et confiteor tibi, deus meus, in quibus lau-
dabar ab eis, quibus placere tunc mihi erat honeste uiuere.
non enim uidebam uoraginem turpitudinis in quam proiectus
eram ab oculis tuis. nam in illis iam quid me foedius fuit, ubi
etiam talibus displicebam fallendo innumerabilibus mendaciis
et paedagogum et magistros et parentes amore ludendi, studio
spectandi nugatoria et imitandi ludicra inquietudine? furta
etiam faciebam de cellario parentum et de mensa, uel gula
imperitante uel ut haberem quod darem pueris, ludum suum
mihi, quo pariter utique delectabantur, tamen uendentibus. in
quo etiam ludo fraudulentas uictorias ipse uana excellentiae
cupiditate uictus saepe aucupabar. quid autem tam nolebam
pati atque atrociter, si deprehenderem, arguebam, quam id
quod aliis faciebam? et, si deprehensus arguerer, saeuire magis quam cedere libebat. istane est innocentia puerilis? non est,
domine, non est, oro te, deus meus. nam haec ipsa sunt, quae
a paedagogis et magistris, a nucibus et pilulis et passeribus,
ad praefectos et reges, aurum, praedia, mancipia, haec ipsa
omnino succedentibus maioribus aetatibus transeunt, sicuti

ferulis maiora supplicia succedunt. humilitatis ergo signum in
statura pueritiae, rex noster, probasti, cum aisti: talium est
regnum caelorum.

31. Sed tamen, domine. tibi excellentissimo atque optimo **20**
conditori et rectori uniuersitatis, deo nostro gratias, etiamsi
me puerum tantum esse uoluisses. eram enim etiam tunc,
uiuebam atque sentiebam meamque incolumitatem, uestigium
secretissimae unitatis ex qua eram, curae habebam, custodiebam interiore sensu integritatem sensuum meorum inque ipsis
paruis paruarumque rerum cogitationibus ueritate delectabar.
falli nolebam, memoria uigebam, locutione instruebar, amicitia mulcebar, fugiebam dolorem, abiectionem, ignorantiam.
quid in tali animante non mirabile atque laudabile? at ista
omnia dei mei dona sunt. non mihi ego dedi haec: et bona
sunt, et haec omnia ego. bonus ergo est qui fecit me, et ipse est
bonum meum et illi exulto bonis omnibus, quibus etiam puer
eram. hoc enim peccabam, quod non in ipso, sed in creaturis
eius me atque ceteris uoluptates, sublimitates, ueritates quaerebam, atque ita inruebam in dolores, confusiones, errores.
gratias tibi, dulcedo mea et honor meus et fiducia mea, deus
meus, gratias tibi de donis tuis; sed tu mihi ea serua. ita enim
seruabis me, et augebuntur et perficientur quae dedisti mihi,
et ero ipse tecum, quia et ut sim tu dedisti mihi.

LIBER SECVNDVS

1   1. Recordari uolo transactas foeditates meas et carnales
corruptiones animae meae, non quod eas amem, sed ut amem
te, deus meus. amore amoris tui facio istuc, recolens uias meas
nequissimas in amaritudine recogitationis meae, ut tu dulcescas mihi, dulcedo non fallax, dulcedo felix et secura, et conligens me a dispersione, in qua frustatim discissus sum dum ab
uno te auersus in multa euanui. exarsi enim aliquando satiari
inferis in adulescentia, et siluescere ausus sum uariis et umbrosis amoribus, et contabuit species mea, et computrui coram
oculis tuis placens mihi et placere cupiens oculis hominum.

2   2. Et quid erat, quod me delectabat, nisi amare et amari?
sed non tenebatur modus ab animo usque ad animum, quatenus est luminosus limes amicitiae, sed exhalabantur nebulae
de limosa concupiscentia carnis et scatebra pubertatis et obnubilabant atque obfuscabant cor meum, ut non discerneretur
serenitas dilectionis a caligine libidinis. utrumque in confuso
aestuabat et rapiebat imbecillam aetatem per abrupta cupiditatum atque mersabat gurgite flagitiorum. inualuerat super
me ira tua, et nesciebam. obsurdueram stridore catenae mortalitatis meae, poena superbiae animae meae, et ibam longius
a te, et sinebas, et iactabar et effundebar et diffluebam et
ebulliebam per fornicationes meas, et tacebas. o tardum gaudium meum! tacebas tunc, et ego ibam porro longe a te in
plura et plura sterilia semina dolorum superba deiectione et
inquieta lassitudine.

3. quis mihi modularetur aerumnam meam et nouissimarum rerum fugaces pulchritudines in usum uerteret earumque
suauitatibus metas praefigeret, ut usque ad coniugale litus exaestuarent fluctus aetatis meae, si tranquillitas in eis non poterat esse fine procreandorum liberorum contenta, sicut praescribit lex tua, domine, qui formas etiam propaginem mortis
nostrae, potens imponere lenem manum ad temperamentum
spinarum a paradiso tuo seclusarum? non enim longe est a no-

bis omnipotentia tua, etiam cum longe sumus a te. aut certe
sonitum nubium tuarum uigilantius aduerterem: tribulationem autem carnis habebunt huius modi. ego autem uobis
parco, et: bonum est homini mulierem non tangere, et: qui
sine uxore est, cogitat ea quae sunt dei, quomodo placeat deo;
qui autem matrimonio iunctus est, cogitat ea quae sunt
mundi, quomodo placeat uxori. has ergo uoces exaudirem
uigilantior et abscisus propter regnum caelorum felicior expectarem amplexus tuos.

4. sed efferuui miser, sequens impetum fluxus mei relicto te,
et excessi omnia legitima tua nec euasi flagella tua: quis enim
hoc mortalium? nam tu semper aderas misericorditer saeuiens,
et amarissimis aspergens offensionibus omnes inlicitas iucun-
ditates meas, ut ita quaererem sine offensione iucundari, et
ubi hoc possem, non inuenirem quidquam praeter te, domine,
praeter te, qui fingis dolorem in praecepto et percutis ut sanes
et occidis nos, ne moriamur abs te. ubi eram et quam longe
exulabam a deliciis domus tuae anno illo sexto decimo aetatis
carnis meae, cum accepit in me sceptrum – et totas manus ei
dedi – uesania libidinis licentiosae per dedecus humanum, in-
licitae autem per leges tuas? non fuit cura meorum ruentem
excipere me matrimonio, sed cura fuit tantum ut discerem
sermonem facere quam optimum et persuadere dictione.

5. Et anno quidem illo intermissa erant studia mea, dum **3**
mihi reducto a Madauris, in qua uicina urbe iam coeperam
litteraturae atque oratoriae percipiendae gratia peregrinari,
longinquioris apud Carthaginem peregrinationis sumptus
praeparabantur animositate magis quam opibus patris, municipis Thagastensis admodum tenuis. cui narro haec? neque
enim tibi, deus meus, sed apud te narro haec generi meo, generi humano, quantulacumque ex particula incidere potest in
istas meas litteras. et ut quid hoc? ut uidelicet ego et quisquis
haec legit cogitemus de quam profundo clamandum sit ad te. et
quid propius auribus tuis, si cor confitens et uita ex fide est? quis
enim non extollebat laudibus tunc hominem, patrem meum,

quod ultra uires rei familiaris suae impenderet filio quidquid
etiam longe peregrinanti studiorum causa opus esset? multo-
rum enim ciuium longe opulentiorum nullum tale negotium
pro liberis erat, cum interea non satageret idem pater qualis
crescerem tibi aut quam castus essem, dummodo essem disertus uel desertus potius a cultura tua, deus, qui es unus uerus
et bonus dominus agri tui, cordis mei.

6. sed ubi sexto illo et decimo anno, interposito otio ex necessitate domestica, feriatus ab omni schola cum parentibus
esse coepi, excesserunt caput meum uepres libidinum, et nulla
erat eradicans manus. quin immo ubi me ille pater in balneis
uidit pubescentem et inquieta indutum adulescentia, quasi
iam ex hoc in nepotes gestiret, gaudens matri indicauit, gaudens uinulentia, in qua te iste mundus oblitus est creatorem
suum et creaturam tuam pro te amauit, de uino inuisibili per-
uersae atque inclinatae in ima uoluntatis suae. sed matris in
pectore iam inchoaueras templum tuum et exordium sanctae
habitationis tuae: nam ille adhuc catechumenus et hoc recens
erat. itaque illa exiliuit pia trepidatione ac tremore et, quamuis mihi nondum fideli, timuit tamen uias distortas, in quibus
ambulant qui ponunt ad te tergum et non faciem.

7. ei mihi! et audeo dicere tacuisse te, deus meus, cum irem
abs te longius? itane tu tacebas tunc mihi? et cuius erant nisi
tua uerba illa per matrem meam, fidelem tuam, quae cantasti
in aures meas? nec inde quidquam descendit in cor, ut facerem illud. uolebat enim illa, et secreto memini ut monuerit
cum sollicitudine ingenti, ne fornicarer maximeque ne adulterarem cuiusquam uxorem. qui mihi monitus muliebres uidebantur, quibus obtemperare erubescerem. illi autem tui erant,
et nesciebam et te tacere putabam atque illam loqui, per quam
mihi tu non tacebas, et in illa contemnebaris a me, a me, filio
eius, filio ancillae tuae, seruo tuo. sed nesciebam et praeceps
ibam tanta caecitate ut inter coaetaneos meos puderet me
minoris dedecoris, quoniam audiebam eos iactantes flagitia
sua et tanto gloriantes magis, quanto magis turpes essent, et

libebat facere non solum libidine facti uerum etiam laudis.
quid dignum est uituperatione nisi uitium? ego, ne uitu-
perarer, uitiosior fiebam, et ubi non suberat quo admisso ae-
quarer perditis, fingebam me fecisse quod non feceram, ne
uiderer abiectior quo eram innocentior, et ne uilior haberer
quo eram castior.

   8. ecce cum quibus comitibus iter agebam platearum Babyloniae et uolutabar in caeno eius tamquam in cinnamis et unguentis pretiosis. et in umbilico eius quo tenacius haererem,
calcabat me inimicus inuisibilis et seducebat me, quia ego se-
ductilis eram. non enim et illa, quae iam de medio Babylonis
fugerat, sed ibat in ceteris eius tardior, mater carnis meae, sicut monuit me pudicitiam, ita curauit quod de me a uiro suo
audierat, iamque pestilentiosum et in posterum periculosum
sentiebat, cohercere termino coniugalis affectus, si resecari ad
uiuum non poterat; non curauit hoc, quia metus erat, ne impediretur spes mea compede uxoria, non spes illa, quam in te
futuri saeculi habebat mater, sed spes litterarum, quas ut nossem nimis uolebat parens uterque, ille, quia de te prope nihil
cogitabat, de me autem inania, illa autem, quia non solum
nullo detrimento, sed etiam nonnullo adiumento ad te adipis-
cendum futura existimabat usitata illa studia doctrinae. ita
enim conicio, recolens, ut possum, mores parentum meorum.
relaxabantur etiam mihi ad ludendum habenae ultra temperamentum seueritatis in dissolutionem affectionum uariarum,
et in omnibus erat caligo intercludens mihi, deus meus, serenitatem ueritatis tuae, et prodiebat tamquam ex adipe iniquitas
mea.

   9. Furtum certe punit lex tua, domine, et lex scripta in cor-   **4**
dibus hominum, quam ne ipsa quidem delet iniquitas: quis
enim fur aequo animo furem patitur? nec copiosus adactum
inopia. et ego furtum facere uolui, et feci nulla compulsus egestate nisi penuria et fastidio iustitiae et sagina iniquitatis. nam
id furatus sum quod mihi abundabat et multo melius, nec ea re
uolebam frui quam furto appetebam, sed ipso furto et peccato.

arbor erat pirus in uicinia nostrae uineae pomis onusta nec
forma nec sapore inlecebrosis. ad hanc excutiendam atque
asportandam nequissimi adulescentuli perreximus nocte intempesta, quousque ludum de pestilentiae more in areis pro-
duxeramus, et abstulimus inde onera ingentia non ad nostras
epulas, sed uel proicienda porcis, etiamsi aliquid inde comedi-
mus, dum tamen fieret a nobis quod eo liberet, quo non liceret. ecce cor meum, deus, ecce cor meum, quod miseratus es in
imo abyssi. dicat tibi nunc, ecce, cor meum, quid ibi quaerebat, ut essem gratis malus et malitiae meae causa nulla esset
nisi malitia. foeda erat, et amaui eam; amaui perire, amaui
defectum meum, non illud ad quod deficiebam, sed defectum
meum ipsum amaui, turpis anima et dissiliens a firmamento
tuo in exterminium, non dedecore aliquid, sed dedecus
appetens.

5   10. Etenim species est pulchris corporibus et auro et
argento et omnibus, et in contactu carnis congruentia ualet
plurimum ceterisque sensibus est sua cuique accommodata
modificatio corporum. habet etiam honor temporalis et impe-
ritandi atque superandi potentia suum decus, unde etiam uindictae auiditas oritur: et tamen in cuncta haec adipiscenda non
est egrediendum abs te, domine, neque deuiandum a lege tua.
et uita, quam hic uiuimus, habet inlecebram suam propter
quendam modum decoris sui et conuenientiam cum his omnibus infimis pulchris. amicitia quoque hominum caro nodo dulcis est propter unitatem de multis animis. propter uniuersa
haec atque huius modi peccatum admittitur, dum immoderata
in ista inclinatione, cum extrema bona sint, meliora et summa
deseruntur, tu, domine deus noster, et ueritas tua et lex tua.
habent enim et haec ima delectationes, sed non sicut deus
meus, qui fecit omnia, quia in ipso delectatur iustus, et ipse
est deliciae rectorum corde.

     11. cum itaque de facinore quaeritur qua causa factum sit,
credi non solet, nisi cum appetitus adipiscendi alicuius illorum
bonorum, quae infima diximus, esse potuisse apparuerit aut

metus amittendi. pulchra sunt enim et decora, quamquam
prae bonis superioribus et beatificis abiecta et iacentia. homicidium fecit. cur fecit? adamauit eius coniugem aut praedium
aut uoluit depraedari unde uiueret, aut timuit ab illo tale aliquid amittere aut laesus ulcisci se exarsit. num homicidium
sine causa faceret ipso homicidio delectatus? quis crediderit?
nam et de quo dictum est uaecordi et nimus crudeli homine,
quod gratuito potius malus atque crudelis erat, praedicta est
tamen causa: ne per otium, inquit, torpesceret manus aut animus. quaere id quoque: cur ita? ut scilicet illa exercitatione
scelerum capta urbe honores, imperia, diuitias assequeretur et
careret metu legum et difficultate rerum propter inopiam rei
familiaris et conscientiam scelerum. nec ipse igitur Catilina
amauit facinora sua, sed utique aliud, cuius causa illa faciebat.

12. Quid ego miser in te amaui, o furtum meum, o facinus **6**
illud meum nocturnum sexti decimi anni aetatis meae? non
enim pulchrum eras, cum furtum esses. aut uero aliquid es, ut
loquar ad te? pulchra erant poma illa quae furati sumus, quoniam creatura tua erat, pulcherrime omnium, creator omnium, deus bone, deus summum bonum et bonum uerum
meum; pulchra erant illa poma, sed non ipsa concupiuit anima
mea miserabilis. erat mihi enim meliorum copia, illa autem
decerpsi tantum ut furarer. nam decerpta proieci, epulatus
inde solam iniquitatem qua laetabar fruens. nam et si quid illorum pomorum intrauit in os meum, condimentum ibi facinus erat. et nunc, domine deus meus, quaero quid me in furto
delectauerit, et ecce species nulla est: non dico sicut in aequi-
tate atque prudentia, sed neque sicut in mente hominis atque
memoria et sensibus et uegetante uita, neque sicut speciosa
sunt sidera et decora locis suis et terra et mare plena fetibus,
qui succedunt nascendo decedentibus; non saltem ut est quaedam defectiua species et umbratica uitiis fallentibus.

13. nam et superbia celsitudinem imitatur, cum tu sis unus
super omnia deus excelsus. et ambitio quid nisi honores quaerit et gloriam, cum tu sis prae cunctis honorandus unus et

gloriosus in aeternum? et saeuitia potestatum timeri uult: quis
autem timendus nisi unus deus, cuius potestati eripi aut sub-
trahi quid potest, quando aut ubi aut quo uel a quo potest?
et blanditiae lasciuientium amari uolunt: sed neque blandius
est aliquid tua caritate nec amatur quicquam salubrius quam
illa prae cunctis formosa et luminosa ueritas tua. et curiositas
affectare uidetur studium scientiae, cum tu omnia summe
noueris. ignorantia quoque ipsa atque stultitia simplicitatis et
innocentiae nomine tegitur, quia te simplicius quicquam non
reperitur. quid te autem innocentius, quandoquidem opera
sua malis inimica sunt? et ignauia quasi quietem appetit: quae
uero quies certa praeter dominum? luxuria satietatem atque
abundantiam se cupit uocari: tu es autem plenitudo et inde-
ficiens copia incorruptibilis suauitatis. effusio liberalitatis ob-
tendit umbram: sed bonorum omnium largitor affluentissimus
tu es. auaritia multa possidere uult: et tu possides omnia.
inuidentia de excellentia litigat: quid te excellentius? ira
uindictam quaerit: te iustius quis uindicat? timor insolita et
repentina exhorrescit rebus, quae amantur, aduersantia, dum
praecauet securitati: tibi enim quid insolitum? quid repenti-
num? aut quis a te separat quod diligis? aut ubi nisi apud te
firma securitas? tristitia rebus amissis contabescit, quibus se
oblectabat cupiditas, quia ita sibi nollet, sicut tibi auferri nihil
potest.

14. ita fornicatur anima, cum auertitur abs te et quaerit extra te ea quae pura et liquida non inuenit, nisi cum redit ad te.
peruerse te imitantur omnes, qui longe se a te faciunt et ex-
tollunt se aduersum te. sed etiam sic te imitando indicant
creatorem te esse omnis naturae, et ideo non esse quo a te
omni modo recedatur. quid ergo in illo furto ego dilexi, et in
quo dominum meum uel uitiose atque peruerse imitatus sum?
an libuit facere contra legem saltem fallacia, quia poten-
tatu non poteram, ut mancam libertatem captiuus imitarer,
faciendo impune quod non liceret tenebrosa omnipotentiae
similitudine? ecce est ille seruus fugiens dominum suum et

consecutus umbram. o putredo, o monstrum uitae et mortis profunditas! potuitne libere quod non licebat, non ob aliud nisi quia non licebat?

15. Quid retribuam domino, quod recolit haec memoria 7 mea et anima mea non metuit inde? diligam te, domine, et gratias agam et confitear nomini tuo, quoniam tanta dimisisti mihi mala et nefaria opera mea. gratiae tuae deputo et misericordiae tuae, quod peccata mea tamquam glaciem soluisti. gratiae tuae deputo et quaecumque non feci mala: quid enim non facere potui, qui etiam gratuitum facinus amaui? et omnia mihi dimissa esse fateor, et quae mea sponte feci mala et quae te duce non feci. quis est hominum qui suam cogitans infirmitatem audet uiribus suis tribuere castitatem atque innocentiam suam, ut minus amet te, quasi minus ei necessaria fuerit misericordia tua, qua donas peccata conuersis ad te? qui enim uocatus a te secutus est uocem tuam et uitauit ea, quae me de me ipso recordantem et fatentem legit, non me derideat ab eo medico aegrum sanari, a quo sibi praestitum est ut non aegrotaret, uel potius ut minus aegrotaret, et ideo te tantundem, immo uero amplius diligat, quia per quem me uidet tantis peccatorum meorum languoribus exui, per eum se uidet tantis peccatorum languoribus non implicari.

16. Quem fructum habui miser aliquando in his, quae nunc 8 recolens erubesco, maxime in illo furto in quo ipsum furtum amaui, nihil aliud, cum et ipsum esset nihil et eo ipso ego miserior? et tamen solus id non fecissem: sic recordor animum tunc meum, solus omnino id non fecissem. ergo amaui ibi etiam consortium eorum cum quibus id feci. non ergo nihil aliud quam furtum amaui; immo uero nihil aliud, quia et illud nihil est. quid est re uera? quis est qui doceat me, nisi qui inluminat cor meum et discernit umbras eius? quid est quod mihi uenit in mentem quaerere et discutere et considerare? quia si tunc amarem poma illa quae furatus sum et eis frui cuperem, possem etiam solus, si satis esset, committere illam iniquitatem qua peruenirem ad uoluptatem meam, nec confricatione

consciorum animorum accenderem pruritum cupiditatis meae. sed quoniam in illis pomis uoluptas mihi non erat, ea erat in ipso facinore quam faciebat consortium simul peccantium.

9   17. Quid erat ille affectus animi? certe enim plane turpis erat nimis, et uae mihi erat qui habebam illum. sed tamen quid erat? delicta quis intellegit? risus erat quasi titillato corde, quod fallebamus eos qui haec a nobis fieri non putabant et uehementer nolebant. cur ergo eo me delectabat, quo id non faciebam solus? an quia etiam nemo facile solus ridet? nemo quidem facile, sed tamen etiam solos et singulos homines, cum alius nemo praesens est, uincit risus aliquando, si aliquid nimie ridiculum uel sensibus occurrit uel animo. at ego illud solus non facerem, non facerem omnino solus. ecce est coram te, deus meus, uiua recordatio animae meae. solus non facerem furtum illud, in quo me non libebat id quod furabar, sed quia furabar: quod me solum facere prorsus non liberet, nec facerem. o nimis inimica amicitia, seductio mentis inuestigabilis, ex ludo et ioco nocendi auiditas et alieni damni appetitus, nulla lucri mei, nulla ulciscendi libidine, sed cum dicitur 'eamus, faciamus', et pudet non esse impudentem.

10   18. Quis exaperit istam tortuosissimam et implicatissimam nodositatem? foeda est; nolo in eam intendere, nolo eam uidere. te uolo, iustitia et innocentia, pulchra et decora honestis luminibus et insatiabili satietate. quies est apud te ualde et uita imperturbabilis. qui intrat in te, intrat in gaudium domini sui et non timebit et habebit se optime in optimo. defluxi abs te ego et erraui, deus meus, nimis deuius a stabilitate tua in adulescentia et factus sum mihi regio egestatis.

LIBER TERTIVS

1. Veni Carthaginem, et circumstrepebat me undique sar- **1**
tago flagitiosorum amorum. nondum amabam et amare amabam et secretiore indigentia oderam me minus indigentem.
quaerebam quid amarem, amans amare, et oderam securitatem et uiam sine muscipulis, quoniam fames mihi erat intus ab
interiore cibo, te ipso, deus meus, et ea fame non esuriebam,
sed eram sine desiderio alimentorum incorruptibilium, non
quia plenus eis eram, sed quo inanior, fastidiosior. et ideo non
bene ualebat anima mea et ulcerosa proiciebat se foras, mise-
rabiliter scalpi auida contactu sensibilium. sed si non haberent
animam, non utique amarentur. amare et amari dulce mihi
erat magis, si et amantis corpore fruerer. uenam igitur amicitiae coinquinabam sordibus concupiscentiae candoremque
eius obnubilabam de tartaro libidinis, et tamen foedus atque
inhonestus, elegans et urbanus esse gestiebam abundanti uanitate. rui etiam in amorem, quo cupiebam capi. deus meus, misericordia mea, quanto felle mihi suauitatem illam et quam
bonus aspersisti, quia et amatus sum et perueni occulte ad
uinculum fruendi et conligabar laetus aerumnosis nexibus, ut
caederer uirgis ferreis ardentibus zeli et suspicionum et timo-
rum et irarum atque rixarum.

2. Rapiebant me spectacula theatrica plena imaginibus mi- **2**
seriarum mearum et fomitibus ignis mei. quid est, quod ibi
homo uult dolere cum spectat luctuosa et tragica, quae tamen
pati ipse nollet? et tamen pati uult ex eis dolorem spectator et
dolor ipse est uoluptas eius. quid est nisi mirabilis insania?
nam eo magis eis mouetur quisque, quo minus a talibus affectibus sanus est, quamquam, cum ipse patitur, miseria, cum
aliis compatitur, misericordia dici solet. sed qualis tandem
misericordia in rebus fictis et scenicis? non enim ad sub-
ueniendum prouocatur auditor, sed tantum ad dolendum
inuitatur, et actori earum imaginum amplius fauet, cum amplius dolet. et si calamitates illae hominum, uel antiquae uel

falsae, sic agantur ut qui spectat non doleat, abscedit inde
fastidiens et reprehendens; si autem doleat, manet intentus et
gaudens lacrimat.

3. ergo amantur et dolores. certe omnis homo gaudere uult.
an cum miserum esse neminem libeat, libet tamen esse miseri-
cordem, quod quia non sine dolore est, hac una causa amantur dolores? et hoc de illa uena amicitiae est. sed quo uadit?
quo fluit? ut quid decurrit in torrentem picis bullientis, aestus
immanes taetrarum libidinum, in quos ipsa mutatur et uertitur per nutum proprium de caelesti serenitate detorta atque deiecta? repudietur ergo misericordia? nequaquam. ergo
amentur dolores aliquando. sed caue immunditiam, anima
mea, sub tutore deo meo, deo patrum nostrorum et laudabili
et superexaltato in omnia saecula, caue immunditiam. neque
enim nunc non misereor, sed tunc in theatris congaudebam
amantibus cum sese fruebantur per flagitia, quamuis haec
imaginarie gererent in ludo spectaculi; cum autem sese amit-
tebant, quasi misericors contristabar, et utrumque delectabat
tamen. nunc uero magis misereor gaudentem in flagitio quam
uelut dura perpessum detrimento perniciosae uoluptatis et
amissione miserae felicitatis. haec certe uerior misericordia,
sed non in ea delectat dolor. nam etsi approbatur officio caritatis qui dolet miserum, mallet tamen utique non esse quod
doleret qui germanitus misericors est. si enim est maliuola
beniuolentia, quod fieri non potest, potest et ille, qui ueraci-
ter sinceriterque misereretur, cupere esse miseros, ut miserea-
tur. nonnullus itaque dolor approbandus, nullus amandus est.
hoc enim tu, domine deus, qui animas amas, longe alteque
purius quam nos et incorruptibilius misereris, quod nullo dolore sauciaris. et ad haec quis idoneus?

4. at ego tunc miser dolere amabam, et quaerebam ut esset
quod dolerem, quando mihi in aerumna aliena et falsa et
saltatoria ea magis placebat actio histrionis, meque alliciebat
uehementius qua mihi lacrimae excutiebantur. quid autem
mirum, cum infelix pecus aberrans a grege tuo et impatiens

custodiae tuae turpi scabie foedarer? et inde erant dolorum amores, non quibus altius penetrarer – non enim amabam talia perpeti, qualia spectare – sed quibus auditis et fictis tamquam in superficie raderer: quos tamen quasi ungues scalpentium feruidus tumor et tabes et sanies horrida consequebatur. talis uita mea numquid uita erat, deus meus?

5. Et circumuolabat super me fidelis a longe misericordia **3** tua. in quantas iniquitates distabui, et sacrilegam curiositatem secutus sum, ut deserentem te deduceret me ad ima infida et circumuentoria obsequia daemoniorum, quibus immolabam facta mea mala, et in omnibus flagellabas me! ausus sum etiam in celebritate sollemnitatum tuarum, intra parietes ecclesiae tuae, concupiscere et agere negotium procurandi fructus mortis: unde me uerberasti grauibus poenis, sed nihil ad culpam meam, o tu praegrandis misericordia mea, deus meus, refugium meum a terribilibus nocentibus, in quibus uagatus sum praefidenti collo ad longe recedendum a te, amans uias meas et non tuas, amans fugitiuam libertatem.

6. habebant et illa studia, quae honesta uocabantur, ductum suum intuentem fora litigiosa, ut excellerem in eis, hoc laudabilior, quo fraudulentior. tanta est caecitas hominum de caecitate etiam gloriantium. et maior iam eram in schola rhetoris, et gaudebam superbe et tumebam typho, quamquam longe sedatior, domine, tu scis, et remotus omnino ab euersionibus, quas faciebant euersores – hoc enim nomen scaeuum et diabolicum uelut insigne urbanitatis est – inter quos uiuebam pudore impudenti, quia talis non eram: et cum eis eram et amicitiis eorum delectabar aliquando, a quorum semper factis abhorrebam, hoc est ab euersionibus, quibus proterue insectabantur ignotorum uerecundiam, quam proturbarent gratis inludendo atque inde pascendo maliuolas laetitias suas. nihil est illo actu similius actibus daemoniorum. quid itaque uerius quam euersores uocarentur, euersi plane prius ipsi atque peruersi, deridentibus eos et seducentibus fallacibus occulte spiritibus in eo ipso, quod alios inridere amant et fallere?

4   7. Inter hos ego imbecilla tunc aetate discebam libros eloquentiae, in qua eminere cupiebam fine damnabili et uentoso
per gaudia uanitatis humanae, et usitato iam discendi ordine
perueneram in librum cuiusdam Ciceronis, cuius linguam fere
omnes mirantur, pectus non ita. sed liber ille ipsius exhor-
tationem continet ad philosophiam et uocatur Hortensius. ille
uero liber mutauit affectum meum, et ad te ipsum, domine,
mutauit preces meas, et uota ac desideria mea fecit alia. uiluit
mihi repente omnis uana spes, et immortalitatem sapientiae
concupiscebam aestu cordis incredibili, et surgere coeperam
ut ad te redirem. non enim ad acuendam linguam, quod uidebar emere maternis mercedibus, cum agerem annum aetatis
undeuicensimum iam defuncto patre ante biennium, non ergo
ad acuendam linguam referebam illum librum neque mihi lo-
cutionem, sed quod loquebatur persuaserat.

8. quomodo ardebam, deus meus, quomodo ardebam reuolare a terrenis ad te, et nesciebam quid ageres mecum!
apud te est enim sapientia. amor autem sapientiae nomen
Graecum habet philosophiam, quo me accendebant illae litterae. sunt qui seducant per philosophiam magno et blan-
do et honesto nomine colorantes et fucantes errores suos, et
prope omnes qui ex illis et supra temporibus tales erant no-
tantur in eo libro et demonstrantur, et manifestatur ibi saluti-
fera illa admonitio spiritus tui per seruum tuum bonum et
pium: uidete, ne quis uos decipiat per philosophiam et ina-
nem seductionem secundum traditionem hominum, secundum elementa huius mundi et non secundum Christum, quia
in ipso inhabitat omnis plenitudo diuinitatis corporaliter. et
ego illo tempore, scis tu, lumen cordis mei, quoniam nondum
mihi haec apostolica nota erant, hoc tamen solo delectabar in
illa exhortatione, quod non illam aut illam sectam, sed ipsam
quaecumque esset sapientiam ut diligerem et quaererem et
assequerer et tenerem atque amplexarer fortiter, excitabar
sermone illo et accendebar et ardebam, et hoc solum me in
tanta flagrantia refrangebat, quod nomen Christi non erat

ibi, quoniam hoc nomen secundum misericordiam tuam, domine, hoc nomen saluatoris mei, filii tui, in ipso adhuc lacte
matris tenerum cor meum pie biberat et alte retinebat, et
quidquid sine hoc nomine fuisset quamuis litteratum et expolitum et ueridicum non me totum rapiebat.

9. Itaque institui animum intendere in scripturas sanctas et **5**
uidere quales essent. et ecce uideo rem non compertam superbis neque nudatam pueris, sed incessu humilem, successu excelsam et uelatam mysteriis, et non eram ego talis ut intrare in
eam possem aut inclinare ceruicem ad eius gressus. non enim
sicut modo loquor, ita sensi, cum attendi ad illam scripturam,
sed uisa est mihi indigna quam Tullianae dignitati compararem. tumor enim meus refugiebat modum eius et acies mea
non penetrabat interiora eius. uerum autem illa erat quae
cresceret cum paruulis, sed ego dedignabar esse paruulus et
turgidus fastu mihi grandis uidebar.

10. Itaque incidi in homines superbe delirantes, carnales ni- **6**
mis et loquaces, in quorum ore laquei diaboli et uiscum confec-
tum commixtione syllabarum nominis tui et domini Iesu Christi
et paracleti consolatoris nostri spiritus sancti. haec nomina non
recedebant de ore eorum, sed tenus sono et strepitu linguae;
ceterum cor inane ueri. et dicebant 'ueritas et ueritas' et multum eam dicebant mihi, et nusquam erat in eis, sed falsa
loquebantur non de te tantum, qui uere ueritas es, sed etiam
de istis elementis huius mundi, creatura tua, de quibus etiam
uera dicentes philosophos transgredi debui prae amore tuo,
mi pater summe bone, pulchritudo pulchrorum omnium. o
ueritas, ueritas, quam intime etiam tum medullae animi mei
suspirabant tibi, cum te illi sonarent mihi frequenter et multi-
pliciter uoce sola et libris multis et ingentibus! et illa erant
fercula, in quibus mihi esurienti te inferebatur pro te sol et
luna, pulchra opera tua, sed tamen opera tua, non tu, nec ipsa
prima. priora enim spiritalia opera tua quam ista corporea
quamuis lucida et caelestia. at ego nec priora illa, sed te ipsam, te, ueritas, in qua non est commutatio nec momenti

obumbratio, esuriebam et sitiebam. et apponebantur adhuc mihi in illis ferculis phantasmata splendida, quibus iam melius erat amare istum solem saltem istis oculis uerum quam illa falsa animo decepto per oculos. et tamen, quia te putabam, manducabam, non auide quidem, quia nec sapiebas in ore meo sicuti es – neque enim tu eras illa figmenta inania – nec nutriebar eis, sed exhauriebar magis. cibus in somnis simillimus est cibis uigilantium, quo tamen dormientes non aluntur: dormiunt enim. at illa nec similia erant ullo modo tibi, sicut nunc mihi locuta es, quia illa erant corporalia phantasmata, falsa corpora, quibus certiora sunt uera corpora ista, quae uidemus uisu carneo, siue caelestia siue terrestria, cum pecudibus et uolatilibus. uidemus haec, et certiora sunt, quam cum imaginamur ea. et rursus certius imaginamur ea quam ex eis suspicamur alia grandiora et infinita, quae omnino nulla sunt. qualibus ego tunc pascebar inanibus, et non pascebar. at tu, amor meus, in quem deficio ut fortis sim, nec ista corpora es quae uidemus quamquam in caelo, nec ea quae non uidemus ibi, quia tu ista condidisti nec in summis tuis conditionibus habes. quanto ergo longe es a phantasmatis illis meis, phantasmatis corporum quae omnino non sunt! quibus certiores sunt phantasiae corporum eorum quae sunt, et eis certiora corpora, quae tamen non es. sed nec anima es, quae uita est corporum – ideo melior uita corporum certiorque quam corpora – sed tu uita es animarum, uita uitarum, uiuens te ipsa, et non mutaris, uita animae meae.

11. ubi ergo mihi tunc eras et quam longe? et longe peregrinabar abs te exclusus et a siliquis porcorum, quos de siliquis pascebam. quanto enim meliores grammaticorum et poetarum fabellae quam illa decipula! nam uersus et carmen et Medea uolans utiliores certe quam quinque elementa uarie fucata propter quinque antra tenebrarum, quae omnino nulla sunt et occidunt credentem. nam uersum et carmen etiam ad uera pulmenta transfero; uolantem autem Medeam etsi cantabam, non adserebam, etsi cantari audiebam, non credebam:

illa autem credidi. uae, uae! quibus gradibus deductus in profunda inferi, quippe laborans et aestuans inopia ueri, cum te,
deus meus – tibi enim confiteor, qui me miseratus es et nondum confitentem – cum te non secundum intellectum mentis,
quo me praestare uoluisti beluis, sed secundum sensum carnis
quaererem. tu autem eras interior intimo meo et superior
summo meo. offendi illam mulierem audacem, inopem prudentiae, aenigma Salomonis, sedentem super sellam in foribus
et dicentem: panes occultos libenter edite et aquam dulcem
furtiuam bibite. quae me seduxit, quia inuenit foris habitantem in oculo carnis meae et talia ruminantem apud me
qualia per illum uorassem.

   12. Nesciebam enim aliud, uere quod est, et quasi acutule **7**
mouebar ut suffragarer stultis deceptoribus, cum a me quaere-
rent unde malum, et utrum forma corporea deus finiretur et
haberet capillos et ungues, et utrum iusti existimandi essent
qui haberent uxores multas simul et occiderent homines et sa-
crificarent de animalibus. quibus rerum ignarus perturbabar,
et recedens a ueritate ire in eam mihi uidebar, quia non noueram malum non esse nisi priuationem boni usque ad quod
omnino non est. quod unde uiderem, cuius uidere usque ad
corpus erat oculis et animo usque ad phantasma? et non noueram deum esse spiritum, non cui membra essent per longum et
latum nec cui esse moles esset, quia moles in parte minor est
quam in toto suo, et si infinita sit, minor est in aliqua parte
certo spatio definita quam per infinitum, et non est tota ubique sicut spiritus, sicut deus. et quid in nobis esset secundum
quod essemus et recte in scriptura diceremur ad imaginem dei,
prorsus ignorabam.

   13. et non noueram iustitiam ueram interiorem, non ex
consuetudine iudicantem sed ex lege rectissima dei omni-
potentis, qua formarentur mores regionum et dierum pro re-
gionibus et diebus, cum ipsa ubique ac semper esset, non alibi
alia nec alias aliter, secundum quam iusti essent Abraham et
Isaac et Iacob et Moyses et Dauid et illi omnes laudati ore dei;

sed eos ab imperitis iudicari iniquos, iudicantibus ex humano
die et uniuersos mores humani generis ex parte moris sui me-
tientibus, tamquam si quis nescius in armamentis quid cui
membro accommodatum sit, ocrea uelit caput contegi et galea
calciari et murmuret quod non apte conueniat, aut in uno die
indicto a promeridianis horis iustitio quisquam stomachetur
non sibi concedi quid uenale proponere, quia mane con-
cessum est, aut in una domo uideat aliquid tractari manibus a
quoquam seruo quod facere non sinatur qui pocula ministrat,
aut aliquid post praesepia fieri quod ante mensam pro-
hibeatur, et indignetur, cum sit unum habitaculum et una fa-
milia, non ubique atque omnibus idem tribui. sic sunt isti qui
indignantur, cum audierint illo saeculo licuisse iustis aliquid
quod isto non licet iustis, et quia illis aliud praecepit deus, istis
aliud pro temporalibus causis, cum eidem iustitiae utrique ser-
uierint, cum in uno homine et in uno die et in unis aedibus ui-
deant aliud alii membro congruere, et aliud iam dudum licuisse, post horam non licere, quiddam in illo angulo permitti
aut iuberi, quod in isto iuxta uetetur et uindicetur. numquid
iustitia uaria est et mutabilis? sed tempora, quibus praesidet,
non pariter eunt; tempora enim sunt. homines autem, quorum
uita super terram breuis est, quia sensu non ualent causas
contexere saeculorum priorum aliarumque gentium, quas experti non sunt, cum his quas experti sunt, in uno autem corpore uel die uel domo facile possunt uidere quid cui membro,
quibus momentis, quibus partibus personisue congruat, in illis
offenduntur, hic seruiunt.

14. haec ego tunc nesciebam et non aduertebam, et ferie-
bant undique ista oculos meos, et non uidebam, et cantabam
carmina et non mihi licebat ponere pedem quemlibet ubilibet,
sed in alio atque alio metro aliter atque aliter et in uno aliquo
uersu non omnibus locis eundem pedem; et ars ipsa qua cane-
bam non habebat aliud alibi, sed omnia simul. et non intuebar
iustitiam, cui seruirent boni et sancti homines, longe excellentius atque sublimius habere simul omnia quae praecipit et

nulla ex parte uariari et tamen uariis temporibus non omnia
simul, sed propria distribuentem ac praecipientem. et repre-
hendebam caecus pios patres non solum, sicut deus iuberet
atque inspiraret, utentes praesentibus, uerum quoque, sicut
deus reuelaret, futura praenuntiantes.

15. Numquid aliquando aut alicubi iniustum est diligere **8**
deum ex toto corde ex tota anima ex tota mente et diligere
proximum tamquam te ipsum? itaque flagitia quae sunt contra
naturam ubique ac semper detestanda atque punienda sunt,
qualia Sodomitarum fuerunt. quae si omnes gentes facerent,
eodem criminis reatu diuina lege tenerentur, quae non sic fecit
homines ut se illo uterentur modo. uiolatur quippe ipsa societas, quae cum deo nobis esse debet, cum eadem natura, cuius
ille auctor est, libidinis peruersitate polluitur. quae autem
contra mores hominum sunt flagitia pro morum diuersitate ui-
tanda sunt, ut pactum inter se ciuitatis aut gentis consuetudine
uel lege firmatum nulla ciuis aut peregrini libidine uioletur.
turpis enim omnis pars uniuerso suo non congruens. cum
autem deus aliquid contra morem aut pactum quorumlibet
iubet, etsi numquam ibi factum est, faciendum est, et si omis-
sum, instaurandum, et si institutum non erat, instituendum est.
si enim regi licet in ciuitate, cui regnat, iubere aliquid, quod
neque ante illum quisquam nec ipse umquam iusserat, et non
contra societatem ciuitatis eius obtemperatur, immo contra
societatem non obtemperatur – generale quippe pactum est
societatis humanae oboedire regibus suis – quanto magis deo
regnatori uniuersae creaturae suae ad ea quae iusserit sine
dubitatione seruiendum est! sicut enim in potestatibus societatis humanae maior potestas minori ad oboediendum praepo-
nitur, ita deus omnibus.

16. item in facinoribus, ubi libido est nocendi siue per con-
tumeliam siue per iniuriam et utrumque uel ulciscendi causa,
sicut inimico inimicus, uel adipiscendi alicuius extra com-
modi, sicut latro uiatori, uel euitandi mali, sicut ei qui timetur,
uel inuidendo, sicut feliciori miserior aut in aliquo prosperatus

ei quem sibi aequari timet aut aequalem dolet, uel sola uoluptate alieni mali, sicut spectatores gladiatorum aut inrisores
aut inlusores quorumlibet. haec sunt capita iniquitatis, quae
pullulant principandi et spectandi et sentiendi libidine aut una
aut duabus earum aut simul omnibus, et uiuitur male aduersus tria et septem, psalterium decem chordarum, decalogum
tuum, deus altissime et dulcissime. sed quae flagitia in te, qui
non corrumperis? aut quae aduersus te facinora, cui noceri
non potest? sed hoc uindicas quod in se homines perpetrant,
quia etiam cum in te peccant, impie faciunt in animas suas,
et mentitur iniquitas sibi siue corrumpendo ac peruertendo
naturam suam, quam tu fecisti et ordinasti, uel immoderate
utendo concessis rebus uel in non concessa flagrando in eum
usum qui est contra naturam; aut rei tenentur animo et uerbis
saeuientes aduersus te et aduersus stimulum calcitrantes, aut
cum diruptis limitibus humanae societatis laetantur audaces
priuatis conciliationibus aut diremptionibus, prout quidque
delectauerit aut offenderit. et ea fiunt cum tu derelinqueris,
fons uitae, qui es unus et uerus creator et rector uniuersitatis,
et priuata superbia diligitur in parte unum falsum. itaque pietate humili reditur in te, et purgas nos a consuetudine mala, et
propitius es peccatis confitentium, et exaudis gemitus compeditorum, et soluis a uinculis quae nobis fecimus, si iam non
erigamus aduersum te cornua falsae libertatis, auaritia plus
habendi et damno totum amittendi, amplius amando proprium nostrum quam te, omnium bonum.

9 17. Sed inter flagitia et facinora et tam multas iniquitates
sunt peccata proficientium, quae a bene iudicantibus et uitu-
perantur ex regula perfectionis et laudantur spe frugis sicut
herba segetis. et sunt quaedam similia uel flagitio uel facinori
et non sunt peccata, quia nec te offendunt, dominum deum
nostrum, nec sociale consortium, cum conciliantur aliqua in
usum uitae congrua et tempori, et incertum est an libidine
habendi, aut puniuntur corrigendi studio potestate ordinata,
et incertum est an libidine nocendi. multa itaque facta, quae

hominibus improbanda uiderentur, testimonio tuo approbata
sunt, et multa laudata ab hominibus te teste damnantur, cum
saepe se aliter habet species facti et aliter facientis animus atque articulus occulti temporis. cum uero aliquid tu repente
inusitatum et improuisum imperas, etiamsi hoc aliquando
uetuisti, quamuis causam imperii tui pro tempore occultes et
quamuis contra pactum sit aliquorum hominum societatis,
quis dubitet esse faciendum, quando ea iusta est societas hominum quae seruit tibi? sed beati qui te imperasse sciunt. fiunt
enim omnia a seruientibus tibi, uel ad exhibendum quod ad
praesens opus est, uel ad futura praenuntianda.

18. Haec ego nesciens inridebam illos sanctos seruos et **10**
prophetas tuos. et quid agebam cum inridebam eos, nisi ut inriderer abs te sensim atque paulatim perductus ad eas nugas,
ut crederem ficum plorare cum decerpitur et matrem eius ar-
borem lacrimis lacteis? quam tamen ficum si comedisset aliquis sanctus, alieno sane, non suo scelere decerptam, misceret
uisceribus et anhelaret de illa angelos, immo uero particulas
dei gemendo in oratione atque ructando: quae particulae
summi et ueri dei ligatae fuissent in illo pomo, nisi electi sancti
dente ac uentre soluerentur. et credidi miser magis esse misericordiam praestandam fructibus terrae quam hominibus,
propter quos nascerentur. si quis enim esuriens peteret qui
manichaeus non esset, quasi capitali supplicio damnanda buccella uideretur, si ei daretur.

19. Et misisti manum tuam ex alto et de hac profunda cali- **11**
gine eruisti animam meam, cum pro me fleret ad te mea
mater, fidelis tua, amplius quam flent matres corporea funera.
uidebat enim illa mortem meam ex fide et spiritu quem habebat ex te, et exaudisti eam, domine, exaudisti eam nec despex-
isti lacrimas eius, cum profluentes rigarent terram sub oculis
eius in omni loco orationis eius: exaudisti eam. nam unde illud
somnium quo eam consolatus es, ut uiuere mecum cederet et
habere mecum eandem mensam in domo? quod nolle coeperat
auersans et detestans blasphemias erroris mei. uidit enim se

stantem in quadam regula lignea et aduenientem ad se iuuenem splendidum hilarem atque adridentem sibi, cum illa esset
maerens et maerore confecta. qui cum causas ab ea quaesisset
maestitiae suae cotidianarumque lacrimarum, docendi, ut adsolet, non discendi gratia, atque illa respondisset perditionem
meam se plangere, iussisse illum, quo secura esset, atque ad-
monuisse, ut attenderet et uideret, ubi esset illa, ibi esse et me.
quod illa ubi attendit, uidit me iuxta se in eadem regula stantem. unde hoc, nisi quia erant aures tuae ad cor eius, o tu bone
omnipotens, qui sic curas unumquemque nostrum tamquam
solum cures, et sic omnes tamquam singulos?

　　20. unde illud etiam, quod cum mihi narrasset ipsum uisum
et ego ad id trahere conarer ut illa se potius non desperaret
futuram esse quod eram, continuo sine aliqua haesitatione:
'non' inquit, 'non enim mihi dictum est: ubi ille, ibi et tu,
sed: ubi tu, ibi et ille'. confiteor tibi, domine, recordationem
meam, quantum recolo, quod saepe non tacui, amplius me isto
per matrem uigilantem responso tuo, quod tam uicina inter-
pretationis falsitate turbata non est et tam cito uidit quod ui-
dendum fuit, quod ego certe, antequam dixisset, non uideram,
etiam tum fuisse commotum quam ipso somnio, quo feminae
piae gaudium tanto post futurum ad consolationem tunc prae-
sentis sollicitudinis tanto ante praedictum est. nam nouem
ferme anni secuti sunt, quibus ego in illo limo profundi ac tene-
bris falsitatis, cum saepe surgere conarer et grauius alliderer,
uolutatus sum, cum tamen illa uidua casta, pia et sobria, quales
amas, iam quidem spe alacrior, sed fletu et gemitu non se-
gnior, non desineret horis omnibus orationum suarum de me
plangere ad te, et intrabant in conspectum tuum preces eius,
et me tamen dimittebas adhuc uolui et inuolui illa caligine.

12　　21. Et dedisti alterum responsum interim quod recolo. nam
et multa praetereo, propter quod propero ad ea quae me magis urguent confiteri tibi, et multa non memini. dedisti ergo
alterum per sacerdotem tuum, quendam episcopum nutritum
in ecclesia et exercitatum in libris tuis. quem cum illa femina

rogasset ut dignaretur mecum conloqui et refellere errores
meos et dedocere me mala ac docere bona – faciebat enim
hoc, quos forte idoneos inuenisset – noluit ille, prudenter sane,
quantum sensi postea. respondit enim me adhuc esse indoci-
lem, eo quod inflatus essem nouitate haeresis illius et nonnullis
quaestiunculis iam multos imperitos exagitassem, sicut illa in-
dicauerat ei. 'sed' inquit 'sine illum ibi. tantum roga pro eo
dominum: ipse legendo reperiet quis ille sit error et quanta
impietas.' simul etiam narrauit se quoque paruulum a seducta
matre sua datum fuisse manichaeis, et omnes paene non le-
gisse tantum uerum etiam scriptitasse libros eorum, sibique
apparuisse nullo contra disputante et conuincente quam esset
illa secta fugienda: itaque fugisse. quae cum ille dixisset atque
illa nollet adquiescere, sed instaret magis deprecando et ubertim flendo, ut me uideret et mecum dissereret, ille iam substomachans taedio: 'uade' inquit 'a me; ita uiuas, fieri non
potest ut filius istarum lacrimarum pereat.' quod illa ita se accepisse inter conloquia sua mecum saepe recordabatur, ac si
de caelo sonuisset.

LIBER QVARTVS

1 1. Per idem tempus annorum nouem, ab undeuicensimo anno aetatis meae usque ad duodetricensimum, seducebamur et seducebamus, falsi atque fallentes in uariis cupiditatibus, et palam per doctrinas, quas liberales uocant, occulte autem falso nomine religionis, hic superbi, ibi superstitiosi, ubique uani, hac popularis gloriae sectantes inanitatem usque ad theatricos plausus et contentiosa carmina et agonem coronarum faenearum et spectaculorum nugas et intemperantiam libidinum, illac autem purgari nos ab istis sordibus expetentes, cum eis qui appellarentur electi et sancti afferremus escas, de quibus nobis in officina aqualiculi sui fabricarent angelos et deos per quos liberaremur. et sectabar ista atque faciebam cum amicis meis per me ac mecum deceptis. inrideant me adrogantes et nondum salubriter prostrati et elisi a te, deus meus, ego tamen confitear tibi dedecora mea in laude tua. sine me, obsecro, et da mihi circumire praesenti memoria praeteritos circuitus erroris mei et immolare tibi hostiam iubilationis. quid enim sum ego mihi sine te nisi dux in praeceps? aut quid sum, cum mihi bene est, nisi sugens lac tuum aut fruens te cibo, qui non corrumpitur? et quis homo est quilibet homo, cum sit homo? sed inrideant nos fortes et potentes, nos autem infirmi et inopes confiteamur tibi.

2 2. Docebam in illis annis artem rhetoricam et uictoriosam loquacitatem uictus cupiditate uendebam. malebam tamen, domine, tu scis, bonos habere discipulos, sicut appellantur boni, et eos sine dolo docebam dolos, non quibus contra caput innocentis agerent, sed aliquando pro capite nocentis. et, deus, uidisti de longinquo lapsantem in lubrico et in multo fumo scintillantem fidem meam, quam exhibebam in illo magisterio diligentibus uanitatem et quaerentibus mendacium, socius eorum. in illis annis unam habebam non eo quod legitimum uocatur coniugio cognitam, sed quam indagauerat uagus ardor inops prudentiae, sed unam tamen, ei quoque seruans

tori fidem; in qua sane experirer exemplo meo quid distaret
inter coniugalis placiti modum, quod foederatum esset gene-
randi gratia, et pactum libidinosi amoris, ubi proles etiam
contra uotum nascitur, quamuis iam nata cogat se diligi.

3. recolo etiam, cum mihi theatrici carminis certamen inire
placuisset, mandasse mihi nescio quem haruspicem, quid ei
dare uellem mercedis ut uincerem, me autem foeda illa sacramenta detestatum et abominatum respondisse, nec si co-
rona illa esset immortaliter aurea muscam pro uictoria mea
necari sinere. necaturus enim erat ille in sacrificiis suis animantia, et illis honoribus inuitaturus mihi suffragatura daemonia uidebatur. sed hoc quoque malum non ex tua castitate
repudiaui, deus cordis mei. non enim amare te noueram, qui
nisi fulgores corporeos cogitare non noueram. talibus enim
figmentis suspirans anima nonne fornicatur abs te et fidit in
falsis et pascit uentos? sed uidelicet sacrificari pro me nollem
daemonibus, quibus me illa superstitione ipse sacrificabam.
quid est enim aliud uentos pascere quam ipsos pascere, hoc est
errando eis esse uoluptati atque derisui?

4. Ideoque illos planos, quos mathematicos uocant, plane **3**
consulere non desistebam, quod quasi nullum eis esset sacrificium et nullae preces ad aliquem spiritum ob diuinationem
dirigerentur. quod tamen christiana et uera pietas conse-
quenter repellit et damnat. bonum est enim confiteri tibi, domine, et dicere: miserere mei: cura animam meam, quoniam
peccaui tibi, neque ad licentiam peccandi abuti indulgentia
tua, sed meminisse dominicae uocis: ecce sanus factus es; iam
noli peccare, ne quid tibi deterius contingat. quam totam illi
salubritatem interficere conantur, cum dicunt: 'de caelo tibi
est ineuitabilis causa peccandi' et 'Venus hoc fecit aut Saturnus
aut Mars', scilicet ut homo sine culpa sit, caro et sanguis et superba putredo, culpandus sit autem caeli ac siderum creator et
ordinator. et quis est hic nisi deus noster, suauitas et origo
iustitiae, qui reddes unicuique secundum opera eius et cor
contritum et humiliatum non spernis?

5. erat eo tempore uir sagax, medicinae artis peritissimus
atque in ea nobilissimus, qui pro consule manu sua coronam
illam agonisticam imposuerat non sano capiti meo, sed non ut
medicus. nam illius morbi tu sanator, qui resistis superbis, humilibus autem das gratiam. numquid tamen etiam per illum
senem defuisti mihi aut destitisti mederi animae meae? quia
enim factus ei eram familiarior et eius sermonibus – erant
enim sine uerborum cultu uiuacitate sententiarum iucundi et
graues – assiduus et fixus inhaerebam, ubi cognouit ex con-
loquio meo libris genethliacorum esse me deditum, benigne ac
paterne monuit ut eos abicerem neque curam et operam rebus
utilibus necessariam illi uanitati frustra impenderem, dicens
ita se illa didicisse, ut eius professionem primis annis aetatis
suae deferre uoluisset qua uitam degeret, et si Hippocraten intellexisset, et illas utique litteras potuisse intellegere: et tamen
non ob aliam causam se postea illis relictis medicinam assecu-
tum, nisi quod eas falsissimas comperisset et nollet uir grauis
decipiendis hominibus uictum quaerere. 'at tu' inquit 'quo te in
hominibus sustentas, rhetoricam tenes, hanc autem fallaciam
libero studio, non necessitate rei familiaris sectaris. quo magis
mihi te oportet de illa credere, qui eam tam perfecte discere
elaboraui, quam ex ea sola uiuere uolui'. a quo ego cum quae-
sissem quae causa ergo faceret ut multa inde uera pronuntiar-
entur, respondit ille ut potuit, uim sortis hoc facere in rerum
natura usquequaque diffusam. si enim de paginis poetae cuius-
piam longe aliud canentis atque intendentis, cum forte quis
consulit, mirabiliter consonus negotio saepe uersus exiret, mi-
randum non esse dicebat, si ex anima humana superiore
aliquo instinctu nesciente quid in se fieret, non arte, sed sorte
sonaret aliquid, quod interrogantis rebus factisque concineret.

6. et hoc quidem ab illo uel per illum procurasti mihi, et
quid ipse postea per me ipsum quaererem, in memoria mea
deliniasti. tunc autem nec ipse nec carissimus meus Nebridius,
adulescens ualde bonus et ualde castus, inridens totum illud
diuinationis genus, persuadere mihi potuerunt, ut haec abice-

rem, quoniam me amplius ipsorum auctorum mouebat auctoritas, et nullum certum quale quaerebam documentum adhuc
inueneram, quo mihi sine ambiguitate appareret, quae ab eis
consultis uera dicerentur, forte uel sorte, non arte inspectorum
siderum dici.

7. In illis annis, quo primum tempore in municipio, quo **4**
natus sum, docere coeperam, comparaueram amicum socie-
tate studiorum nimis carum, coaeuum mihi et conflorentem
flore adulescentiae. mecum puer creuerat et pariter in scholam ieramus pariterque luseramus. sed nondum erat sic amicus, quamquam ne tunc quidem sic, uti est uera amicitia, quia
non est uera nisi cum eam tu agglutinas inter haerentes tibi
caritate diffusa in cordibus nostris per spiritum sanctum, qui
datus est nobis. sed tamen dulcis erat nimis, cocta feruore parilium studiorum. nam et a fide uera, quam non germanitus et
penitus adulescens tenebat, deflexeram eum in superstitiosas
fabellas et perniciosas, propter quas me plangebat mater. mecum iam errabat in animo ille homo, et non poterat anima
mea sine illo. et ecce tu imminens dorso fugitiuorum tuorum,
deus ultionum et fons misericordiarum simul, qui conuertis
nos ad te miris modis, ecce abstulisti hominem de hac uita,
cum uix expleuisset annum in amicitia mea, suaui mihi super
omnes suauitates illius uitae meae.

8. quis laudes tuas enumerat unus in se uno, quas expertus
est? quid tunc fecisti, deus meus, et quam inuestigabilis abyssus iudiciorum tuorum? cum enim laboraret ille febribus,
iacuit diu sine sensu in sudore laetali et, cum desperaretur,
baptizatus est nesciens, me non curante et praesumente id
retinere potius animam eius quod a me acceperat, non quod
in nescientis corpore fiebat. longe autem aliter erat. nam recreatus est et saluus factus, statimque, ut primo cum eo loqui
potui – potui autem mox, ut ille potuit, quando non discede-
bam et nimis pendebamus ex inuicem – temptaui apud illum
inridere, tamquam et illo inrisuro mecum baptismum, quem
acceperat mente atque sensu absentissimus. sed tamen iam se

accepisse didicerat. at ille ita me exhorruit ut inimicum ad-
monuitque mirabili et repentina libertate, ut, si amicus esse
uellem, talia sibi dicere desinerem. ego autem stupefactus
atque turbatus distuli omnes motus meos, ut conualesceret
prius essetque idoneus uiribus ualetudinis, cum quo agere possem quod uellem. sed ille abreptus dementiae meae, ut apud
te seruaretur consolationi meae: post paucos dies me absente
repetitur febribus et defungitur.

9. quo dolore contenebratum est cor meum, et quidquid
aspiciebam mors erat. et erat mihi patria supplicium et paterna
domus mira infelicitas, et quidquid cum illo communicaue-
ram, sine illo in cruciatum immanem uerterat. expectabant
eum undique oculi mei, et non dabatur; et oderam omnia,
quod non haberent eum. nec mihi iam dicere poterant, 'ecce
ueniet', sicut cum uiueret, quando absens erat. factus eram
ipse mihi magna quaestio et interrogabam animam meam
quare tristis esset et quare conturbaret me ualde, et nihil
nouerat respondere mihi. et si dicebam 'spera in deum', iuste
non obtemperabat, quia uerior erat et melior homo quem ca-
rissimum amiserat, quam phantasma in quod sperare iubeba-
tur. solus fletus erat dulcis mihi et successerat amico meo in
deliciis animi mei.

5   10. Et nunc, domine, iam illa transierunt, et tempore lenitum est uulnus meum. possumne audire abs te, qui ueritas es,
et admouere aurem cordis mei ori tuo, ut dicas mihi cur fletus
dulcis sit miseris? an tu, quamuis ubique adsis, longe abiecisti a
te miseriam nostram, et tu in te manes, nos autem in experimentis uoluimur? et tamen nisi ad aures tuas ploraremus,
nihil residui de spe nostra fieret. unde igitur suauis fructus de
amaritudine uitae carpitur gemere et flere et suspirare et
conqueri? an hoc ibi dulce est, quod speramus exaudire te?
recte istuc in precibus, quia desiderium perueniendi habent.
num in dolore amissae rei et luctu, quo tunc operiebar? neque enim sperabam reuiuescere illum aut hoc petebam lacrimis, sed tantum dolebam et flebam. miser enim eram et

amiseram gaudium meum. an et fletus res amara est et prae
fastidio rerum, quibus fruebamur, et tunc ab eis abhorremus,
delectat?

11. Quid autem ista loquor? non enim tempus quaerendi **6**
nunc est, sed confitendi tibi. miser eram, et miser est omnis
animus uinctus amicitia rerum mortalium, et dilaniatur cum
eas amittit, et tunc sentit miseriam qua miser est et antequam
amittat eas. sic ego eram illo tempore et flebam amarissime et
requiescebam in amaritudine. ita miser eram et habebam ca-
riorem illo amico meo uitam ipsam miseram. nam quamuis
eam mutare uellem, nollem tamen amittere magis quam illum,
et nescio an uellem uel pro illo, sicut de Oreste et Pylade traditur, si non fingitur, qui uellent pro inuicem uel simul mori,
qua morte peius eis erat non simul uiuere. sed in me nescio
quis affectus nimis huic contrarius ortus erat et taedium
uiuendi erat in me grauissimum et moriendi metus. credo, quo
magis illum amabam, hoc magis mortem, quae mihi eum ab-
stulerat, tamquam atrocissimam inimicam oderam et timebam, et eam repente consumpturam omnes homines putabam,
quia illum potuit. sic eram omnino, memini. ecce cor meum.
deus meus, ecce intus; uide, quia memini, spes mea, qui me
mundas a talium affectionum immunditia, dirigens oculos
meos ad te et euellens de laqueo pedes meos. mirabar enim
ceteros mortales uiuere, quia ille, quem quasi non moriturum
dilexeram, mortuus erat, et me magis, quia ille alter eram,
uiuere illo mortuo mirabar. bene quidam dixit de amico
suo dimidium animae suae. nam ego sensi animam meam et
animam illius unam fuisse animam in duobus corporibus, et
ideo mihi horrori erat uita, quia nolebam dimidius uiuere,
et ideo forte mori metuebam, ne totus ille moreretur, quem
multum amaueram.

12. O dementiam nescientem diligere homines humaniter! **7**
o stultum hominem immoderate humana patientem! quod ego
tunc eram. itaque aestuabam, suspirabam, flebam, turbabar,
nec requies erat nec consilium. portabam enim concisam et

cruentam animam meam impatientem portari a me, et ubi
eam ponerem non inueniebam. non in amoenis nemoribus,
non in ludis atque cantibus, nec in suaue olentibus locis, nec in
conuiuiis apparatis, neque in uoluptate cubilis et lecti, non de-
nique in libris atque carminibus adquiescebat. horrebant omnia et ipsa lux, et quidquid non erat quod ille erat improbum
et odiosum erat praeter gemitum et lacrimas: nam in eis solis
aliquantula requies. ubi autem inde auferebatur anima mea,
onerabat me grandi sarcina miseriae. ad te, domine, leuanda
erat et curanda, sciebam, sed nec uolebam nec ualebam, eo
magis quia non mihi eras aliquid solidum et firmum, cum de te
cogitabam. non enim tu eras, sed uanum phantasma et error
meus erat deus meus. si conabar eam ibi ponere, ut requie-
sceret, per inane labebatur et iterum ruebat super me, et ego
mihi remanseram infelix locus, ubi nec esse possem nec inde
recedere. quo enim cor meum fugeret a corde meo? quo a me
ipso fugerem? quo non me sequerer? et tamen fugi de patria.
minus enim eum quaerebant oculi mei ubi uidere non sole-
bant, atque a Thagastensi oppido ueni Carthaginem.

8   13. Non uacant tempora nec otiose uoluuntur per sensus
nostros: faciunt in animo mira opera. ecce ueniebant et
praeteribant de die in diem, et ueniendo et praetereundo
inserebant mihi spes alias et alias memorias, et paulatim
resarciebant me pristinis generibus delectationum, quibus
cedebat dolor meus ille; sed succedebant non quidem dolores
alii, causae tamen aliorum dolorum. nam unde me facillime
et in intima dolor ille penetrauerat, nisi quia fuderam in harenam animam meam diligendo moriturum ac si non moriturum? maxime quippe me reparabant atque recreabant aliorum
amicorum solacia, cum quibus amabam quod pro te amabam, et hoc erat ingens fabula et longum mendacium, cuius
adulterina confricatione corrumpebatur mens nostra pruriens
in auribus. sed illa mihi fabula non moriebatur, si quis amicorum meorum moreretur. alia erant quae in eis amplius capiebant animum, conloqui et conridere et uicissim beniuole

obsequi, simul legere libros dulciloquos, simul nugari et simul
honestari, dissentire interdum sine odio tamquam ipse homo
secum atque ipsa rarissima dissensione condire consensiones
plurimas, docere aliquid inuicem aut discere ab inuicem,
desiderare absentes cum molestia, suscipere uenientes cum
laetitia: his atque huius modi signis a corde amantium et
redamantium procedentibus per os, per linguam, per oculos et
mille motus gratissimos quasi fomitibus conflare animos et ex
pluribus unum facere.

14. Hoc est quod diligitur in amicis, et sic diligitur ut rea **9**
sibi sit humana conscientia si non amauerit redamantem aut si
amantem non redamauerit, nihil quaerens ex eius corpore
praeter indicia beniuolentiae. hinc ille luctus si quis moriatur,
et tenebrae dolorum et uersa dulcedine in amaritudinem cor
madidum et ex amissa uita morientium mors uiuentium. beatus qui amat te et amicum in te et inimicum propter te. solus
enim nullum carum amittit cui omnes in illo cari sunt, qui non
amittitur. et quis est iste nisi deus noster, deus, qui fecit caelum et terram et implet ea, quia implendo ea fecit ea? te nemo
amittit, nisi qui dimittit, et quia dimittit, quo it aut quo fugit
nisi a te placido ad te iratum? nam ubi non inuenit legem
tuam in poena sua? et lex tua ueritas et ueritas tu.

15. Deus uirtutum, conuerte nos et ostende faciem tuam, et **10**
salui erimus. nam quoquouersum se uerterit anima hominis,
ad dolores figitur alibi praeterquam in te, tametsi figitur in
pulchris extra te et extra se. quae tamen nulla essent, nisi
essent abs te. quae oriuntur et occidunt et oriendo quasi esse
incipiunt, et crescunt ut perficiantur, et perfecta senescunt et
intereunt: et non omnia senescunt, et omnia intereunt. ergo
cum oriuntur et tendunt esse, quo magis celeriter crescunt ut
sint, eo magis festinant ut non sint. sic est modus eorum. tantum dedisti eis, quia partes sunt rerum, quae non sunt omnes
simul, sed decedendo ac succedendo agunt omnes uniuersum,
cuius partes sunt. ecce sic peragitur et sermo noster per signa
sonantia. non enim erit totus sermo, si unum uerbum non

decedat, cum sonuerit partes suas, ut succedat aliud. laudet te
ex illis anima mea, deus, creator omnium, sed non in eis figatur
glutine amore per sensus corporis. eunt enim quo ibant, ut
non sint, et conscindunt eam desideriis pestilentiosis, quoniam
ipsa esse uult et requiescere amat in eis quae amat. in illis autem non est ubi, quia non stant: fugiunt, et quis ea sequitur
sensu carnis? aut quis ea comprehendit, uel cum praesto sunt?
tardus est enim sensus carnis, quoniam sensus carnis est: ipse
est modus eius. sufficit ad aliud, ad quod factus est, ad illud
autem non sufficit, ut teneat transcurrentia ab initio debito usque ad finem debitum. in uerbo enim tuo, per quod creantur,
ibi audiunt: 'hinc et huc usque.'

11   16. Noli esse uana, anima mea, et obsurdescere in aure cordis tumultu uanitatis tuae. audi et tu: uerbum ipsum clamat ut
redeas, et ibi est locus quietis imperturbabilis, ubi non deseri-
tur amor si ipse non deserat. ecce illa discedunt ut alia suc-
cedant, et omnibus suis partibus constet infima uniuersitas.
'numquid ego aliquo discedo?' ait uerbum dei. ibi fige mansionem tuam, ibi commenda quidquid inde habes, anima mea,
saltem fatigata fallaciis. ueritati commenda quidquid tibi est
a ueritate, et non perdes aliquid, et reflorescent putria tua, et
sanabuntur omnes languores tui, et fluxa tua reformabuntur et
renouabuntur et constringentur ad te, et non te deponent quo
descendunt, sed stabunt tecum et permanebunt ad semper
stantem ac permanentem deum.

17. ut quid peruersa sequeris carnem tuam? ipsa te sequatur
conuersam. quidquid per illam sentis in parte est, et ignoras
totum cuius hae partes sunt, et delectant te tamen. sed si ad
totum comprehendendum esset idoneus sensus carnis tuae, ac
non et ipse in parte uniuersi accepisset pro tua poena iustum
modum, uelles ut transiret quidquid existit in praesentia, ut
magis tibi omnia placerent. nam et quod loquimur per eundem sensum carnis audis, et non uis utique stare syllabas, sed
transuolare, ut aliae ueniant et totum audias. ita semper omnia, quibus unum aliquid constat – et non sunt omnia simul ea

quibus constat – plus delectant omnia quam singula, si possint
sentiri omnia. sed longe his melior qui fecit omnia, et ipse est
deus noster, et non discedit, quia nec succeditur ei.

18. Si placent corpora, deum ex illis lauda et in artificem **12**
eorum retorque amorem, ne in his quae tibi placent tu
displiceas. si placent animae, in deo amentur, quia et ipsae
mutabiles sunt et in illo fixae stabiliuntur: alioquin irent et
perirent. in illo ergo amentur, et rape ad eum tecum quas
potes et dic eis: 'hunc amemus: ipse fecit haec et non est
longe. non enim fecit atque abiit, sed ex illo in illo sunt. ecce
ubi est, ubi sapit ueritas. intimus cordi est, sed cor errauit ab
eo. redite, praeuaricatores, ad cor, et inhaerete illi qui fecit
uos. state cum eo et stabitis, requiescite in eo et quieti eritis.
quo itis in aspera? quo itis? bonum, quod amatis, ab illo est:
sed quantum est ad illum, bonum est et suaue; sed amarum erit
iuste, quia iniuste amatur deserto illo quidquid ab illo est. quo
uobis adhuc et adhuc ambulare uias difficiles et laboriosas?
non est requies ubi quaeritis eam. quaerite quod quaeritis, sed
ibi non est ubi quaeritis. beatam uitam quaeritis in regione
mortis: non est illic. quomodo enim beata uita, ubi nec uita?

19. 'et descendit huc ipsa uita nostra, tulit mortem nostram
et occidit eam de abundantia uitae suae, et tonuit clamans ut
redeamus hinc ad eum in illud secretum unde processit ad
nos in ipsum primum uirginalem uterum, ubi ei nupsit humana creatura, caro mortalis, ne semper mortalis; et inde uelut sponsus procedens de thalamo suo exultauit ut gigans ad
currendam uiam. non enim tardauit, sed cucurrit clamans dic-
tis, factis, morte, uita, descensu, ascensu, clamans ut redeamus
ad eum. et discessit ab oculis, ut redeamus ad cor et inuenia-
mus eum. abscessit enim et ecce hic est. noluit nobiscum diu
esse et non reliquit nos. illuc enim abscessit unde numquam
recessit, quia mundus per eum factus est, et in hoc mundo
erat et uenit in hunc mundum peccatores saluos facere. cui
confitetur anima mea, et sanat eam, quoniam peccauit illi.
fili hominum, quo usque graues corde? numquid et post

descensum uitae non uultis ascendere et uiuere? sed quo ascenditis, quando in alto estis et posuistis in caelo os uestrum? descendite, ut ascendatis, et ascendatis ad deum. cecidistis enim ascendendo contra deum.' dic eis ista, ut plorent in conualle plorationis, et sic eos rape tecum ad deum, quia de spiritu eius haec dicis eis, si dicis ardens igne caritatis.

13 20. Haec tunc non noueram, et amabam pulchra inferiora et ibam in profundum, et dicebam amicis meis: 'num amamus aliquid nisi pulchrum? quid est ergo pulchrum? et quid est pulchritudo? quid est quod nos allicit et conciliat rebus, quas amamus? nisi enim esset in eis decus et species, nullo modo nos ad se mouerent.' et animaduertebam et uidebam in ipsis corporibus aliud esse quasi totum et ideo pulchrum, aliud autem quod ideo deceret quoniam apte accommodaretur alicui, sicut pars corporis ad uniuersum suum aut calciamentum ad pedem et similia. et ista consideratio scaturriuit in animo meo ex intimo corde meo, et scripsi libros de pulchro et apto, puto, duos aut tres; tu scis, deus: nam excidit mihi. Non enim habemus eos, sed aberrauerunt a nobis nescio quo modo.

14 21. Quid est autem quod me mouit, domine deus meus, ut ad Hierium, Romanae urbis oratorem, scriberem illos libros? quem non noueram facie, sed amaueram hominem ex doctrinae fama, quae illi clara erat, et quaedam uerba eius audieram et placuerant mihi. sed magis, quia placebat aliis et eum efferebant laudibus, stupentes quod ex homine Syro, docto prius Graecae facundiae, post in Latina etiam dictor mirabilis extitisset et esset scientissimus rerum ad studium sapientiae pertinentium, mihi placebat. laudatur homo et amatur absens. utrumnam ab ore laudantis intrat in cor audientis amor ille? absit! sed ex amante alio accenditur alius. hinc enim amatur qui laudatur, dum non fallaci corde laudatoris praedicari creditur, id est cum amans eum laudat.

22. sic enim tunc amabam homines ex hominum iudicio; non enim ex tuo, deus meus, in quo nemo fallitur. sed tamen cur non sicut auriga nobilis, sicut uenator studiis popularibus

diffamatus, sed longe aliter et grauiter et ita, quemadmodum et me laudari uellem? non autem uellem ita laudari et amari me ut histriones, quamquam eos et ipse laudarem et amarem, sed eligens latere quam ita notus esse et uel haberi odio quam sic amari. ubi distribuuntur ista pondera uariorum et diuersorum amorum in anima una? quid est quod amo in alio, quod rursus nisi odissem, non a me detestarer et repellerem, cum sit uterque nostrum homo? non enim sicut equus bonus amatur ab eo qui nollet hoc esse, etiamsi posset, hoc et de histrione dicendum est, qui naturae nostrae socius est. ergone amo in homine quod odi esse, cum sim homo? grande profundum est ipse homo, cuius etiam capillos tu, domine, numeratos habes et non minuuntur in te: et tamen capilli eius magis numerabiles quam affectus eius et motus cordis eius.

23. at ille rhetor ex eo erat genere, quem sic amabam ut uellem esse me talem; et errabam typho et circumferebar omni uento et nimis occulte gubernabar abs te. et unde scio et unde certus confiteor tibi, quod illum in amore laudantium magis amaueram quam in rebus ipsis de quibus laudabatur? quia si non laudatum uituperarent eum idem ipsi et uituperando atque spernendo ea ipsa narrarent, non accenderer in eo et non excitarer, et certe res non aliae forent nec homo ipse alius, sed tantummodo alius affectus narrantium. ecce ubi iacet anima infirma nondum haerens soliditati ueritatis: sicut aurae linguarum flauerint a pectoribus opinantium, ita fertur et uertitur, torquetur ac retorquetur, et obnubilatur ei lumen et non cernitur ueritas, et ecce est ante nos. et magnum quiddam mihi erat, si sermo meus et studia mea illi uiro innotescerent: quae si probaret, flagrarem magis; si autem improbaret, sauciaretur cor uanum et inane soliditatis tuae. et tamen pulchrum illud atque aptum, unde ad eum scripseram, libenter animo uersabam ob os contemplationis meae et nullo conlaudatore mirabar.

24. Sed tantae rei cardinem in arte tua nondum uidebam, **15** omnipotens, qui facis mirabilia solus, et ibat animus per

formas corporeas et pulchrum, quod per se ipsum, aptum autem, quod ad aliquid accommodatum deceret, definiebam et
distinguebam et exemplis corporeis astruebam. et conuerti me
ad animi naturam, et non me sinebat falsa opinio, quam de spiritalibus habebam, uerum cernere. et inruebat in oculos ipsa
uis ueri, et auertebam palpitantem mentem ab incorporea re
ad liniamenta et colores et tumentes magnitudines et, quia non
poteram ea uidere in animo, putabam me non posse uidere
animum. et cum in uirtute pacem amarem, in uitiositate autem odissem discordiam, in illa unitatem, in ista quandam
diuisionem notabam, inque illa unitate mens rationalis et natura ueritatis ac summi boni mihi esse uidebatur, in ista uero
diuisione inrationalis uitae nescio quam substantiam et naturam summi mali, quae non solum esset substantia sed omnino
uita esset, et tamen abs te non esset, deus meus, ex quo sunt
omnia, miser opinabar. et illam monadem appellabam tamquam sine ullo sexu mentem, hanc uero dyadem, iram in facinoribus, libidinem in flagitiis, nesciens quid loquerer. non enim
noueram neque didiceram nec ullam substantiam malum esse
nec ipsam mentem nostram summum atque incommutabile
bonum.

25. sicut enim facinora sunt, si uitiosus est ille animi motus
in quo est impetus et se iactat insolenter ac turbide, et flagitia,
si est immoderata illa animae affectio qua carnales hauriuntur
uoluptates, ita errores et falsae opiniones uitam contaminant,
si rationalis mens ipsa uitiosa est qualis in me tunc erat nesciente alio lumine illam inlustrandam esse, ut sit particeps
ueritatis, quia non est ipsa natura ueritatis, quoniam tu inluminabis lucernam meam, domine; deus meus, inluminabis
tenebras meas, et de plenitudine tua omnes nos accepimus.
es enim tu lumen uerum quod inluminat omnem hominem
uenientem in hunc mundum, quia in te non est transmutatio
nec momenti obumbratio.

26. sed ego conabar ad te et repellebar abs te, ut saperem

mortem, quoniam superbis resistis. quid autem superbius,
quam ut adsererem mira dementia me id esse naturaliter,
quod tu es? cum enim ego essem mutabilis et eo mihi mani-
festum esset, quod utique ideo sapiens esse cupiebam, ut ex
deteriore melior fierem, malebam tamen etiam te opinari
mutabilem quam me non hoc esse, quod tu es. itaque repellebar, et resistebas uentosae ceruici meae, et imaginabar formas
corporeas et caro carnem accusabam et spiritus ambulans
nondum reuertebar ad te, et ambulando ambulabam in ea
quae non sunt, neque in te neque in me neque in corpore, neque mihi creabantur a ueritate tua, sed a mea uanitate fingebantur ex corpore. et dicebam paruulis fidelibus tuis, ciuibus
meis, a quibus nesciens exulabam, dicebam illis garrulus et
ineptus: 'cur ergo errat anima, quam fecit deus?' et mihi nolebam dici: 'cur ergo errat deus?' et contendebam magis incommutabilem tuam substantiam coactam errare quam meam
mutabilem sponte deuiasse et poena errare confitebar.

27. et eram aetate annorum fortasse uiginti sex aut septem cum illa uolumina scripsi, uoluens apud me corporalia
figmenta obstrepentia cordis mei auribus, quas intendebam,
dulcis ueritas, in interiorem melodiam tuam, cogitans de pulchro et apto, et stare cupiens et audire te et gaudio gaudere
propter uocem sponsi, et non poteram, quia uocibus erroris
mei rapiebar foras et pondere superbiae meae in ima decidebam. non enim dabas auditui meo gaudium et laetitiam, aut
exultabant ossa, quae humiliata non erant.

28. Et quid mihi proderat quod annos natus ferme uiginti, **16**
cum in manus meas uenissent Aristotelica quaedam quas
appellant decem categorias – quarum nomine, cum eas rhetor Carthaginiensis, magister meus, buccis typho crepantibus
commemoraret et alii qui docti habebantur, tamquam in nescio quid magnum et diuinum suspensus inhiabam – legi eas
solus et intellexi? quas cum contulissem cum eis qui se dicebant uix eas magistris eruditissimis non loquentibus tantum,

sed multa in puluere depingentibus, intellexisse, nihil inde
aliud mihi dicere potuerunt quam ego solus apud me ipsum
legens cognoueram; et satis aperte mihi uidebantur loquentes
de substantiis, sicuti est homo, et quae in illis essent, sicuti
est figura hominis, qualis sit, et statura, quot pedum sit, et
cognatio, cuius frater sit, aut ubi sit constitutus aut quando
natus, aut stet aut sedeat, aut calciatus uel armatus sit, aut
aliquid faciat aut patiatur aliquid, et quaecumque in his
nouem generibus, quorum exempli gratia quaedam posui, uel
in ipso substantiae genere innumerabilia reperiuntur.

29. quid hoc mihi proderat, quando et oberat, cum etiam
te, deus meus, mirabiliter simplicem atque incommutabilem,
illis decem praedicamentis putans quidquid esset omnino com-
prehensum, sic intellegere conarer, quasi et tu subiectus esses
magnitudini tuae aut pulchritudini, ut illa essent in te quasi
in subiecto sicut in corpore, cum tua magnitudo et tua
pulchritudo tu ipse sis, corpus autem non eo sit magnum et
pulchrum quo corpus est, quia etsi minus magnum et minus
pulchrum esset, nihilominus corpus esset? falsitas enim erat
quam de te cogitabam, non ueritas, et figmenta miseriae
meae, non firmamenta beatitudinis tuae. iusseras enim, et ita
fiebat in me, ut terra spinas et tribulos pareret mihi et cum
labore peruenirem ad panem meum.

30. et quid mihi proderat quod omnes libros artium, quas
liberales uocant, tunc nequissimus malarum cupiditatum seruus per me ipsum legi et intellexi, quoscumque legere potui?
et gaudebam in eis, et nesciebam unde esset quidquid ibi
uerum et certum esset. dorsum enim habebam ad lumen, ad
ea quae inluminantur faciem: unde ipsa facies mea, qua in-
luminata cernebam, non inluminabatur. quidquid de arte
loquendi et disserendi, quidquid de dimensionibus figurarum
et de musicis et de numeris, sine magna difficultate nullo
hominum tradente intellexi, scis tu, domine deus meus, quia
et celeritas intellegendi et dispiciendi acumen donum tuum
est. sed non inde sacrificabam tibi. itaque mihi non ad usum,

sed ad perniciem magis ualebat, quia tam bonam partem substantiae meae sategi habere in potestate et fortitudinem meam non ad te custodiebam, sed profectus sum abs te in longinquam regionem, ut eam dissiparem in meretrices cupiditates. nam quid mihi proderat bona res non utenti bene? non enim sentiebam illas artes etiam ab studiosis et ingeniosis difficillime intellegi, nisi cum eis eadem conabar exponere, et erat ille excellentissimus in eis, qui me exponentem non tardius sequeretur.

31. sed quid mihi hoc proderat, putanti quod tu, domine deus ueritas, corpus esses lucidum et immensum et ego frustum de illo corpore? nimia peruersitas! sed sic eram nec erubesco, deus meus, confiteri tibi in me misericordias tuas et inuocare te, qui non erubui tunc profiteri hominibus blasphemias meas et latrare aduersum te. quid ergo tunc mihi proderat ingenium per illas doctrinas agile et nullo adminiculo humani magisterii tot nodosissimi libri enodati, cum deformiter et sacrilega turpitudine in doctrina pietatis errarem? aut quid tantum oberat paruulis tuis longe tardius ingenium, cum a te longe non recederent, ut in nido ecclesiae tuae tuti plumescerent et alas caritatis alimento sanae fidei nutrirent? o domine deus noster, in uelamento alarum tuarum speremus, et protege nos et porta nos. tu portabis et paruulos et usque ad canos tu portabis, quoniam firmitas nostra quando tu es, tunc est firmitas, cum autem nostra est, infirmitas est. uiuit apud te semper bonum nostrum, et quia inde auersi sumus, peruersi sumus. reuertamur iam, domine, ut non euertamur, quia uiuit apud te sine ullo defectu bonum nostrum, quod tu ipse es, et non timemus ne non sit quo redeamus, quia nos inde ruimus; nobis autem absentibus non ruit domus nostra, aeternitas tua.

COMMENTARY

Book I

Chapters 1–5 of book 1 establish the themes of the *C.* The book begins with the impulse to praise God. A. is aware that a human being who has the impulse to praise is both 'a bit of your creation' (*aliqua portio creaturae tuae*) and alienated from God by sin; and that it is God who 'stirs up' (*tu excitas*) this bit of creation to praise God whom he does not yet know. Without someone to tell him about God (*sine praedicante*), he might invoke *aliud pro alio*, 'one thing in place of another', as A. did when he was a Manichaean and then a Platonist (see Introd. §3*a*, *b*) with an inadequate concept of God. But he must make the attempt at invocation, because 'you have made us for yourself, and our heart is restless until it rests in you'.

The problems raised in 1.2.2–4.4 are those which had chiefly obstructed A.'s understanding of God. As a Manichaean, and until he read Platonist books, he could not think of God except in physical terms, and therefore could not understand how God could be present throughout the universe (1.2.2–3.3). When he was convinced by Platonist arguments, he could not believe that God created the world and intervenes to help those trapped in their own confusion (1.4.4–5.6).

Finally, the opening paragraphs are a spectacular display of the styles and registers A. will use: exegesis of Scripture, philosophical analysis, brilliant rhetorical technique and evocation of intense feeling.

1.1.1 A. praises God and asks the help of God whom he does not yet know. **magnus es ... sapientiae tuae non est numerus:** a reworking of phrases from the Psalms, here addressed directly to God. *magnus dominus et laudabilis ualde* is a version of Psalms 47: 2, 95: 4 and 144: 3. (In *On the Psalms* 95.4 A.'s text is *laudabilis nimis*, as in the Vulgate: see Introd. §4*b* on A. and texts of the Bible.) *magnus dominus noster et magna uirtus eius et sapientiae eius non est numerus* occurs in Psalm 146: 5. A. interpreted *sapientiae eius non est numerus* to mean that God is not limited by number, that is, God's wisdom is infinite (cf. *On the Gospel of John* 39.4 *deus nec recedit a numero, nec capitur numero*).   **et laudare te uult homo:** introductory *et* (three times in this sentence), derived from Hebrew and Greek through the Latin Bible, is often used in the *C.* (see further Introd. §2*a*).   **testimonium quia superbis resistis:** mortality is the evidence that God 'resists the proud' because human self-assertion cannot overcome death. *quia*, as often in post-classical Latin, is here equivalent to *quod*, and means 'that'; in the next sentence, in *quia fecisti nos ad te*, it means 'because'. *deus superbis resistit, humilibus autem dat gratiam* (Proverbs 3: 34, *VL*) is a key text for A. *superbia*, for him, was the root of sin, the basic tendency of human beings to want their own way in disregard of God, just as Adam and Eve disregarded God's warning that they would die if they ate fruit from the tree of the knowledge of good and evil (Genesis 2: 17). A. says, in a section of *On Christian Teaching* (3.23.33) written when he was probably starting work on the *C.*, that *deus superbis resistit, humilibus autem dat gratiam* sounds on every page of the Scriptures. It reappears in the first chapter of the *City of God*, where it is juxtaposed with the proud claim of the earthly city *parcere subiectis et debellare superbos* (Virgil, *Aeneid* 6.853). In the *C.* it recurs at 4.3.5, when the doctor Vindicianus cannot heal A.'s diseased understanding; at 4.15.6 it is used of A.'s Manichaean arrogance in supposing that he is of the same nature as God; and at 7.9.13 it introduces the gift of the 'Platonic books' and the effect they had on A. At 10.36.59 it challenges A.'s wish to be loved and feared for his own sake, not for God's.   **ut laudare te delectet:** *delectatio* is a key word of the *C.* A. insists that the love of God, whom he loves to praise, is a greater delight than any of the lesser loves he pursued before his conversion.   **quomodo credent sine praedicante?:** O'D. *credent*, V. *credunt*. A. is quoting (from *quomodo autem* to *praedicante*) Romans 10: 14; the Greek text does not settle the question of the tense, but the parallel with *inuocabunt* supports the future tense here.   **quaerentes ... inueniunt eum:** from the words of Jesus in Matthew 7: 7, 'Ask, and it shall be given you; seek, and you shall find; knock, and the door will be opened to you.' A. here asks that he should be able to ask (*quaeram ... inuocem*), and echoes this first prayer in the final words of the *C.* (13.38.53), a prayer for fuller understanding of God: *a te petatur, in te quaeratur, ad te pulsetur: sic, sic accipietur, sic inuenietur, sic aperietur*.   **praedicatus enim es**

nobis: the *praedicator* is sometimes identified as Ambrose, bishop of Milan, whose preaching made it possible for A. to read the Bible as authoritative (5.13.23–14.24); but the reference may be to the Bible as a whole, or to St Paul whose words prompted A.'s 'conversion' (Introd. §3*c*).   **per humanitatem filii tui:** *humanitas*, like English 'humanity', has a double meaning. In classical Latin it is the quality of a civilised human being, who has a cultivated mind and is kindly towards other people. The humanity of Christ is Christ's being human in the Incarnation.

1.2.2 'Invoke' means 'call in', but how can A. call into himself God who made all that is? Everything must contain (*capere*) God in the sense that God must be in it, or it would not exist at all; but nothing can contain God in the sense of enclosing God.   **utique** 'necessarily', that is, logically necessary, because *inuoco* means 'I call in'.   **quoniam itaque et ego sum:** the strong sense of *sum*, 'I too exist'.   **non enim ego iam inferi:** understand *sum*. C. 'I am not now possessed by Hades', which allows for different interpretations of the Latin. G–M take *inferi* as nominative plural, 'I am not hell (and even if I were, God is present there too)'. Alternatively, *inferi* might be genitive singular with the meaning 'I am not of hell', i.e. I do not belong to hell; the singular is used in Psalm 138: 8 which A. goes on to quote, *si descendero in infernum, ades.* V. emends to *in* ⟨*profundis*⟩ *inferi* as at 3.6.11 (see note there). *iam*, 'now', probably marks a stage in the argument (*OLD* s.v. 7), but could imply 'no longer' or 'not yet'. In classical Latin *inferi* means the people living in the underworld, i.e. the dead, but A. elsewhere takes it to mean 'where the (unredeemed) dead are'. In *Literal Interpretation of Genesis* 12.33.62 he argues that this place is a spiritual, not a physical, location, but acknowledges that there are unresolved questions about the scriptural use of *inferi*. A. seems consistently to have held that Scripture taught the eternal punishment of some human beings; in *City of God* 21.17–27 he discusses, and rejects, several attempts to mitigate this belief.   **deus meus, qui dixit: caelum et terram ego impleo:** direct quotation of the words of God through the prophet Jeremiah (23: 24).

1.3.3 What exactly does it mean to say that God 'fills' heaven and earth? God is not contained by anything, nor is part of God in one place and part in another. But God *continet*, literally 'holds

together', everything which would otherwise be dispersed in transient existence.

As in 1.2.2, A. asks a series of questions exploring the implications
of words and images: in 1.2.2 'I invoke God', in 1.3.3 'I fill heaven
and earth'. The questions are addressed to God, who does not
answer, but they constrain the reader to answer *etiam sic, domine* (as
in 1.2.2) to the last question. 1.2.2 and 1.3.3 include far less biblical
material than 1.1.1, and far more reminiscence of Plotinus' philosophy, both in style and in content (especially *Ennead* 5.5.9; see further Introd. §3*b*). Here A. raises philosophical problems as he did
in the days before his conversion, just as in 1.1.1 he presents a man
who might not even be able to get started on praising God.   **non
enim uasa:** with the image of liquid filling a container, A. can exploit both the philosophical point that God, so to speak, overflows
all containers, and the contrast between God-given stability (*continentia*) and the human tendency to dissipation among many things.
Cf. 2.10.18 *defluxi abs te ego et erraui, deus meus, nimis deuius a stabilitate
tua*, and 10.29.40 *per continentiam quippe colligimur et redigimur in unum,
a quo in multa defluximus*, and see further on 2.1.1.   **partem tui
capiunt:** the first three possibilities considered depend on thinking
of God in material terms, and A. explicitly rejects them in 7.1.1–2,
where he presents this habit of thought as one of the barriers between him and God. The right answer (not marked with *etiam sic* as
in 1.2.2) is the last, *ubique totus es*.

1.4.4 A. confronts the problem of God and change, using biblical
quotation and a series of paradoxes in highly wrought language.

The problem, not fully stated here, is how God can be present in a
changing world and yet be unchanging (see further Sorabji (1983);
Kirwan (1989) 151–66). If God is perfectly good, all change must be
for the worse; alternatively, something less than the best must have
been allowed to exist before. So when the Bible says that (for instance) God repents of his anger, was God wrong to be angry? Is
God subject to moods? A.'s spectacular use of rhetorical technique
suggests that philosophical puzzle (as in 1.2.2–3.3) and biblical affirmation cannot yet be integrated: they will not be until his exegesis of
Genesis 1–3 in books 11–13 of the *C*.

1.4.4 begins with four rhetorical questions, *quid ... quid, rogo ...
quis ... aut quis?*, of which the second pair is a biblical quotation

(Psalm 17: 32). Then comes an ever-increasing string of Latin superlatives: *summe, optime, potentissime, omnipotentissime* (logically nonsense);
a string of paired superlatives, *misericordissime et iustissime, secretissime et
praesentissime, pulcherrime et fortissime*; then a change from the *-issime*
endings to *stabilis et incomprehensibilis*; then a series of present par-
ticiples; and so on to a further series of paradoxes, carefully organised to avoid monotony, and reinforced by biblical quotation and
allusion. A. ends with the near-jingle *reddis debita nulli debens, donas
debita nihil perdens*, which is characteristic of his preaching style: his
congregation liked word-play and strong rhythm. For the technical-
ities of rhetoric, see Introd. §2c.   **zelas:** a rare word, used in the
Latin Bible of strongly possessive love (e.g. Joel 2: 18). At 3.1.1 A.
suffers from *zelus* in a love-affair.   **paenitet te et non doles:**
Genesis 6: 6–7 *paenituit eum quod hominem fecisset in terra. et tactus dolore
cordis intrinsecus, Delebo, inquit, hominem* ... So far, A. has only paradox
to oppose to the problem that God, according to the Bible, is vulnerable to pain, distress and regret for past actions.   **usuras exigis:** a reminiscence of the parable of the Talents (Matthew 25: 27),
'you should have put my money with the bankers, and I would have
got back my own with interest'.   **supererogatur tibi** 'payment
is made to you above what was expected', an allusion to the parable
of the Good Samaritan (Luke 10: 35): 'whatever you have paid out
above that, I will repay you when I return'. (Hence the technical
term 'a work of supererogation', i.e. more than one was asked to
do.) A.'s magnificent burst of language ends with an acknowledgement that he has not really said anything, because language is
wholly inadequate to express the greatness of God. Yet the silence
of those who have something to say (the *tacentes*) is bad, because the
'people who talk', the *loquaces*, are *muti*: they fail to say anything. A.
uses *loquaces* of people who have much to say, like the Manichaeans
(3.6.10), but all of it mistaken or trivial: almost 'the chattering
classes'.   **deus meus, uita mea, dulcedo mea sancta:** these
exclamations addressed to God, as in the Psalms, are one of the
most distinctive (and most imitated) features of the *C*.

1.5.5 begins with a plea for rest and oblivion of troubles, and, re-
markably, uses the image of a man getting drunk, embracing his beloved who makes angry scenes if he fails to show love, and at a loss
for words to say what the beloved means to him. In 1.3.3 A. used the

language of the philosophical puzzles he has now learned to reject; here he uses the language of the romantic drama which filled his head in adolescence (see on 3.1.1). In 1.4.4 all the superlatives and structured sentences he can muster fail to give voice to the greatness of God; here, short impassioned cries fail to express his love.   **inebries illud, ut obliuiscar mala mea:** there may be an allusion to the Song of Songs (1.1–3), in which love of the Bridegroom (allegorised as Christ) is sweeter than wine. The Song of Songs was much used in the late fourth century to express an intense love of God (E. A. Clark (1986) 386–410), but is not a key text for the *C.* More simply, for drunken forgetfulness of troubles, cf. 6.6.9–10, where A. first contrasts his own anxiety with the happiness of a drunken beggar, then compares the beggar's brief intoxication with his own long-lasting intoxication by worldly fame. *mala mea* means both 'the evils I suffer' and 'the evils I have done'.   **paruane ipsa est:** understand *miseria*, which means 'wretchedness', either in the sense of unhappiness or in the sense of a condition which should provoke pity, so *misereri* is to take pity on someone and *miseratio* a response of pity. A. exploits the double sense of *miseria* to make the point that people are unhappy about trivialities and fail to realise their true wretchedness (cf. 1.6.7, 1.13.21, 3.2.2–3).   **miserationes:** the plural derives from Hebrew usage, but post-classical Latin increasingly uses abstract nouns in the plural.   **aures cordis mei:** cf. 4.5.10 *possumne ... admouere aurem cordis mei ori tuo?* A. likes these very physical metaphors, derived from Hebrew poetry but startling in Latin (although *oculi mentis* was an accepted phrase, *OLD* s.v. *oculus* 7). One reason may be that the rule of life he followed as an ascetic Christian aimed to transform the body as well as the soul. *cor*, 'heart', is the seat of human feeling, and therefore of love for God. A. identifies himself with his *cor* in 10.3.4: he says of those who do not know him *auris eorum non est ad cor meum, ubi ego sum quicumque sum.* Compare Platonist emphasis on the mind, *nous*, as the true human identity, and the aspect of human beings which is closest to God. The heart affects understanding: Jesus (Matthew 13: 15) quoted Isaiah 6: 9–10 on those who hear but do not understand, look but do not see, because their heart is gross, and A. says (7.1.2) that his *cor incrassatum* prevented him from thinking of God except as something material.   **noli abscondere a me faciem tuam: moriar, ne**

moriar, ut eam uideam 'do not hide your face from me: let me die in order to see it, lest I should die [for ever, by not seeing it]'. O'D. compares *Sermon* 231.3.3 *qui autem nondum mortuus est, nec resurrexit, male adhuc uiuit: et si male uiuit, non uiuit: moriatur, ne moriatur. quid est, moriatur, ne moriatur? mutetur, ne damnetur,* 'he who is not yet dead and has not yet risen again still lives badly; and if he lives badly, he does not live; let him die, lest he die. What is this: let him die, lest he die? Let him change, lest he be damned.' He interprets as 'let me die [to sin], so that I may see your face, lest I die [without hope of redemption].' Cf. 2.2.4 *percutis ut sanes et occidis nos, ne moriamur abs te.* In Exodus 33: 20 God says to Moses that a human being cannot see the face of God and live: *non poteris uidere faciem meam; non enim uidebit me homo et uiuet.*

1.5.6 A. acknowledges his state of sin. The language here is cramped and fractured like the *angusta et ruinosa domus animae,* but A. has shored fragments of Scripture against his ruin.   **angusta est domus animae meae quo uenias ad eam** 'the house is (too) narrow that you should come to it'. *quo* introduces a final clause without a preceding comparative: this is rare but not unparalleled. This is not the familiar image (see Kenney (1984) on Lucretius 3.774) of the body as a crumbling house for the soul: *domus animae* means 'the house of [i.e. which is] my soul'. *animae* is an 'epexegetic genitive', common in Hebrew metaphor.   **alienis:** other people's sins. A. is adapting Psalm 18: 13–14 *delicta quis intellegit? ab occultis meis munda me, et ab alienis parce seruo tuo.* In his *On the Psalms* he interpreted *aliena* in this passage as sins into which others lead us. Cf. 2.9.17 on the effect of people saying 'let's go, let's do it', where A. also cites *delicta quis intellegit?*   **non iudicio contendo tecum** evokes a sequence of biblical allusions, beginning with Jeremiah 2: 29 *quid uultis mecum iudicio contendere? omnes dereliquistis me, dicit Dominus* (cf. Job 9: 3 for the impossibility of challenging God's judgement). *ego nolo fallere me ipsum,* adapted from *fallentes uosmetipsos* in James 1: 22, is a very emphatic refusal to deceive himself. *ne mentiatur iniquitas mea sibi* (Psalm 26: 12, with *mea* added), means, for A., that his wickedness might deceive itself about what it is: in 3.8.16 he interprets this as human nature corrupting itself. *iniquitas* makes the link to Psalm 129: 3, of which A. quotes only the beginning; but the end of the verse, though unspoken, brings him back to his starting-point: *si iniquitates* *obseruaueris, domine, domine, quis sustinebit?* [*ne intres in iudicium cum seruo tuo, quia non iustificabitur in conspectu tuo omnis uiuens*].

1.6.7 A. begins to speak to God about himself: but what is his own beginning? A. does not explain why his first need is to say 'I do not know whence I came here, to this life which dies or death which lives'. In terms of writing an account of his life, he does not know where the beginning is. In terms of what he is as a human being, there were divergent theories about the union of soul and body, and each would imply something different about human life. Plato had argued for a pre-existent soul which fell away from closeness to the One God and became trapped in a mortal body, but still remembered enough to recognise goodness and beauty in this changing world: so, if A. knew where he came from, he would know something about what he is, namely, a rational soul still in touch with God. (Cf. 10.20.29, where A. considers the possibility that we recognise the *beata uita* because we remember it.) Platonist philosophers debated whether the soul remained uncontaminated by the changeable and vulnerable body which it inhabits. A further problem, which preoccupied A. throughout his life as a Christian, was whether the soul is inherited from the parents and the child is therefore born infected with human sinfulness, or whether each baby starts fresh with a newly created soul. In *On the Soul and its Origin* 4.6.8 A. makes the same point that he does not know what the answer is, and does not even know whether he did know and has forgotten. See further E. A. Clark (1992) 227–44; O'Daly (1987) 15–20. **me terram et cinerem:** compare Abraham's words to God (Genesis 18: 27 *VL*), pleading with him to spare the city of Sodom: *quia semel coepi, loquar ad dominum meum, cum sim terra et cinis*, and Job's final words (Job 42: 6 *VL*) *despexi memetipsum et distabui et aestimaui me terram et cinerem*. **inrisor:** human mockery worries A. Cf. 3.8.16, where *inrisores et inlusores quorumlibet* are grouped with the spectators at gladiatorial games as those who take pleasure in another's pain; and compare 5.10.20, where A. envisages the kindly laughter of a charitable Christian reader. For the implied audience of the *C.*, see 2.3.5. **et tu fortasse inrides me, sed conuersus misereberis mei:** the reference is probably to God 'laughing down' the proud as in Psalm 2: 4 *qui habitat in caelis inridebit eos, et dominus subsannabit eos* (a text familiar from Handel's *Messiah*: 'he that

dwelleth in Heaven shall laugh them to scorn; the Lord shall have
them in derision'). But A. is also conscious of the absurdity that he
is telling God what God knows and made possible. A. does not hesi-
tate, here, to impute emotional change to God (cf. 1.4.4). *miseria*
and its cognates echo through this paragraph, as in 1.5.5.   **uitam
mortalem an mortem uitalem:** one of A.'s favourite word-
plays, here neatly presented as a *commutatio*. Each of the pairs is an
oxymoron, a deliberate juxtaposition of contraries (Greek *oxymoron*
means 'sharp-dull'), and the second reverses the first.   **nescio ...
non enim ego memini:** cf. 1.6.8 *nam ista mea non memini*; 1.6.9–10
generalises the point that all A. knows of his own beginnings comes
from observation of other babies and from other people, so far as
their knowledge goes. But if he does not remember infancy, is it part
of his identity? (See further O'Daly (1987) 148–51.) At 6.5.7 he notes
that he depends on what others have told him even to know who his
parents were: this becomes one example of how life would be impossible if we did not take on trust some claims which (like Christian
teaching) cannot be proved. For the reiterated *nescio*, cf. the repeated
Nesciebam ... non noueram which begins at 3.7.12 (q.v.).   **ex quo et
in qua:** i.e. from his father and in his mother.   **nutrices:** wet-
nurses, commonly used to substitute for, or to supplement, breast-
feeding by the mother. Soranus' *Gynaecology* (an early second-century
textbook for midwives, which A. had read by the time he wrote *City
of God*) devotes as much attention to the choice of a wet-nurse as
modern babycare manuals do to bottle-feeding.   **diuitias usque
ad fundum rerum dispositas:** the image suggests buried treas-
ure even in the lowest, or remotest, parts of the creation (cf. 3.3.5,
4.11.16 for *ima* used of this world).   **tu etiam mihi dabas ...
ex te quippe bona omnia:** the interwoven language of this section conveys the interrelatedness of the infant and his world. His
satisfaction is also the satisfaction of the women who feed him, and
he has no further unmet need. This is *ordinatus affectus*, feeling which
is ordered according to God's intention, and also the *alimentum* suited
to his need (book 3 takes up the theme of proper food). So his delight, *delectatio*, is quite proper.   **intus et foris:** inner awareness
of God, and the external world created by God. A. usually regards
what is *foris* as a distraction from what is *intus* (see 3.1.1, 3.6.11), but
here he sees both as God's gift.   **adquiescere delectationibus,**

flere autem offensiones carnis meae: according to Epicurus, the infant's desire for tranquil pleasure and avoidance of physical distress is a demonstration of what human beings really want; according to the Stoics, it is a first manifestation of *oikeiosis*, human recognition of what 'belongs' to humans, which will develop into the recognition of all rational beings as kin. A. could have found both theories in Cicero, *On Ends*, which he probably read at Milan (6.16.26) if not earlier. He goes on to advance his own theory about infant behaviour.

1.6.8 A. deduces his own infancy from watching babies: he first smiled, then tried to make other people do what he wanted.

This paragraph, which does not include biblical material, uses the 'cradle argument', the belief that the very young child displays the basic characteristics of human nature (see Brunschwig (1986) for Stoic and Epicurean versions). In A.'s version, the infant becomes aware of the world around and tries to express wants, but the wants are not understood or satisfied by others, and the infant tries to impose his will on those who are not his subordinates. Frustrated and inappropriate wants, failure of communication, misplaced attempts to dominate – such are human relationships after the Fall. For A.'s account of infancy, see further Miles (1982), who emphasises *concupiscentia*, the anxious grasping at objects which might be missed: the objects change but the drive continues.   **iactabam membra et uoces:** another word-play (syllepsis), bringing together the literal and non-literal senses of *iactare*.   **ueresimilia:** so most manuscripts, followed by V. and by O'D., who divides as *uere similia*, arguing that A. wants to say that the signs were not 'really like' the infant A.'s wants, not that they lacked verisimilitude. Other editors emend to *uerisimilia*, which is the standard form (*OLD* s.v. *uerus* 7b has *ueri similia* as standard). The gap between signs and the truth to which they point is important to A., who argued that all knowledge of things depends on interpretation of signs: *ea demum est miserabilis animi seruitus, signa pro rebus accipere* (*On Christian Teaching* 3.5.9). He was also aware of the gaps between words, the thoughts of the person who uses them, and the understanding of the person who hears or reads them (see further *On the Teacher*, especially 38–44). On his treatment of language as a sign-system, see Markus (1957); Kirwan (1989) 33–59; Rist (1994) 21–40; and cf. 1.8.13 on language as human convention.

1.6.9 A.'s infancy is long past; but was there a stage of his
life before infancy?   **et ecce infantia mea olim mortua
est et ego uiuo:** cf. below *alicui iam aetati meae mortuae*, a 'dead'
phase of life which might have existed before infancy, and 7.1.1 *iam
mortua erat adulescentia mea.*   **ante omne quod uel ante dici
potest, tu es** 'before everything that can even be called "before",
you exist'. A. discusses God's relation to time in *C.* book 11; see on
1.6.10.   **apud te ... uiuunt rationes:** a spectacular example of
'rising *tricolon*' (Introd. §2c). This is a deliberate shift of register from
the much less dramatic language of 1.6.8, as A. moves from himself
to God. As in 1.4.4, he insists on the unchanging nature of God who
makes the changing world, and as in 1.1.1, his thunderous invocation
leads to an unexpected question: was there a phase of my life before
infancy? (see on 1.6.7 for the reason).   **omnium inrationalium
et temporalium sempiternae uiuunt rationes:** the *rationes* are
the basic principles of being, established by God in the act of creation, which develop at the right moment. In *Literal Interpretation of
Genesis* 9.17.32 A. compared them to seeds, and they became known
as *rationes seminales.*   **laudari a me iubes et confiteri me tibi:**
A.'s first use of *confiteor*.

1.6.10 A. praises God who created him, and who, existing beyond time, makes it possible for things to exist in time.   **confiteor
tibi, domine caeli et terrae:** Jesus' words to God, in Matthew 11:
25. As often in the *C.*, the unstated context of the quotation is important. Matthew continues 'that you have hidden these things from
the wise and understanding, and revealed them to babes', and A.
makes a confession of praise for the babyhood he does not remember but is able to conjecture.   **auctoritatibus etiam mulier-
cularum** is consciously paradoxical: *muliercula* is a pitying or con-
temptuous diminutive of *mulier*, and women were not acknowledged
as authoritative.   **eram enim et uiuebam:** the distinction is
between existence as part of God's creation (*eram*, cf. *sum* 1.2.2) and
transient mortal life (*uiuebam*, cf. 1.7.12 *adnumerare huic uitae meae quam
uiuo in hoc saeculo*). But, A. says, life at its highest (*summe uiuere*) is not
distinct from existence at its highest (*summe esse*), so there is for God
no distinction between *esse* and *uiuere*. He is probably remembering
the argument of Plotinus, *Ennead* 3.6.6, that Being has no need of
anything to keep it in existence; it must therefore be fully alive, or it

would not be existent rather than non-existent. **in fine infantiae:** strictly, *infantia* is a time of 'not speaking', but neither *infantia*
nor *pueritia* has a precise time-reference (see on 1.8.13). **idipsum
est:** literally 'life at its highest and existence at its highest are the
very same thing' (*id ipsum*). But A. uses *idipsum* as a name for God, for
instance in his account of the vision he and Monnica shared at
Ostia: *erigentes nos ardentiore affectu in idipsum*, 9.10.24. He explains it, in
On the Psalms 121.5, in terms of God's self-description to Moses
(Exodus 3: 14), 'I am that I am'. See further O'D. on 9.4.11. **in
te sunt et ista omnia:** *ista* probably here means 'the well-known
. . .', almost 'as Paul said, everything'. The reference is to Romans 11:
35 *et in ipso sunt omnia*. **non enim haberent uias transeundi,
nisi contineres ea:** A. continues the paradox *neque peragitur in te
hodiernus dies, et tamen in te peragitur*. God does not experience the passing of time (*neque peragitur in te*), but the passing of time is possible
only because God has created things which change over time. If God
did not hold things in being (*nisi contineres ea*, cf. 1.3.3 *continet*), they
could not pass away (*non haberent uias transeundi*). **anni tui hodiernus dies:** A. develops his theories on time in book 11, and this
phrase is elaborated in 11.13.16. Here, he is concerned to make the
contrast between time-bound human existence and God's existence
which transcends time and in which all things are eternally present.
In 11.29.39 A. characterises human experience of time as *distentio*, a
stretching between remembrance of what has happened and expectation of what will happen, unable to measure the present moment
until it has become past (cf. 1.8.13 on the end of *infantia*). See further
Sorabji (1983), Kirwan (1989) 167–86, Rist (1994) 79–85. **acceperunt modos et utcumque extiterunt** 'they received their limits
and however they were' (C. 'the measure and condition of their
existence') – awkward phrasing to express the claim that God gives
defined existence to all creation (cf. Genesis 1: 2 'the earth was a
formless void'). **quid ad me, si quis non intellegat?:** cf. 1.6.7
for awareness of an unsympathetic audience. **quid est hoc?:**
probably a reminiscence of Sirach (Ecclesiasticus) 39: 26 *non est dicere,
quid est hoc, aut quid est istud? omnia enim in tempore suo quaerentur*; but
possibly also of Exodus 16: 15, in which the Israelites ask *quid est
hoc?* and the answer is 'the bread which the Lord has given you to
eat', that is, manna in the wilderness. **amet non inueniendo**

inuenire potius quam inueniendo non inuenire te: someone
who claims to have found (out about) God has failed to realise that
God is beyond human understanding, and therefore has not found
God; so by failing to find God one does find God.

1.7.11 God made human beings, but did not make sin in them;
yet even the youngest child manifests sin.   **peccatum non fecisti
in eo:** A. affirms here that God is not responsible for sin, but people
are. See on 3.7.12 and 4.15.26 for his earlier, Manichaean, beliefs
about the origin of evil.   **quis me commemorat peccatum:**
someone else would need to bring A.'s sins of infancy to his mind,
because he cannot himself remember.   **nemo mundus a peccato:** a reminiscence of Job 14: 4–5 (*VL*) *quis enim erit mundus absque
sorde? nec unus quidem, etiamsi unius diei fuerit uita eius super terram.* This
text, and Psalm 50: 7 *in iniquitate conceptus sum et in peccatis mater mea me
in utero aluit* (quoted in 1.7.12), are central to A.'s reflections on the
sinfulness of very young children. See further O'D. II 42–4; G. Clark
(1994) for the social context.   **quid ergo tunc peccabam?:** A.
is aware (1.6.8, 1.6.10) that babies have few ways of expressing what
they want, and he does not say that they cannot yet reason 'there
is plenty for both' as an older person can. Both points damage his
argument that behaviour which is acknowledged as bad in an adult
must also be bad in a baby. But what he sees in babies is greed, jeal-
ousy, frantic attempts to impose the will and to get what is bad for
one – in other words the basic human sinful disposition which A.
thought was transmitted in the procreation of children. He does
not here call it 'original sin', that is, sin acquired at the origin of
a human being. The phrase *originalis peccati uinculum quo omnes in
Adam morimur* occurs at 5.9.16, but this paragraph, like 1.6.8, has
no biblical material. See further Bonner (1986) 370–8.   **repre-
hendar iustissime:** the heavy verb *reprehendere* is three times
repeated in the next sentence.   **imbecillitas membrorum infantilium innocens est, non animus infantium:** a word-play
to make a moral point. *in-nocentia* is literally 'harmlessness' or 'not
harming', but that, A. says, is because babies' limbs cannot inflict
serious harm, not because their souls are innocent.   **expiare
se dicunt ista matres:** *expiare* here may be a dead metaphor
(cf. C. 'charm it away'), but G–M suggest the use of traditional
charms.   **nisi uero et ista innocentia est:** cf. 1.19.30 *istane est*

innocentia puerilis?   **quod licet probes** 'which you may prove',
not 'even though you approve'.

1.7.12 The creation of a human infant is a proof of God's power
and goodness, which A. celebrates with a spectacular passage of
rhetoric. But he does not want to spend longer on the infancy he
does not remember.   **proque eius uniuersitate atque incolumitate omnes conatus animantis insinuasti:** Stoic terminology for the primary human impulse for self-preservation and
completeness (*uniuersitas*).   **quia deus es omnipotens et bonus,
etiamsi sola ista fecisses:** i.e. you would still be all-powerful
and good if human infants were your only creation.   **une** is the
vocative of *unus*: see further Introd. §3*b* for God as One contrasted
with Many.   **formosissime, qui formas omnia:** a word-play
(*figura etymologica*) on *formosus*, which means 'well-formed' therefore
'beautiful'. On the triad *modus, forma, ordo*, which gives structure to
all creation, see further O'D. II 46–51.   **in iniquitate conceptus sum et in peccatis mater mea me in utero aluit:** Psalm
50: 7 (see on 1.7.11).   **quid mihi iam cum eo est:** C. 'I feel no
sense of responsibility', but A. does think he sinned in infancy. He
wants to say that, because he has no memory of his infancy, it is not
part of his present identity, so perhaps 'what have I to do with it
now?'

1.8.13 In learning to speak A. becomes a child, not an infant.
pueritia is distinguished from *infantia*, literally 'not-speaking'; a child
might be considered an *infans* up to age seven. The next stage, *adulescentia*, begins at 2.1.1, when A. is 15, and ends at 7.1.1 *iam mortua
erat adulescentia mea mala et nefanda et ibam in iuuentutem*. A. was then
thirty-one. On the 'ages of man' see further O'D. II 52–6: there
is no consistent scheme. The cliché that life-stages merge into one
another, and we cannot explain where infancy has gone, makes in
simple form a point about time which A. develops in book II (see on
1.6.10). A period of time is not discernible until it ceases to be present, and then it is no longer there to be considered.   **huc pergens:** to this time (at which he is speaking).   **farer** is the imperfect subjunctive from *fari*, not found elsewhere; it is used here for
the contrast with *infans*.   **et memini hoc, et unde loqui didiceram post aduerti:** A. can remember being a child who speaks;
he does not claim to remember how he learned to speak, but has

realised what happened. *didiceram*: the use of the indicative instead
of the subjunctive in indirect questions, found occasionally in classical Latin, is common in post-classical Latin.   **prensabam
memoria** 'I would grasp with my memory' (imperfect tense used
of repeated action). *prensabam* is the reading of the ninth-century MS
O, which is generally careful. S (the Sessorianus, see Introd. §4*a*)
has *pensabam*, 'I would weigh/consider', which is possible but less
vivid. The Benedictine editors suggested *praesonabam*, but A. is not
talking about trying out words. There is also a problem of punctuation, which cannot be settled from the MSS because ancient punctuation, to judge from surviving material and from comments
by grammarians, was variable (see further Habinek (1985) 42–88;
Parkes (1992)). Each of the two main possibilities has merit, but each
produces a somewhat awkward sentence. O'D. has a full stop after
prensabam memoria, taking *ego ipse* as the subject of the verb *prensabam*.
This brings the sentence to an abrupt conclusion, but the long
sequence of subordinate clauses between subject and verb perhaps
conveys something of the child's frustration in giving voice to his
wishes. Alternatively, V. puts a full stop after *quibus uolebam omnibus*.
This leaves *ego ipse* without a verb, unless *me docebam* is taken to be
implicit in *non enim docebant me maiores homines* ('my elders did not
teach me: I taught myself'), but gives a powerful sequence of verbs
prensabam . . . uidebam . . . tenebam explaining how A. acquired language. There is a minor problem about *ceterorumque membrorum actu*:
V., following S, reads *cetero*, but the sense, the balance of the sentence and several MSS support *ceterorum*. Cf. 1.6.8 for words as signs;
on A.'s theory of language (and Wittgenstein's use of it) see further
Burnyeat (1987). A., like Wittgenstein, is interested in language com-
munities, but his emphasis throughout this paragraph is on language
as an attempt to express and impose will (*uellem . . . uoluntati . . . uolebam . . . uolebam*), not on the development of the self in the process of
language learning. When A. does learn how to express *uoluntates*, he
goes further into a human society which is stormy (*procellosa*) and in
which he is dependent and subordinate.

1.9.14 A. did not understand why he should learn to read and
write; he began to pray because he was afraid of beatings.   **quas
ibi miserias expertus sum:** a quotation from one of the four
classic authors studied in schools (Introd. §2*b*, and see on 1.16.26),

Terence, *The Brothers* 867. The words are spoken by Demea, who thinks, looking back, that he had lived his life badly.   **ludificationes** 'mockeries' or 'delusions', like those caused by the demons who make people believe what is false (cf. 3.5.6).   **recte mihi uiuere puero id proponebatur, obtemperare monentibus ut in hoc saeculo florerem** 'to me, as a boy, this was presented as living rightly: to obey those who instructed me so that I should flourish in this world'. *id* is in apposition to *recte uiuere*; *ut in saeculo florerem* could depend either on *obtemperare* ('to obey those who advised me so that I should flourish') or on *monentibus* ('to obey those who advised me to flourish').   **linguosis artibus** 'arts of the tongue'. *linguosa* is not a neutral word, but implies that rhetoric tells lies. Cf. Psalm 139: 12 *uir linguosus non dirigetur super terram*, and A.'s comment in *On the Psalms* 139.5 *uir linguosus amat mendacia*. For the general feeling, cf. 3.3.6 (A. as student) and 4.2.2 (A. as teacher).   **ad honorem ... famulantibus:** in classical Latin *famulor* takes a dative. See further Campbell and McGuire (1931) 35–6 for A.'s uses of *ad*.   **labore et dolore:** A.'s suffering at school is linked with the punishment imposed on the descendants of Adam and Eve (*in dolore paries filios ... in laboribus comedes*, Genesis 3: 16–17), just as his immediate experience of human relationships demonstrates the oppressiveness and conflict of fallen human society.   **homines rogantes te** 'people praying to you'. A.'s childhood experiences include calling to God, but with an inadequate idea of God and asking for the wrong thing.   **ut poteramus** 'so far as we were able'.   **rumpebam nodos linguae meae** 'I broke the knots that held my tongue'.   **quod non erat ad insipientiam mihi:** an allusion to Psalm 21: 3 *deus meus, clamabo ad te per diem et non exaudies, et nocte et non ad insipientiam mihi*. A. probably interpreted this difficult phrase as 'by not hearing my prayer you did not make me a fool' (as you would have done if you had heard it), i.e. God was teaching him to pray for his real needs, rather than granting prayers which would not benefit him. Another possibility is 'and this will not count as folly in me', i.e. that I cry out even though you do not hear: adults laughed at his suffering, but at least he was trying to do the right thing in calling upon God.

   1.9.15 A. compares his childhood fear of beatings with an adult's fear of torture, and compares his childish games with the concerns

of adults.   **estne quisquam:** the first sentence shows A. strug-
gling to imagine the kind of indifference with which adults respond
to their children's fear of punishment. Beatings at school were a literary cliché: Prudentius (*Preface* 7–9) uses beating as shorthand for
'my time at school', and Ausonius (*Letter* 22.29) tells his grandson to
be brave, because his father and mother went through it. But from
the child's perspective remembered by A., being beaten at school is
as painful and terrifying a prospect as, for an adult, the kind of torture which might be inflicted by those in authority.   **facit enim
hoc quaedam etiam stoliditas:** A. interrupts his own rhetorical
question *estne quisquam*, 'is there anyone' (i.e. who could be indifferent) with the reflection that 'a certain stolidity of character' might
have this effect, so there is someone (*est ergo*). The punctuation here
followed from *facit enim* to *est ergo* is O'D.'s: the question *estne … quisquam* is resumed after the parenthesis at *qui tibi pie cohaerendo*. Alternatively, the parenthesis could end at *stoliditas* and *est ergo* could
be taken as a resumption of the question, 'so is there anyone …?'
eculeos et ungulas: the rack (*eculeus*), and the metal claws (*ungulae*)
which tore the flesh, had been used on Christian martyrs only two
generations previously, and were still within the repertory of Roman
judicial punishments. Martyrs were believed to have been indifferent
to torture because their love of God was so strong. But, A. asks,
could persons indifferent to their own suffering remain indifferent to
the terror of those they love?   **puerorum autem talia cum
sint:** either 'but when such things are of children', i.e. done by children, or 'but although such things are of children', i.e. characteristic
of children.   **nemo miseratur pueros uel illos uel utrosque** 'no one takes pity on the children or the adults or both'. The
adults are pitiable (see on 1.6.7 for *miseria*) because they are concerned with trivialities. The theme of false adult values appears
in moral philosophy as a reproach to adults, but A. is exceptional
both in showing intense awareness of the child's perspective and in
being prepared to think it important instead of dismissing it as
childish.   **nisi uero** '(this is deplorable) unless, of course …'
quaestiuncula: a minor scholarly dispute, but the vocabulary of
quaestio and *torqueretur* adds the schoolteacher to those who (from
their own perspective) undergo torture.

        1.10.16 A. thinks that, even though adults are unjust to children, he too was at fault as a child, because his disobedience was not a choice of better things. This paragraph establishes themes of great importance to the *C.*: the will to dominate, already present in infancy and early childhood (1.7.11, 1.8.13); *curiositas*, the wish to know what one cannot or should not know; and scratching the itch of desire. These categories of sinfulness, derived from 1 John 2: 16, recur in the adult A.'s self-examination at 10.30.41, and help him to organise his confessions in books 1–4: *concupiscentia carnis et concupiscentia oculorum et ambitio saeculi* ('the lust of the flesh, and the lust of the eyes, and the pride of life', AV).   **ordinator et creator rerum omnium naturalium, peccatorum autem tantum ordinator:** a favourite contrast for A. (cf. 1.7.11 *tu fecisti eum et peccatum non fecisti in eo*). Sin disrupts the divine ordering of the world, but God restores order.   **amans ... scalpi aures meas falsis fabellis, quo prurirent ardentius:** the 'itchy ears' come from 2 Timothy 4: 3–4 *erit enim tempus, cum sanam doctrinam non sustinebunt, sed ad sua desideria coaceruabunt sibi magistros, prurientes auribus; et a ueritate quidem auditum auertent, ad fabulas autem conuertentur*. The image is developed at 3.2.4 (q.v.); the 'itchy ears' recur at 4.8.13, when the unsound teaching of the Manichaeans proves to be no comfort. **spectacula:** races and fights and theatre shows, financed, in return for civic honour, by local notables. A. described them, and the transient glory they offered, in *Against the Academics* 1.2: he was writing for his patron Romanianus, who had financed *spectacula* at Thagaste. There is a similar evocation in John Chrysostom, *On Vainglory* 4–6; see further Brown (1992) 78–89. A.'s *curiositas* is not satisfied by stories: he wants to see what he should not. His disapproval of *spectacula*, which is shared by many Christian writers, may seem excessive, but they included not only explicit sexual representations, but extreme violence and cruelty inflicted on animals and people. The effect on a crowd of spectators was known to A. from his own experience and that of his close friend Alypius (6.8.13), who was unable to keep away from gladiator shows; the effect on a spectator who takes pleasure in experiencing pity is discussed in 3.2.2–3.   **libera etiam eos qui nondum te inuocant, ut inuocent te et liberes eos:** cf. 1.1.1.

1.11.17 A. was a catechumen as a child, and asked for baptism when he was seriously ill; but he recovered and his mother decided to defer baptism.   **humilitatem ... superbiam:** for human *superbia* see on 1.1.1; the *humilitas domini dei nostri* is the Incarnation of Christ (cf. 12.43.68), and the use of *descendens* is deliberate paradox (cf. 4.12.19). For A.'s audience, *humilitas* had a social resonance: the *humiliores* were the 'lower classes' who were vulnerable not only to contempt and neglect, but to brutal physical punishments which were not prescribed for the *honestiores*, the more respectable.   **condiebar eius sale:** a reference to the rite of 'seasoning with salt' which marked A. as a catechumen, i.e. a member of the church who was undergoing instruction but was not yet baptised, and who therefore did not share in the Eucharist. Catechumens received the sign of the cross on the forehead and a laying-on of hands; they were given bread which had been blessed, and salt which was perhaps placed on the tongue (see further van der Meer (1961) 353–7, who suggests that most catechumens thought of the salt as an 'antedemonic specific'). The imperfect tenses *signabar* and *condiebar* indicate a repeated rite. Monnica was not unusual in wishing to delay A.'s baptism for fear of post-baptismal sin: the emperor Constantine, like A.'s father Patricius, was baptised only on his deathbed. In the next paragraph A. reports the reaction 'let him do it, he's not baptised yet'. Many fourth-century Christians believed that since baptism cleanses from sin, and cannot be repeated, post-baptismal sin is difficult or impossible to absolve. A., by the time he wrote the *C.*, regarded baptism as a cleansing (*mundatio*) from past sin and as a major commitment, but thought that human beings cannot at any time in their lives be free from sin, because human nature retains its basic sinful drive (*concupiscentia*). He had begun to use the image, derived from Romans 9: 20–1, of human beings made out of potter's clay, a *massa luti* (lump of mud) which is also a *massa peccati* (lump of sin). See further Bonner (1986) 378–83. **pressu stomachi repente aestuarem:** it is not clear whether this boyhood illness was commonplace stomach trouble and fever, or a precursor of the chest pains and breathing problems which affected A. in Milan (9.2.4).   **salutem meam carius parturiebat:** Monnica's physical motherhood and maternal concern (*conturbata mater carnis meae*), already emphasised by *ab utero matris meae*, is contrasted with her spiritual childbearing, an image which was often used of women (and of men) who had renounced childbearing

for celibacy.   **nisi statim recreatus essem:** an ironic end to a
dramatic sentence. A. was restored to health, and therefore was not
'created anew' by baptism. Cf. 4.4.8 for A.'s *alter ego*, the friend who
was baptised in a critical illness: *recreatus est et saluus factus*.   **mundatio mea:** baptism is, literally, washing (*lauacrum*), and the spiritual cleansing of baptism is expressed as removing dirt (*sordes*) –
another maternal task.   **ius maternae pietatis:** C. 'my right
to follow my mother's devotion', but perhaps rather the rightful
claims of Monnica's piety, even against the legal authority of the *pater-
familias*.   **illa satagebat ut tu mihi pater esses:** Monnica's
efforts to make God, not Patricius, the true father of A. were, on
the evidence of the *C.*, successful. Patricius appears rarely, and then
little to his credit: here he is inferior to his wife; in 2.3.6 (q.v.) he
rejoices in his son's virility; at 9.9.19 it is only Monnica's tact which
stops her being a battered wife; and his death is reported at 3.4.7
(q.v.) out of sequence and in a parenthesis which displaces him.
melior seruiebat 'she served him, though better than he'. O'D.
notes (on 13.32.47) that A. uses *seruiebat* in preference to the biblical
subdita est, 'she was subject'. A. makes it clear that God helped her
to overcome her husband in this matter because she was serving
God, not because a morally superior wife should not be subject to
her husband; but the imagery used in this paragraph transforms the
wife and mother into a person of spiritual authority.

    1.11.18 A. asks why he was not baptised in childhood.   **uellem
scire, si tu etiam uelles** 'I should like to know, if you also were
willing' – but the answer is only in terms of human confusion, not in
terms of God's purpose.   **sine illum, faciat** 'let him be, let
him do it'; in classical Latin *sine faciat* (cf. *sine uulneretur* below) would
be expected, but cf. 3.12.21, 4.1.1 for *sine* with an accusative.   **id
ageretur mecum meorum meaque diligentia ... salus ani-
mae meae tuta esset tutela tua:** these intense groupings of
words perhaps suggest the intense (but misdirected) anxiety of his
family.   **terram per eos, unde postea formarer, quam
ipsam iam effigiem committere uolebat:** the word *terra* at first
suggests land in sight from the waves of temptation, but *unde postea
formarer* shows that A. is using imagery from the creation-narratives
in Genesis: the earth which was 'without form and void' (Genesis
1: 2), which was separated from the waters (*ibid.* 9–10), and from

which God made the first human being (Genesis 2: 7), is formed into humanity made in God's image and likeness (Genesis 1: 26–7), which A. interprets as the earth shaped by God into its proper form, *effigies*. A. uses the same metaphor at 13.12.13: 'before our earth received the form given by teaching it was invisible and unorganised, and we were covered by the darkness of ignorance'. In 1.11.18 the *effigies* is made by God in baptism, which restores the image of God in a human being, so A. before baptism is the *terra . . . unde postea formarer*. On the development of A.'s thought about image and likeness, see further Markus (1964): he was reluctant to call anyone but Christ the image of God, but came to think that God's image is never lost from the human soul. But the image may be either more like or less like the original: it may be deformed and in need of reformation. *per eos* i.e. *fluctus*, an odd usage with *committere*, but perhaps suggesting that he would come through the waters of temptation.

1.12.19 A. resented being compelled to learn, but God ensured that it did him good, despite the mistaken motives of those who made him do it. The paragraph is full of word-play, perhaps because the boy A. is discovering the skills of rhetoric. **me in eas urgeri oderam, et urgebar tamen et bene mihi fiebat:** see Introd. §2*a* on parataxis and on clauses linked with *et*. *bene mihi fiebat* 'good was being done to me', despite the constraints he suffered and the false standards of those in authority. In this paragraph A. is always passive or compelled. **nemo autem inuitus bene facit, etiamsi bonum est quod facit** 'no one does right against his will, even if what he does is good', because if he acted under compulsion, he did not choose to do right. *autem* is used to mark the second premise of the argument: 'I would not have learned unless I had been forced; but (*autem*) no one does right against his will; so I did not do right in learning'. **quo referrem** 'to what use I would put'. **copiosae inopiae et ignominiosae gloriae:** two oxymorons (see on 1.6.7) reinforced by the similar vowel-patterns *copiosae . . . inopiae*. A. particularly likes *copia–inopia*, cf. 2.4.9, and *TLL* s.v. *inopia* for other authors who use the contrast. The sentence *illi enim . . . gloriae* is in the classical style which A. was being made to learn, but its meaning is a rejection of the style. **cui numerati sunt capilli nostri:** used again at 4.14.22. The unstated context in Matthew 10: 30 is illuminating. 'Do not fear those who kill the body but cannot destroy the soul; rather fear him who can destroy body and soul in Hell. Are not sparrows sold two for a penny? Yet not one of them falls to the ground without your father. As for you, even the hairs of your head are numbered. So do not be afraid: you matter more than sparrows.' **tantillus puer et tantus pecca- tor** 'so small a child yet so great a sinner'. This seems wild ex- aggeration, but A. is thinking of his *inordinatus animus* (cf. 1.10.16 and compare 1.6.7 *ordinatus affectus*) with its mistaken loves and its wilful disobedience – the basic ingredients of sin, whether in the garden of Eden or in fourth-century Africa. Cf. 1.7.11 for sinful babies. **ita de non bene facientibus tu bene faciebas mihi** 'so you brought about good for me from those who were not doing good'. Almost all MSS have *non de bene facientibus*, which would make a quite different (and wrong) point, namely that God brought about good for A., but not from those who were doing good.

1.13.20 A. considers his dislike of Greek, and his preference for Latin literature over basic skills of literacy.

Greek was the first 'foreign language' for a Latin-speaking school- boy, and north African inscriptions show that people took pride in being *utraque lingua eruditus*, 'educated in both languages'. It was the official language of the east Mediterranean half of the Roman empire, and was essential for literary culture and for the most in- teresting work being done in philosophy and theology. A. probably improved his Greek during his years at Hippo, where there were many Greek speakers: around 400 he wrote that he could not read Greek theological works properly, but by about 415 he was able to com- ment on the Greek text of the Bible and to read Greek treatises if there was a translation (see further Marrou (1938) 27–37, (1949) 631–7). He rightly ascribes his problem with Greek to idleness at school, but does not, as he reasonably might, put some of the blame on the teaching methods (see 1.14.22–3). **non quas primi magistri, sed quas docent qui grammatici uocantur:** 'pri- mary' teachers taught basic reading, writing and number skills; some of their texts and exercises survive. See further Dionisotti (1982), Kaster (1983). *grammatici*, on whom see Kaster (1988), taught close attention to the style and vocabulary of texts and to any literary or historical allusions, much like a school commentary on a clas- sical text in the earlier years of the twentieth century. A. himself, according to his biographer Possidius, was a *grammaticus* at Thagaste (see on 4.2.2). A.'s chief objection to grammarians is that they said nothing about the moral content of the texts (see on 1.17.27).   **uanitate uitae:** the phrase *uanitas uitae* is another possible translation of 'the pride of life' in 1 John 2: 16 (see on 1.10.16).   **caro eram et spiritus ambulans et non reuertens:** Psalm 77: 39 'I was flesh, and a breath which goes and does not return', a mortal being. The context (not quoted, cf. 1.12.19) is important: God is merciful to sinners, remembering what they are. *spiritus* here means not an immortal spirit, but breath, which (for a time) animates the body. A. uses the same verse, slightly modified, at 4.15.26 (q.v.).   **tenere cogebar Aeneae nescio cuius errores:** i.e. to keep in memory the *Aeneid* of Virgil, which was the basic text of Latin literary education. *nescio cuius* probably implies (cf. *cuiusdam Ciceronis* 3.4.7 and note, *Manichaeum nescio quem* 5.5.8) that Aeneas, the hero and founder of Rome, is not of great importance. The *errores* of Aeneas are literally wanderings, those of A. are faults; the theme of weeping for fictional characters instead of one's own spiritual destitution is developed in 3.2.4 (q.v.). **a te morientem** 'dying away from you', i.e. turning away from God and on course for death (cf. 1.5.5).   **siccis oculis ferrem miserrimus:** 'most wretched' in the sense 'pitiable', not the sense 'miserable' (see on 1.5.5).

1.13.21 The double meaning of *miseria* is brought into relation with two directions for love: human passion and desire for God. **lumen cordis mei et panis oris intus animae meae et uirtus maritans mentem meam et sinum cogitationis meae:** images for the beloved, namely God. On *cor* see 1.5.5. *panis* derives from John 6: 35 'I am the bread of life: who comes to me shall not go hungry'; the imagery of spiritual food is central to book 3. As in 1.5.5, A. offers strongly physical images for spiritual and intellectual aspects of humanity: *anima* has a mouth, *mens* has a husband, and *cogitatio* has a *sinus* (C. 'innermost recesses'), a more common image which derives from the deep fold of a tunic over the breast. **fornicabar abs te:** an Old Testament image ('whoring after strange gods') reinforced by the language of *amor*.   **euge, euge:** Greek for 'Very good!' (cf. Italian 'Bravo!'); in Psalm 39: 15–16, the false praise of those 'who seek my soul to carry it away' (echoed at 10.36.59).   **dicitur, ut pudeat, si non ita homo sit** 'it is said so that he should be ashamed, if he is not that kind of person', i.e. the kind who pursues worldly goals.   **Didonem extinctam ferroque extrema secutam:** Virgil, *Aeneid* 6.457 *uenerat extinctam ferroque extrema secutam*. A.'s version is a complete hexameter, unexpected in a prose text but perhaps not much more disconcerting in rhythm than some of his biblical citations (Introd. §2*b*).   **sequens ipse extrema condita tua** 'myself pursuing the furthest things of your creation'. The *extrema* sought by Dido are the last things, i.e. the end of life; those sought by A. are the most remote from God.   **terra iens in terram:** Genesis 3: 19 'dust thou art, and to dust shalt thou return'.   **si prohiberer ea legere, dolerem, quia non legerem quod dolerem** 'if I had been forbidden to read these things, I should have felt pain, because I was not reading that which would cause me pain'. A. contrasts misplaced *dolor* (pain, grief, resentment) with the real pain caused to his soul by reading damaging literature. The contrast is exploited further in 3.2.2–4.   **litterae:** usually 'literature' (as in English 'a man of letters'), but also the letters of the alphabet; cf. Kaster (1988) 35–47 on the various meanings of 'literacy' and 'letters'.

1.13.22 A. decides that basic literacy is more important than the literature he loved.   **non est ita, non est ita: melior est prorsus doctrina illa prior:** 'that earlier teaching' (not here 'doctrine') is reading and writing. See on 1.13.20. It is unclear how much of this God is being asked to say (*ueritas tua dicat mihi*): probably *non est ita, non est ita*, contradicting the claim of the last sentence in 1.13.21 that *honestiores et uberiores litterae putantur*, then A. restates the point, *melior est prorsus doctrina illa prior*.   **at enim uela pendent liminibus grammaticarum scholarum:** *at enim* introduces a possible objection to A.'s argument that basic literacy is more valuable than training in literature. Curtained doorways (like offices reached only through a secretary's office) were a mark of importance, and the *grammaticus* in his professorial chair (*cathedra*) was a person of status. Only privileged boys could attend his classes. But, according to A., the curtain which apparently confers status also conceals error.   **non clament aduersus me quos iam non timeo:** understand *ei quos non timeo*, i.e. the 'buyers and sellers of literature'. A. is not now afraid of schoolmasters.   **secundum id pactum et placitum quo inter se homines ista signa**

firmarunt: see on 1.6.8. A. thinks that language (spoken and written) is a human convention.   **ipsius umbra Creusae:** Virgil, *Aeneid* 2.772 *infelix simulacrum atque ipsius umbra Creusae.* A. as a boy wept for the suicide of Dido (1.13.20–1) and the loss of Creusa: Creusa was the wife of Aeneas and Dido had considered herself to be his wife. The *Aeneid* supplies images of loss and wandering (see Introd. §2*b*); perhaps it too is an *infelix simulacrum* as well as a *dulcissimum spectaculum uanitatis.*

1.14.23 A. contrasts his learning of Greek with his learning of Latin, and reflects that it was good for him not to enjoy Greek literature too much.   **talia cantantem:** basic arithmetic (like multiplication tables) was an *odiosa cantio*, but A. also hated Greek which sang the stories of Homer, *oderam … (Graecam) cantantem.* **difficultas omnino ediscendae linguae peregrinae** 'the difficulty of learning a foreign language at all'.   **instabatur mihi:** the verb is used impersonally.   **inter … ioca adridentium et laetitias adludentium:** the preposition *ad-* suggests that the jokes and games were shared with the infant A.   **et qua non esset:** this is the reading of almost all the MSS, but is difficult to interpret. O'D. marks *et qua* as a crux. V. suggests understanding *qua uia*: 'my heart urged me to give birth to its concepts, and by a way which would not have existed, had I not learned some words'. The Benedictine editors emended the text to *quae non possem*, 'which I could not have done'. This must be A.'s meaning, but it is not clear what exactly he said.   **a loquentibus, in quorum et ego auribus parturiebam quidquid sentiebam:** a word-order designed to emphasise the child's breaking into the conversation, and A.'s love of physical imagery, together produce a strange effect. The image of giving birth to ideas derives from Plato, *Theatetus* 150, in which Socrates describes himself as a midwife like his mother, but giving birth in people's ears seems to be A.'s own idea.   **illius fluxum haec restringit:** fearful necessity (*haec*) restricts the flow of free curiosity (*illius*). In present-day educational theory this is obviously a bad thing – no wonder A. failed to learn Greek. But, for A., *fluxus* connotes instability and dispersal (see on 1.3.3), and *curiositas* is the desire to know what one should not know (see on 1.10.16). So even unjust human coercion (beating for the schoolboy, torture for the martyr, as in 1.9.15) is a salutary constraint, as A. insists by the

threefold repetition of *legibus tuis*. See further Markus (1988) 94–
100.   **salubres amaritudines ... iucunditate pestifera:**
oxymoron (see on 1.12.19) to sharpen the point that it was good for
A. to have gall sprinkled on 'Greek sweetness' (*suauitates Graecas*,
above) by the requirement to learn grammar. For salutary bitterness, cf. 2.2.4.

1.15.24 A. interrupts the account of his schooling to reflect on
God's help and pray that his studies may be used in God's service.
Exaudi, domine, deprecationem meam: Psalm 60: 2.   **sub
disciplina tua:** cf. below *cum uana discerem, tu disciplinam dabas
mihi.*   **ut ... amplexer manum tuam totis praecordiis
meis:** this looks bizarre even for A. (cf. *aures cordis mei*, 1.5.5), but
praecordia may have been dead metaphor. *praecordia* are the regions
below the heart and near the diaphragm, thought of as the site of
emotion (like the solar plexus).   **ea uia tuta est, in qua pueri
ambularent:** some attempts were made, in the fourth century, to
provide alternative Christian classics for the education of children.
They were not successful. For the debate on Christianity and the
classics, see Kaster (1988) 70–95.

1.16.25 The literature studied in schools is corrupting.   **flumen
moris humani:** cf. 1.14.23 *fluxus*, but a river also has a current
which sweeps people along. See Markus (1988) 10 for further examples of river and sea imagery.   **Euae filios:** probably Eve's
children here (but Adam's at 1.9.14) because the emphasis is on
succumbing to temptation as Eve did first.   **qui lignum conscenderint:** *lignum* is literally a piece of wood, on which one might
safely cross the sea, but it also connotes the cross and therefore the
saving power of Christ.   **in te legi:** it is not specified where in
the 'river of human custom' A. read about Jupiter's adulteries, but
the next paragraph (q.v.) cites Terence, *Eunuchus.*   **actum est,
ut haberet auctoritatem ad imitandum uerum adulterium
lenocinante falso tonitru:** the word-order is ambiguous, but in
this context the sense is probably *ut uerum adulterium haberet auctoritatem ad imitandum*, i.e. that Jupiter was thus presented so that real
adultery could have an authoritative example to imitate. Thunder,
falsely said to be caused by Jupiter, acts as a pander (*leno*) by declaring Jupiter's authority.   **paenulatorum magistrorum:** bar-
risters, who wore a *paenulus* (originally a hooded cloak designed to

keep out rain, just as a scholar's gown once kept out cold) to address the court.   **ex eodem puluere** probably refers to the dust
of the (metaphorical) arena in which lawyers contend, rather than
to the creation of human beings from the dust of the earth, but A.
is quite capable of having both in mind.   **fingebat haec Homerus et humana ad deos transferebat; diuina mallem ad
nos:** quoted from Cicero, *Tusculan Disputations* 1.26.65 (see Hagendahl (1967) 510–6 for A.'s use of this text). In *City of God* 4.26,
writing for a predominantly non-Christian audience, A. uses the
same quotation, but names Cicero and praises his disapproval of
Homer's immoral gods. Plato is not yet a presence in the *C.* (Introd.
§3*b*), and A. does not comment that the passage from Terence neatly
illustrates Plato's arguments about art in the *Republic*: the young
man, looking at a representation (a picture) of a representation (a
story about Jupiter), acquires wrong beliefs about the gods and bad
models of conduct.   **sed uerius dicitur:** A. argues that Homer
does not ascribe human characteristics to gods, but divine characteristics to wicked humans.   **flagitia**, in books 1–4, are predominantly sexual sins (see further O'D. on 3.8.16).

1.16.26 A literary education is sanctioned by custom and by
law; but words need not be learned from corrupting literature.   **o
flumen tartareum:** Tartarus, a river of the underworld in Greco-
Roman myth, reappears in 3.1.1.   **iactantur in te fili hominum cum mercedibus:** *iactantur in te* could mean 'are thrown into
you' or 'are tossed about in you'. The *mercedes* are their school fees.
Some teachers were paid a public salary (*salarium*), either from the
local authority or from imperial funds; others depended entirely on
fees and presents from their pupils. There were (at intervals) laws
establishing both fees and salaries (evidence in Kaster (1988) 114–21,
and specifically for north Africa in Lepelley (1979) 228–31).   **hoc
agitur publice in foro, in conspectu legum supra merce-
dem salaria decernentium:** A. emphasises the weight of official
backing for this corrupting educational system. Inscriptions in the
forum displayed the texts of the laws on salaries, and teachers em-
ployed by the state might be assigned a lecture room nearby. The
rhetor Libanius had a room in the town hall at Antioch, and
Alypius, when he was A.'s student at Carthage, is described (6.9.14)
revising a speech in the forum, outside the lawcourts.   **saxa tua**

percutis: the sense of being dominated by human custom is re-inforced by the metaphor of the fast-flowing river which roars and crashes against its rocks. *saxa* are probably small enough to be rolled along by the torrent.   **hinc** 'this is why' (C.).   **imbrem au-reum ... illud uero feci ac libens:** first paraphrase, then quota-tion, from Terence, *Eunuchus* 583–91, which describes a young man justifying his sexual misconduct by the example of Jupiter. Terence (a second-century B.C. dramatist who came from north Africa) was a standard school author and example of Latin eloquence, together with Virgil and Cicero whom A. has already quoted, and Sallust who is quoted in 2.5.11 (q.v.). His style and characterisation were much admired; A., disingenuously, speaks as if all that is in question is learning words. But the passage from Terence provides both an image of A. the schoolboy learning from his set texts about illicit love, and a parallel to A. the young man modelling his conduct on representations of illicit love (see on 3.1.1).   **uerba quasi uasa electa atque pretiosa:** words are here presented not as signs (see on 1.6.8) but as precious containers which may be used to hold error or truth (cf. 1.15.24). This image does not offer a theory of language: its purpose is to show the teaching A. was given as enforced in-toxication. The phrase *uasa electa atque pretiosa* may be influenced by Acts 9: 15, where Paul is called *uas electionis*, a 'vessel of choice' or 'chosen vessel', and by Proverbs 20: 15, where the 'lip which speaks wisdom' is a *uas pretiosum*.   **bonae spei puer** 'a promising boy', literally 'a boy of good hope': cf. 2.3.8 for the contrast between the hope of Heaven and the hope of success.

1.17.27 A. won the prize for a speech expressing the rage of Juno.

Prose adaptations of poetry were a familiar school exercise (Quintilian, *Institutes of Oratory* 1.9.2). A. was challenged to express the damaging emotions, *ira et dolor*, which Virgil ascribed to the queen of the gods when she was unable to frustrate the divine will by preventing Aeneas from reaching Italy. The words were to be *quae numquam Iunonem dixisse audieram*: in one sense, not just copied from Virgil, though the speech had to follow Virgil (*uestigia ... sequi cogeba-mur*); in another sense, sheer invention, something never said by a (non-existent) goddess. A.'s critique of the educational system is exemplified in the commentary on this section of the *Aeneid* by his near-contemporary Servius, a respected grammarian who was teaching in Rome by the 390s (see further Kaster (1988) 169–97). On *saeuae memorem Iunonis ob iram* (*Aeneid* 1.4) Servius comments that many people ask why Juno is called *saeua*, because her name derives from *iuuare*, to help; they reply that she is *saeua* at this time, but they are wrong, because 'the ancients' (*ueteres*) used *saeua* to mean 'big' – he offers an example from Ennius. He also explains that *memorem* means not *quae meminerat* but *quae in memoria erat*, adds some other Virgilian examples of active for passive and vice versa, and warns his pupils not to follow this example. He offers no moral or religious comment on the anger and resentment shown by a god.   **non posset Italia Teucrorum auertere regem:** almost a complete hexameter, adapted from Virgil, *Aeneid* 1.38 where the first two words are *nec posse*.   **ille dicebat laudabilius ... congruenter uestientibus:** an elaborate Ciceronian structure, in the style the young A. was expected to imitate, and concerned with suiting expression to subject in accordance with Ciceronian teaching.   **ut quid mihi illud ... quod** can be interpreted both as 'what was it to me then, that I was acclaimed?' and 'what is it to me now?' *ut quid* (cf. 2.3.5), 'why?' or, as here, 'for what?' translates the Greek *hina ti* in Latin versions of the Bible.   **laudes tuae per scripturas tuas suspenderent palmitem cordis mei** 'praise of you, through your scriptures, should have supported the vine-shoot of (i.e. which is) my heart'. That is, A.'s education ought to have been based on the Scriptures. The image is derived from John 15: 4 'a vine-shoot cannot bear fruit of itself, unless it remains on the vine; it is the same for you, unless you remain in me. I am the vine, you are the vine-shoots.' A. then develops the scriptural image with the help of Virgil on plants which are not cultivated, *et turpis auibus praedam fert uua racemos* (*Georgics* 2.60). But whereas Virgil has the vine bearing (inferior) grapes which are carried off by birds, in A. it appears to be the vine-shoot which is carried off: *et non raperetur per inania nugarum turpis praeda uolatilibus* '(if praise of you had supported the vine-shoot), it would not have been snatched away through the emptiness of trifles as the shameful spoil of birds'. The allusion to Virgil is very discreet, perhaps suggesting that the proper role of classical literature is to lend occasional elegance to a scripturally trained mind.   **non enim uno modo sacrificatur transgressoribus angelis** 'not in one way [only] is sacrifice offered to the rebel angels'. The angels who refused obedience to God (see on 2.4.9), and became agents of evil, were identified with *daimones*, supernatural powers which in Greco-Roman religious thought might be benign or malevolent, but in Christian terminology became simply demons. A. argued in *City of God* 2.24 that the gods of Greco-Roman religion were in fact *daimones* who deluded people into worshipping them. By composing a speech in the character of Juno, A. was making an offering to false gods and to the demon-inspired values of secular culture. Cf. 3.3.5.

1.18.28 The people who taught A. were more concerned about correct language than about correct morality. A. thanks God for rescuing him from his alienation.   **barbarismo aut soloecis-mo:** A. explains in *On Christian Teaching* 2.13.19 that *barbarismus* is incorrect pronunciation, for instance a long *e* in the third syllable of *ignoscere*, and *soloecismus* is a grammatical mistake, for instance *inter hominibus* instead of *inter homines* (exploited in 1.18.29). Compare the (professed) anxiety of his fellow-countryman Apuleius (*Florida* 9): *quis enim uestrum mihi unum soloecismum ignouerit? quis uel unam syllabam barbare pronuntiatam donauerit?*   **copiose ornateque:** Ciceronian terms of approval.   **longanimis et multum misericors et uerax:** Psalm 85: 15.   **numquid semper tacebis?:** the immediate suggestion is that God will speak in condemnation of sinners, but A. moves on to his own yearning for God who remains silent. **cuius cor dicit tibi: quaesiui uultum tuum:** Psalm 26: 8 *tibi dixit cor meum, quaesiui uultum tuum; uultum tuum, domine, requiram.* A. interpreted Psalm 104: 4 *quaerite faciem eius semper* as 'seek the presence of God'.   **nam longe a uultu tuo in affectu tenebroso:** understand *eram*, or perhaps *sum*, because A. is still aware of distance although God rescues his soul (*nunc eruis*). In what follows, A. explains distance from God, *longe a uultu tuo*, with the help of Plotinus and the New Testament.   **non enim pedibus:** from Plotinus, *Ennead* 1.6.8, a passage which made a deep impression on A. 'Let us escape to our homeland ... Our homeland is where we came from, and where our father is. What then is this expedition, this flight? You must not hurry on foot, for feet carry us everywhere from one land to another; nor should you arrange transport by horse or ship; you must let all that go, and not look, but, as if shutting your eyes, you must make an exchange and awaken another seeing, which everyone has but few use.' **filius ille tuus mi-nor** is the younger son in Jesus' story of the Prodigal Son (Luke 15: 11–32), *tuus* (and subsequent second-person verbs) because the father in that story stands for God, to whom A. speaks. The story, here briefly evoked in relation to Plotinus on returning to God, is essential to A.'s self-understanding and to the imagery of the *C*. The younger son asked for his share of the inheritance and travelled into a far country, where he wasted it; famine came, he was reduced to working as a swineherd, and 'would fain have filled his belly with the husks that the swine did eat' (AV). Then, coming to himself, he decided 'I will arise and go to my father, and will say to him, Father, I have sinned against heaven and before thee, and am no more worthy to be called thy son: make me as one of thy hired servants. And he arose and came to his father. But while he was still a great way off, his father saw him, and had compassion, and ran, and fell on his neck, and kissed him.' **in affectu ergo libidi-noso:** A. returns (*ergo*, 'then') to what he said before his explanation of distance from God, and this time interprets *in affectu tenebroso* as *libidinoso*, the darkness of lust which keeps him from God. *libido* is wider in range than sexual lust: A. uses the word of any evil desire. See further Bonner (1986) 398–401.

1.18.29 A. returns to the subject of orators who are more concerned to pronounce *homines* correctly than to avoid doing harm to their fellow human beings.

The word *homo* echoes through this paragraph, in which human conventions are contrasted with God's laws, but the value of a human being is affirmed. A. emphasises language as an entry into human social corruption (cf. 1.8.13), whereas many philosophers saw it as proof of human co-operation (*pactum*) in place of violence. For a more positive account of human social bonds cf. 3.8.15–16. **quasi uero ... uastat inimicando:** Stoic and Platonist philosophers agreed that anger does more damage to the soul of the angry person than to the victim of anger. **scripta conscientia:** *conscientia* is in classical Latin 'awareness of doing wrong', as here awareness of doing to others what we do not want them to do to us. But *scripta* suggests 'written in our hearts' as in Romans 2: 15 'these people demonstrate the work of the law written in their hearts, their *conscientia* (Greek *syneidesis*) bearing witness for them', where *conscien-*

tia seems to mean 'conscience' as an inner awareness of right and wrong (cf. 4.9.14, and 10.2.2 *cuius oculis nuda est abyssus humanae conscientiae*).   **inimicum ... insectans:** in 4.2.2 A. allows himself some merit as a teacher in that he discouraged his students from prosecution of the innocent.   **inter hominibus:** a solecism (see on 1.18.28).

1.19.30 A., as a child, told lies, stole food and cheated in games. **Horum ego puer morum in limine iacebam:** like an abandoned child left on a doorstep (many Christian writers pointed out that an abandoned child is likely to be raised in a brothel).   **in illis:** i.e. those whose approval he wanted at the time.   **studio spectandi nugatoria et imitandi ludicra inquietudine:** the last three words are (deliberately) ambivalent. *ludicra* could be accusative plural neuter, so that the phrase would mean 'restless wish to imitate performances', or *ludicra* could be ablative singular feminine with *inquietudine*, so that the phrase would mean 'absurd restless desire to imitate'. The careful balance of the complete phrase supports the first interpretation.   **furta enim faciebam ... saeuire magis quam cedere libebat:** again the three fundamental sins (see on 1.10.16): lust of the flesh (greed), lust of the eyes (watching and imitating *spectacula*), desire to dominate; and, A. adds, doing to others exactly what he did not want them to do to him (that is, cheating).   **istane est innocentia puerilis?:** cf. 1.7.11 on infant innocence.   **talium est regnum caelorum:** Matthew 19:14 'let the children come to me, for of such is the kingdom of heaven'. The most common interpretation of this saying was in terms of the innocence of children, in particular their freedom from the desires which beset older people. A. sees a continuity from childish to adult desires and a change only in their objects, not their nature. He interprets the saying in terms of the humility – literally the low standing – of children. See further G. Clark (1994).

1.20.31 God would deserve thanks even if A. had not lived beyond childhood; God's gifts were very great, but A. sinned by looking for pleasure and for truth in himself and others of God's creation, not in the Creator.

This is consciously an end-of-book section, bringing together themes from book 1. A.'s presentation of himself as a lying, stealing, cheating child, and of his education as a training in corruption, is countered by reflection on the child as a wonderful work of God: compare 1.7.12 on the infant.   **incolumitatem:** as in 1.7.12, but now awareness of oneself as whole is interpreted not only as a gift of God, but as a trace of God who is One, *uestigium secretissimae unitatis.* The child's concern for *integritas sensuum* and for truth in *cogitatio* also suggests the 'ascent of reason' towards the One, 'from bodies to the soul that senses through the body, thence to its inner force to which the bodily senses report external things – thus far the animals can go – and again from there to the reasoning power to which is referred for judgement what is taken from the bodily senses' (7.17.23). Reason's reflection on truth and on its own activity will lead to awareness of God: compare 1.9.14 for A.'s childish awareness, *esse magnum aliquem qui posses etiam non apparens sensibus nostris exaudire nos et subuenire nobis,* and see further 3.6.11.   **falli nolebam ... ignorantiam:** the positive aspects of social experience and education.   **et bona sunt, et haec omnia ego:** i.e. 'I am all these good things'.   **hoc enim peccabam:** an unusually mild statement of A.'s concern for created things rather than their creator, followed by a carefully balanced contrast of what he wanted with what he got. Book 1 ends in gratitude and confidence.

Book II

The first sentence is programmatic: book 2 is concerned with 'foulnesses and carnal corruptions', narrated 'not so that I may love them, but so that I may love you, my God'. A.'s account of his early adolescence – half the length of book 1 on his infancy and childhood – deals with his critical sixteenth year. He was idle and at home between school and further study; he had reached puberty. He and his friends stole pears from a neighbour's tree, and this apparently trivial episode becomes an image of the unexplained evil in human nature.

2.1.1 A. contrasts the love he now feels for God with the wild and self-destructive loves of his adolescence.   **amore amoris tui:** both 'by love of your love' and 'by love for love of you'. A. has just said he is recalling past sins *ut amem te,* 'so that I may love you'.   **ut tu dulcescas mihi, dulcedo non fallax, dulcedo**

felix et secura: *dulcedo* is a favourite image for God (cf. 1.20.31, and 1.15.24 *ut dulcescas mihi*), and A. makes a favourite contrast with bitterness, *amaritudo*; but the contrast is usually between salutary bitterness and dangerous sweetness, as e.g. at 1.14.23 and 2.2.4. **conligens me a dispersione, in qua frustatim discissus sum dum ab uno te auersus in multa euanui:** cf. 1.3.3. Plotinus, *Ennead* 6.9.1, points out that if something is divided into very small pieces it loses its identity. Similarly, the human mind is capable of focussing on God and learning to ignore distractions, but also of dividing its attention among many things, so that it has no coherence (*Ennead* 6.9.8). A. experiences this as fragmentation almost to vanishing-point (cf. 11.29.39).   **exarsi:** immediately after *euanui*, 'I faded out', comes *exarsi*, 'I blazed up', followed by a pile-up of diverse metaphors which convey the turmoil of adolescence.   **satiari inferis:** the infinitive *satiari* depends on *exarsi*, 'I was on fire to be satiated with hell'. Hell is the condition of being unredeemed from sin (cf. 1.2.2 on A.'s use of *inferi*), here specifically sexual sin: this is made explicit in the metaphor which follows.   **siluescere ausus sum uariis et umbrosis amoribus:** *siluescere* is what happens when a vine runs to wood and leaves instead of bearing fruit; cf. 1.17.27 for A. as a young vine. *umbrosis*, an epithet transferred from the thick foliage, has here almost the same overtones as English 'shady'; cf. 2.2.2 for the clear light of friendship.   **contabuit species mea, et computrui coram oculis tuis:** *species* is the outward and pleasing appearance, but also the form which shapes matter into a created being (see further O'D. on 1.7.12). As A. was 'fragmented' in the pursuit of many things, this *species* wasted away and rotted. There is an allusion to Daniel 10: 8 *et species mea immutata est in me, et emarcui, nec habui quidquam uirium*.

2.2.2 A.'s delight was in loving and being loved, but love was contaminated by the wish to possess.

concupiscentia (see on 1.10.16) here becomes specifically *concupiscentia carnis*, the 'lust of the flesh' expressed as sexual desire. The desire for physical possession clouds human friendship, *amicitia*, just as the infant's wish to grasp and dominate manifested the corruption of human relationships (see on 1.7.11). Consequently, *dilectio* – the kind of love, as between parents and children, which shows affectionate commitment rather than desire – cannot be distinguished from *libido*, the desire to possess. (For A.'s use of *libido* and *concupiscentia*, see Bonner (1986) 398–401.) A. does not give any sympathy to his adolescent perceptions of human relationships, as he did (see on 1.9.15) to his childhood perceptions of schooling: all he sees is lust and confusion. **non tenebatur modus ab animo usque ad animum, quatenus est luminosus limes amicitiae:** literally, 'the limit was not maintained from mind to mind, as far as the shining frontier of friendship is'. *modus* is the limit or defining line which makes something what it is (cf. 1.7.12). A. implies that he crossed the boundary of non-possessive friendship. He uses *amicitia* as a general word for human ties of affection, including the proper relationship between husband and wife (*On the Good of Marriage* 9.9). So, although his most intense human relationships were with other young men (see on 4.4.7 and 4.7.12), this passage does not show that he is acknowledging homosexual relationships; and 3.8.15 uses sodomy as the obvious example of a sin against nature, with no suggestion that A. has anything to repent. He seems rather to have made a distinction (see on 4.7.12) between sexual pleasure and the delights of friendship with a (male) intellectual equal: his friendships failed to stay within their proper limits in that he cared too much for the created human being (1.20.31, 2.5.10). In the paragraphs which follow the account of his friend's death (4.8.13–14), he describes the pleasures of friendship, and concludes 'seeking nothing from [the friend's] body except the manifestations of goodwill' (*indicia beneuolentiae*). **luminosus:** clear, rather than brilliant, light (cf. *serenitas dilectionis*, the 'clear sky' of *dilectio*, and in 2.3.8 *serenitatem ueritatis tuae* obscured by *caligo*). Here the one word *luminosus* makes the contrast with the exhalations, cloud and fog which are about to overwhelm it with language (*obnubilabant atque obfuscabant*); the sound of *luminosus limes* is echoed in *limosa* (*concupiscentia*), which suggests mud contaminating clear water. **scatebra pubertatis:** the 'bubbling up' of puberty, as in the metaphors of seething waters in the next sentence. There may be another overtone: the fourth-century medical writer Oribasius uses *scatebra* of a skin eruption (adolescent acne?), cf. 2.8.16 (q.v.) where A. speaks of scratching the itch of desire, *confricatione consciorum animorum accenderem pruritum cupiditatis meae*; the metaphor recurs in 3.2.4 (q.v.) and in 9.1.1 *scabiem libidinum*. **utrumque:** both things, i.e. love and lust in their confused state.

aestuabat ... rapiebat ... mersabat gurgite: cf. the *flumen tartareum* of worldly custom in 1.16.26. **obsurdueram stridore catenae mortalitatis meae** 'I had been deafened by the clanking of the chain of my mortality', that is, by the demands of his mortal body. Mortality is itself the penalty for human *superbia* (see on 1.1.1). **ibam longius a te ... ego ibam porro longe a te:** see on 1.18.28 for the Prodigal Son's journey into a far country. **iactabar et effundebar et diffluebam et ebulliebam:** again the seething waters and the fear of dispersal; the sequence of four verbs joined only by *et* conveys the sense of being tossed by a flood (cf. *iactantur in te* 1.16.26). **sterilia semina:** almost certainly a double meaning. The seeds (like wild oats) bear nothing to eat, and A.'s seed begets no children.

2.2.3 A. ought either to have married or to have chosen celibacy. The paragraph offers another series of metaphors (as in 2.2.2), this time concerned with bringing order to the confusion of desire. **quis mihi modularetur aerumnam meam** 'who could have harmonised my wretchedness?'. The all-important *modus*, limit, here appears as a musical mode, which determines the acceptable relationships of sounds and thus provides structure for a rhythm or a melody. **nouissimarum rerum:** *nouissima*, 'newest', has the sense 'most remote from God', cf. 5.2.2 *a caelis usque in nouissima*, and the comparable use of *extrema* in 1.13.21. The underlying image is of the fall from unity with God into multiplicity (Introd. §3*b*). **metas praefigeret** 'set boundary-markers'; a familiar image (*OLD* s.v. *meta* 2), not a live metaphor. **fluctus:** A.'s favourite image for turbulent desires (cf. 1.11.18), which are seen as waves breaking in foam (*exaestuarent*) on the shore of marriage. **si tranquillitas in eis non poterat esse:** there are two ways of taking this. If the sentence continues from *usque ad coniugale litus exaestuarent fluctus*, A. means that if there could not be calm in the waves of desire – a calm which would be satisfied with the procreation of children – the waves could at least have spent their force on the shore of marriage, that is, not in fornication. There is a similar contrast in a sermon written probably in 397 (Dolbeau (1992) 279–81), and in *On the Good of Marriage* (written in 401): the procreation of children within marriage is good; conjugal intercourse not intended for procreation is not commendable, because it is a surrender to desire, but is pardonable because it avoids the danger of fornication. Thus at 4.2.2 (q.v.) A. contrasts marriage for the purpose of procreation with a *pactum libidinosi amoris* in which children are not wanted; and at 6.12.22 he acknowledges that he and his friend Alypius, a decade earlier, had thought of marriage chiefly as a legitimate sexual relationship. O'D. interprets 2.3.3 differently, in order to make a clear contrast between marriage (for the sake of children) and celibacy. He begins a new sentence at *si tranquillitas* and continues it to *placeat uxori*, the end of A.'s quotations in support of celibacy (beginning at *tribulationem*) from 1 Corinthians 7. This entails accepting *aut certe* as an anacoluthon after the long parenthesis *sicut praescribit ... longe sumus a te.* When he wrote the *C.*, A. thought that sexual relationships, and procreation, are a consequence of the Fall. According to the story in Genesis 3: 1–8, when Adam and Eve disobeyed God and ate fruit from the tree of knowledge of good and evil, they were at once aware of themselves as sexual beings, and because they now knew death, they were mortal. But, it was argued, God mercifully ordained a proper use for sexual desire (cf. *in usum uerteret* in the first sentence of 2.2.3), namely the procreation of children within marriage, which ensures that the human race shall continue in spite of mortality. Cf. 13.20.28 *a quo* [sc. *Deo*] *si non esset lapsus Adam, non diffunderetur ex utero eius salsugo maris, genus humanum profunde curiosum et procellose tumidum et instabiliter fluidum.* A. later changed his mind, and came to think that sex is part of God's original plan for human nature, but has been disordered by the Fall. In *City of God* 14.26 he imagined what intercourse might have been like without the Fall: sexual response would be under rational control, and the decision to beget a child would be carried out as calmly as any other movement of the body – shaking hands, for instance.

propaginem mortis nostrae: cf. 1.6.7 for human life as death. **potens imponere** 'powerful [enough] to impose'.   **spinarum a paradiso tuo seclusarum:** when Adam and Eve were expelled from Paradise, God said that the earth would bear thorns (Genesis 3: 17–18). A. uses the 'thorns excluded from Paradise' as an image for human sexuality (cf. *uepres libidinum* 2.3.6).   **sonitum nubium tuarum:** God's 'clouds', which according to *On the Psalms* 35.8, bring thunder, lightning, fear and rain, are God's voice heard in Scripture.   **abscisus propter regnum caelorum** 'castrated for the sake of the kingdom of heaven', as in Matthew 19: 12 'there are some eunuchs who were born that way, others who were made so by people, and there are eunuchs who have castrated themselves for the sake of the kingdom of heaven'. In the early centuries of the Church, a few interpreters took this literally, but the preferred reading was that it is a powerful metaphor for renouncing the distractions of marriage and parenthood. **felicior expectarem amplexus tuos:** cf. 1.5.5 for the language of love applied to God.

2.2.4 God ensured that A. found no pleasure unmixed with bitterness (cf. 1.14.23); but in his sixteenth year desire took control. **efferuui ... excessi ... euasi:** a reminiscence of Cicero's speech when Catiline left Rome, *abiit, excessit, euasit, erupit* (*Against Catiline* 2.1.1). See further on 2.4.9. **quis enim hoc mortalium?:** understand *quis mortalium hoc* (i.e. *flagella tua*) *potest euadere?* For the *flagella*, cf. 3.3.5. **qui fingis dolorem in praecepto:** Psalm 93: 20. In his commentary on this passage, *On the Psalms* 93.24, A. interpreted *in praecepto* to mean 'as instruction': God teaches us by causing us to feel pain and fear in the midst of pleasure. **percutis ut sanes et occidis nos, ne moriamur abs te:** cf. Deuteronomy 32: 39 (the song of Moses to the Israelites about God) *ego occidam, et ego uiuere faciam; percutiam, et ego sanabo; non est qui de manu mea possit eruere.* For dying in order to live, see on 1.5.5. **quam longe exulabam:** once again the Prodigal Son (see on 1.18.28). **anno illo sexto decimo aetatis carnis meae:** the first precise indication of age as distinct from the generalising *infantia* and *pueritia.* (The year was 369–70.) This age is emphasised at 2.3.6 and again at 2.6.12. A. did not think that sin began only when sexual sin was possible (see on 1.7.11 and 1.19.30; he makes this point explicitly in *Literal Interpretation of Genesis* 10.13.23), and book 1 of the *C.* insists that *concupiscentia* is present from the beginning of life. Nevertheless, he regards fifteen as a critical age for him, the time when lust took over. Legal and medical texts assume that boys reach puberty at fourteen. **cum accepit in me sceptrum:** the subject of *accepit* is *uesania libidinis.* **licentiosae:** sexual freedom for males was sanctioned both by law and by custom (provided they did not approach married or marriageable women), but A. chooses a word which discredits 'licence'. **ruentem excipere me matrimonio:** marriage was legal, for a boy, at fourteen. There is not enough evidence to show how many men married in their teens. It happened in the case of one famous couple known (later) to A.: Pinianus, husband of the younger Melania, married at seventeen, but he was heir to a great fortune and did not have a career to make. Marriage in the twenties was (as far as the evidence goes) more usual, and A.'s family did not want his career held back by an early and probably inferior marriage (cf. 2.3.8 *ne impediretur spes mea compede uxoria*). See further Saller (1987).

2.3.5 A. had a year out between school at Madauros and higher study at Carthage. The previous paragraph gave a first indication of age; here for the first time is a geographical and social location, very briefly noted. Thagaste, Madauros and Carthage – home town, school town, university town – are the only places in north Africa named by A. in the *C.*, and he is not interested in setting the scene. (For evocations, see Brown (1967) 19–27, van der Meer (1961) 16–28; for the cities of north Africa, Lepelley (1979), and an updated brief survey in Lepelley (1992); detailed information on Thagaste and Madauros in Lepelley (1981) 175–84, 127–40.) A.'s father Patricius is not named until book 9 of the *C.*, and then in relation to his wife. **longinquioris apud Carthaginem peregrationis:** another allusion to the Prodigal Son, wanting funds for a long journey. There is no mention of the local great man Romanianus, who was almost certainly helping to pay the bills (cf. 6.14.24).   **animositate:** a rare word which could mean 'high spirit' or 'courage'; the adjective *animosus* is usually positive. But in Galatians 5: 19–21 *animositas* occurs between 'rivalry' and 'dissension', translating Greek *eritheiai*, in a list of the works of the flesh: it seems to mean 'animosity'. Perhaps A. implies that his father was out to show the neighbours? **municipis ... admodum tenuis:** a *municeps* was someone liable for civic *munera* or obligations, even if not very rich.   **cui narro haec?:** A. speaks in God's presence (*apud te*), but to the human audience (see on 1.6.7) which may happen upon his book.   **ut quid hoc?:** so why (see on 1.17.27 for *ut quid*) is A., now, telling this audience something about his background? His answer is, as usual, in terms of his spiritual condition: it is to show from how great depths one must cry to God (Psalm 129: 1 *de profundis clamaui ad te domine*, 'out of the depths have I cried to thee, O Lord'). But in terms of narrative, the question remains unanswered. Why tell the reader now what social class A. comes from and where he was at school? The information is not strictly necessary to explain why he had a year at home – the first sentence of 2.3.6 covers that. Perhaps it is another example of A.'s remembering what a particular age felt like. At fifteen, he was aware of himself as having a recognisable social and educational status, and perhaps he was also aware of a mismatch between the two.   **patrem meum:** by ordinary human standards, as A. admits, Patricius was doing far more than could be expected for his son. But A. can see no merit in his father (see further on 3.4.7), and here blames him as concerned only for his son's education. For A.'s experience of family life, see further Shaw (1987).   **disertus uel desertus** 'cultivated or rather uncultivated'. A. uses an image of himself as land reverting to the wild, *ager desertus*, for lack of cultivation from the *bonus dominus agri*. The *dominus* is God, displacing A.'s landowning father (see on 1.11.17). *agri deserti* were a recurrent concern of late Roman law, and Africa, according to figures compiled in the 420s, had a particularly serious problem: see further Jones (1964) II 813–23, challenged by Whittaker (1976) 161. There may also be an allusion to Jesus' parable of the farmer who allowed both wheat and tares to grow in his field until harvest-time (Matthew 13: 24–30).

2.3.6 A.'s father was delighted to discover that his son had reached puberty; his mother was alarmed.   **uepres libidinum:** cf. 2.1.1 *siluescere* and 2.2.3 *spinae*. A. continues the image of himself as a field neglected by those who should cultivate it: *nulla erat eradicans manus*.   **gaudens matri indicauit:** O'D. notes the parallel between Patricius' announcement of A.'s virility here, and A.'s announcement, much later, of his intention to live in chastity, *inde ad matrem ingredimur, indicamus: gaudet* (8.12.30).   **gaudens uinulentia:** A. allows the reader to think that his father was drunk before explaining that the drunkenness is a metaphorical intoxication with lowly created things. A. himself (1.20.31) had loved created beings rather than their Creator.   **mihi nondum fideli:** i.e. not yet a full member of the church (see O'D. for A.'s use of *fidelis* in *C.* books 1 to 9), although he was a catechumen of longer standing than his father (cf. 1.11.17).   **qui ponunt ad te tergum et non faciem:** the context in Jeremiah 2: 27 is important. 'Saying to wood "You are my father" and to stone "You begot me", they have turned their back to me, not their face.' A.'s father seems to be assimilated to the idols of wood and stone.

2.3.7 God was not silent (contrast 2.2.2), but spoke through Monnica's warnings, which A. dismissed. A. pretended to be worse than he was, so that his friends would not despise him.   **secreto memini:** the *secretum* is A.'s inner self. Monnica's anxiety clearly did affect him, even though he dismissed it.   **maximeque ne adulterarem cuiusquam uxorem:** in Roman law, adultery was a sexual relationship with a married or marriageable woman; the marital status of the man was irrelevant. It was a very serious offence, because it cast doubt on the legitimacy of the woman's children, and was therefore a ground for divorce. A. comments in sermons on the scandal caused by a woman's adultery (e.g. *Sermon* 9.4). Like other Christian preachers he attempted – without much success – to challenge the double standard, arguing that a married man's infidelity was just as bad as a married woman's.   **inter coaetaneos meos puderet me minoris dedecoris:** this theme occurs at 1.13.21 and is developed at 2.9.17.   **iactantes flagitia sua:** *flagitia* (see on 2.5.11) are usually sexual sins. A., despite his self-reproach, makes it clear that he was *innocentior* and *castior* than most (cf. 3.3.6 on the Wreckers). The elaborately balanced series of word-plays after *nesciebam* is perhaps another kind of showing off, a display of the rhetorical skill which mattered to A.'s parents.

2.3.8 A.'s parents did not try to arrange an early marriage: they were more concerned (though for different reasons) that his studies should be successful.   **iter agebam platearum Babyloniae:** Babylon, to which the people of Israel were deported in the sixth century B.C., became an image for the corrupt earthly city which is not the true home of God's people. In the book of Revelation (not always accepted in the early church as part of the canon of Scripture) it is 'Babylon the great, the mother of fornications' (Revelation 17: 5). A. developed, especially in *City of God*, the contrast between Jerusalem the heavenly city and Babylon the earthly city: see further Markus (1988) 45–71.   **in cinnamis et unguentis pretiosis:** a reminiscence of the Song of Songs (4: 14), which in the late fourth century was generally interpreted as an allegory of the soul's love for God (see further E. A. Clark (1986) 401–7).   **in umbilico eius**

quo tenacius haererem: the *umbilicus*, 'navel', is the centre of Babylon; the 'invisible enemy', i.e. the devil, trampled on A. (*calcabat*) and led him astray (*seducebat*, cf. *uias distortas* 2.3.6).   **mater carnis meae:** the phrase, which contrasts Monnica with A.'s spiritual mother, the church (cf. 1.11.17), emphasises Monnica's responsibility for A.'s sexual wrongdoing. In 2.3.6 she was established as spiritually more advanced than her husband and son, and in 2.3.8 she has escaped from the centre of Babylon. But she had not been as concerned to restrain A.'s sexuality by marriage (cf. 2.2.3) as she had been to advise chastity. The sentence perhaps imitates Monnica's hesitant approach to the problem: its main thread is *mater non curauit cohercere quod de me audierat.*   **resecari ad uiuum** 'to be cut back to the quick', a phrase used by Cicero, *On Friendship* 5.18. Here it probably has the double meaning that A. would be alive (*uiuus*), not on the road to death, if he could restrain sexual desire. The image of 'cutting back' may recall the vine run to wood in 2.1.1, and even the 'eunuch for the kingdom of heaven' in 2.2.3.   **compede uxoria:** once A. was further up the ladder, as professor of rhetoric at Milan, Monnica did work (6.13.23) to arrange a marriage, and A. says she hoped he would then be baptised. But he was aware (6.11.19) that he needed a wife with money.   **spes litterarum:** cf. 1.16.26 for A. as *bonae spei puer.*   **relaxabantur ... habenae:** cf. 1.11.18, *laxata ... lora peccandi.* As in 2.2.2 and 2.2.3, A. piles up metaphors to show his undisciplined state.   **ultra temperamentum seueritatis in dissolutionem affectionum uariarum:** *temperamentum seueritatis* is the moderation or regulation imposed by strictness (cf. 2.3.5 *quis mihi modularetur ...?*); the relaxation of discipline went beyond this and led *in dissolutionem affectionum uariarum*, to dissipation which consisted of various emotional states. (For A.'s uses of the genitive, see Campbell and McGuire (1931) 32–4.)   **caligo intercludens ... serenitatem:** cf. 2.2.2.   **prodiebat tamquam ex adipe iniquitas mea:** Psalm 72: 7. A. explains this 'wrongdoing as if from fatness' as sin without the excuse of poverty (*On the Psalms* 72.12); the theme is continued in the next paragraph. As in 2.3.6, the unstated context of the quotation is important: *ideo tenuit eos superbia; operti sunt iniquitate et impietate sua. prodiit quasi ex adipe iniquitas eorum; transierunt in affectum cordis.* Here in two verses of Hebrew poetry are pride, wickedness blocking off the light of God, fat insulating the sinner from awareness of God (cf. 7.1.2 *cor incrassatum*), and the heart going wrong.

2.4.9 A. stole fruit not because he needed it, or even wanted it, but for the sheer satisfaction of doing wrong.

A. uses this episode as a case-history of human wickedness, linked with the story of the Fall (Genesis 3: 1–8), the archetypal theft of forbidden fruit. Like Adam and Eve, A. knew what the rule was. Both Scripture and innate moral sense forbid theft. The pears, unlike the fruit in Genesis, were not beautiful or delicious. A. was not driven by need (*egestas*), except in that he had a need of which he was not aware: he was destitute not in terms of money or food, but in terms of *iustitia*, 'righteousness', a word which covers both doing what is right and wanting to do what is right. Like Adam and Eve, he found that forbidden fruit was connected with sexual awareness, although in book 2 sexual awareness precedes theft. Readers commonly think that A. is making far too much fuss about a minor adolescent rebellion, which he wants the reader to assimilate to Catiline's rebellion against the state (see below), just as he made far too much fuss (1.7.11) about a baby who resents seeing another fed first. He devotes the rest of book 2 to analysing this theft. Has he transferred sexual guilt to another episode of transgression, or is he using the theft of fruit as an image for sexual sin (cf. 2.6.12 *o facinus illud meum nocturnum*)? But he raises a real problem about human nature. Why should anyone deliberately do wrong for nothing but the satisfaction of doing wrong, *quid ibi quaerebat [cor meum] ut essem gratis malus et malitiae meae causa nulla esset nisi malitia*? Why should wrongdoing as such be satisfying, *non dedecore aliquid, sed dedecus amans*? **nec copiosus adactum inopia:** understand *patitur*. The 'law written in our hearts' (Romans 2: 14–15) against theft is so strong that even a thief does not tolerate a thief; not even (*nec*) if the first thief is prosperous and the second driven by need. For *copia* ... *inopia* see on 1.12.19.   **nulla compulsus egestate nisi penuria et fastidio iustitiae:** comparison with 3.1.1 *quo inanior, fastidiosior* (q.v.) suggests that A. has in mind the distaste (*fastidium*) for proper food which can result from undernourishment or from eating the wrong foods (*sagina iniquitatis*, 'bursting with wickedness').   **quousque** 'until which time'. Cicero's most famous speech against Catiline (an alleged conspirator against the Roman state in 63 B.C.) begins *quousque tandem abutere, Catilina, patientia nostra?*, and *quousque* is one of many words and phrases in this paragraph which evoke Cicero's denunciation of Catiline as the wantonly malicious destroyer of Roman social order, and Sallust's treatment of Catiline's conspiracy, in *Catiline's War*, as a case-study of the factors which caused the collapse of the Roman republic. Both Cicero and Sallust were set authors in the school curriculum. Sallust represented Catiline as driven by *inopia* and *egestas*, and Catiline's fellow-conspirators were *adulescentuli* who met *intempesta nocte* – 'that is, the middle of the night, when people should be asleep', as A. explains in his comments on Psalm 118 (*On the Psalms* 118, sermon 29.3).   **de pestilentiae more:** literally 'as a plague does'; C. 'in our usual pestilential way', with the emphasis on *mos* as 'accustomed behaviour'. **uel proicienda porcis** has biblical overtones, both of Jesus' warning 'do not cast your pearls before swine' (Matthew 7: 6) and of the pigs fed by the Prodigal Son.   **dum tamen fieret ... non liceret** 'provided that there should be done by us that which pleased for this reason, that it was not allowed'.   **miseratus es in imo abyssi:** both this phrase, and *dissiliens a firmamento tuo in exterminium* below, sound very much like biblical Latin, but neither appears to be a quotation (unless, as O'D. suggests, there was a *VL* text). A. seems here to evoke the rebel angels (cf. 1.17.27), who wanted nothing except to rebel against God, and fell from heaven to the lowest depths. He discusses faithful and rebel angels in book 2 of *City of God*, in connection with the creation narrative of Genesis 1. In the first verses of Genesis, the *abyssus* is (as A. explains in *City of God* 11.9) a confused mass of land and sea, covered in darkness; the *firmamentum* is the heaven which separates the upper and lower waters, and in which the stars were made. In *City of God* 11.33, A. uses 2 Peter 2: 4 as evidence for the claim that, because God resists the proud but gives favour to the humble (see on 1.1.1), 'the one [company of faithful angels] dwells in the heaven of heavens, the other [the rebels] has been cast down from there and riots in this lowest aerial region of the sky': *illam [angelicam societatem] in caelis caelorum habitantem, istam inde deiectam in hoc infimo aerio caelo tumultuantem.* The principal text for the fall of the angels is Isaiah 14: 12–14 'how art thou fallen from heaven, O Lucifer!', a song of triumph over the king of Babylon which was interpreted as an account of the fall of Satan.

2.5.10 There is usually something understandable in the excessive desire for lesser goods which leads to sin: even lesser goods have beauty.

A. again uses the threefold division *concupiscentia oculorum, concupiscentia carnis, ambitio saeculi* (see on 1.10.16), but this time acknowledges that sensual pleasures and honour are in some ways 'fitting', and adds to them the beauty and harmony of life and the unifying force of friendship. The emphasis throughout is not on turbulence and disruption, but on order (*decus* contrasted with *dedecus* in 2.4.9) and harmony, most clearly expressed in the appeal of this life *propter quendam modum decoris sui et conuenientiam cum his omnibus infimis pulchris*, 'because of a certain measure in its beauty and its harmony with all these inferior objects that are beautiful' (C.). A.'s very first book (which he had mislaid by the time he wrote the *C.*) was a treatise *De pulchro et apto, On the Beautiful and Fitting*. He argued, he says in 4.13.20 and 4.15.24 (q.v.), that we love only what is beautiful, and that its appeal consists in its being pleasing in itself (the beautiful) or in its being well adapted to something else (the fitting). See further Harrison (1992). The style of this paragraph is predominantly Ciceronian, as the *De pulchro et apto* probably was in style as well as theme; but three of its sentences end with an invocation of God and a shift to more biblical Latin. 2.5.11 is philosophical discussion without biblical material; in 2.6.12–13 A. contrasts the true beauty of God's creation and the true good to be found in God with the imitations pursued by sin, but still makes little use of biblical quotation.   **modificatio corporum:** 'modality' rather than 'modification', a way of being which is suited to the various senses.   **uindictae auiditas:** *uindicta* is claiming something as one's own; it may be revenge.   **amicitia … caro nodo dulcis est:** in the *C.*, *nodus* is usually a hampering, not a uniting, bond (cf. 1.9.14 *rumpebam nodos linguae meae*, and 2.10.18 *nodositatem*). C. reads *nidus*, nest (cf. 4.16.31).   **extrema bona:** see on 1.13.21.   **ipse est deliciae rectorum corde:** the phrase *recti corde*, 'upright in heart', occurs in Psalm 63: 11.

2.5.11 People are assumed to commit crimes for a reason; even Catiline is not an example of motiveless malice.   **facinore:** *facinus* is often linked with *flagitium*, but, according to A. in *On Christian*

Teaching 3.10.16, the distinction is that *flagitium* is the effect of desire which drives one to corrupt one's soul and body, *facinus* is the effect of desire which drives one to harm another. In his lectures on Romans (given in 395), A. said that the pursuit of *flagitia* leads to *facinus* when one tries to remove people who are in the way. See further O'D. on 3.8.16.   **esse potuisse:** a Ciceronian rhythm. A. must have liked the juxtaposition with *apparuerit*, but it makes the sentence difficult to follow; the basic structure is *credi non solet* [sc. that someone has committed a crime] *nisi cum apparuerit esse potuisse appetitus ... aut metus,* 'unless it seems possible that there was a desire or fear'. A. uses other favourite devices of Cicero here: a long and elaborately structured sentence (*cum itaque ... amittendi*); a simpler sentence which is still 'abundant' in style, with pairs of adjectives (*pulchra ... et decora ... prae ... superioribus et beatificis abiecta et iacentia*); and two *pugiunculi,* 'stiletto-sentences': *homicidium fecit. cur fecit?* The alliteration of *appetitus adipiscendi alicuius* suggests a greedy mouth.   **uoluit depraedari unde uiueret** 'he wanted to take away property from which he might (himself) live'.   **quis crediderit?:** present-day readers will not find it difficult to believe that someone might murder *ipso homicidio delectatus.* But when such crimes are committed, there is an eager search for explanation, usually in terms of psychological disturbance or social deprivation; this confirms A.'s claim that people cannot believe in motiveless malice.   **de quo dictum est ... praedicta est tamen causa:** the man is Catiline, named at the end of the paragraph after a series of allusions (in 2.4.9) and two quotations from Sallust, who is not named. The first, which gives the *praedicta causa,* that is the reason already given by Sallust for Catiline's behaviour, is slightly adapted: Sallust wrote *ne per otium torpescerent manus aut animus, gratuito potius malus atque crudelis erat* (*Catiline's War* 16.3). The second is almost verbatim: *inopia rei familiaris et conscientia scelerum* (*ibid.* 5.7). **quaere id quoque: cur ita?** 'ask this too: why is it so?' The manuscripts are divided between *quaere,* 'ask', and *quare,* 'why', but *quare* appears to duplicate the question *cur ita?* The further question 'ask this too' reveals that even Catiline had understandable motives of the kind A. has listed: he wanted to acquire status and wealth and to escape punishment and poverty. He did not love crime for itself.

2.6.12 This makes A.'s theft all the more baffling. The pears were beautiful as being part of God's creation, but only the theft was attractive to him.   **aut uero aliquid es, ut loquar ad te?:** A. uses a favourite stylistic trick, invocation (statistics in O'D. on 1.16.26), then uses it to raise a philosophical question (cf. 1.1.1): he is speaking to his theft as if it exists, but was the theft anything at all? On the question whether evil is only the negation or absence of good, see further Evans (1982).   **ecce species nulla est:** *species* (see on 2.1.1) is a pleasing appearance, but also (like Greek *morphē*) a form or structure.   **defectiua species et umbratica:** O'D. cites *City of God* 12.7, where A. argues that one should not look for the 'efficient cause' of an evil will (i.e. the cause that makes it happen), but for a deficient cause, because deficiency is a movement from what is best to what is less. Trying to find deficient causes is like trying to see darkness or hear silence: we can do it only with eyes or ears, but we perceive it by lack of *species* not by *species*. So, here, vices have a defective *species* which is shadow (*umbratica*) not substance (C. 'a flawed reflection of beauty').

2.6.13 All sins are a misguided attempt to achieve some good which is to be found only in God. A. uses a traditional pattern of philosophical definition, each time making the contrast with God. **te simplicius quicquam non reperitur:** A. is playing on the double meaning of *simplicitas*. It can mean 'simpleness' in the sense of naivety, and such simplicity can be approved because a simple person is not trying to deceive (hence the pair *simplicitas et innocentia*). But in philosophical discussion about God, *simplicitas* is single-ness or integrity, contrasted with multiplicity: where there are many things, everything both is (itself) and is not (other things).   **tristitia ... nihil potest:** only *tristitia*, sadness, is not in pursuit of something; but sadness for things lost is, like the other vices, a 'flawed reflection', namely of a yearning for God, who loses nothing. **ita sibi nollet:** understand *auferri*.

2.6.14 Sins, then, are either love of some apparent good, or a perverse imitation of God: but how does this explain A.'s theft? Did he take pleasure in doing something forbidden because doing what he chose was a pale imitation of God's omnipotence?   **ita fornicatur anima:** see on 1.13.21 for the image. The soul turns away from its commitment to God in pursuit of lesser loves.   **peruerse**

te imitantur: people try to be like God by setting themselves up against God (as the rebel angels did, and as in the serpent's words to Eve in Genesis 3: 5: 'you shall be like gods'). But even this attempt to imitate is an acknowledgement of God's power: 'all who make themselves distant from you, and raise themselves up against you, are perversely imitating you'. C. sees a contrast here: 'In their perverted way all humanity imitates you. Yet they put themselves at a distance . . . '   **non esse quo a te omni modo recedatur:** cf. 1.2.2. A. speaks of making oneself remote from God, *longe se a te faciunt*, but there is nowhere to go to retreat wholly from God. **mancam libertatem** 'a defective freedom'. O'D. points out that A. distrusts freedom: at 3.3.5 it is *fugitiua libertas*, the freedom of a slave on the run, when A. loves his own ways and not God's; at 3.8.16 it is *falsa libertas*, the deceptive freedom of resisting God; only at 4.4.8 (q.v.) is it positive, when A.'s friend who was baptised when unconscious rebukes A. *mirabili et repentina libertate* for not taking this seriously. Here, A. is like a *captiuus*, a slave captured in war, who lacks the power to do what he wants (which is in any case a defective freedom) and therefore tries to get his own way by dishonesty (*fallacia*, cf. 1.19.30 for the boy A. pilfering, cheating and lying). Petty theft was notoriously a form of resistance practised by slaves.   **ecce est ille seruus fugiens dominum suum et consecutus umbram:** almost direct quotation from Job 7: 2 (*VL*) *seruus metuens dominum suum et consecutus umbram*. In his *Notes on Job*, written in the same years as the *C*. (399), A. interprets this verse as Adam's attempt to hide from God among the trees of Paradise (Genesis 3: 8). So, again, A.'s theft is presented as comparable (*ecce est ille seruus*) to the sin of Adam.   **o putredo:** cf. 2.1.1 *computrui*. **o monstrum uitae:** a *monstrum* is a portent, especially a living creature born grossly deformed from its proper shape (or *species*). **mortis profunditas:** cf. 2.4.9 *in imo abyssi*: A. could not be further from God, and thereby more in danger of final death (see on 1.5.5) than by wanting something not for any semblance of good, but only because it is forbidden.

2.7.15 A. pauses in his analysis of sin to thank God for forgiving the sins he now remembers and for having safeguarded him from committing others.   **Quid retribuam domino:** Psalm 115: 2 *quid retribuam domino pro omnibus quae retribuit mihi?*   **anima mea**

non metuit inde: *inde* 'from it', i.e. from what A. recollects. He discusses in 10.14.21–2 the experience of remembering past states of mind, e.g. that one was sad or happy, without feeling them. **tamquam glaciem:** *sicut in sereno glacies, ita soluentur peccata tua,* Sirach (Ecclesiasticus) 3: 17. The preceding verses promise this as a reward for care given to elderly parents; cf. 2.3.6 for an unstated context which is important for the full meaning of the passage. **gratiae tuae deputo et quaecumque non feci mala:** God's grace not only forgave A. for sins committed, but also protected him from committing others. A. says that no one who has avoided sin should claim to have done so by his own powers; and no one who has listened to God's voice and thereby avoided sin should mock A. for being more in need of the 'doctor', for it was that doctor who ensured that the other person should not be ill, or at least should be less ill. For the image of Christ as doctor, a favourite with A. and in north African tradition, see Arbesmann (1954). A.'s emphasis is on giving thanks (*gratiae*) to God: we should recognise that we cannot take the credit for avoiding sin, but should be grateful, as if we had escaped a serious illness. But total dependence on God's grace raises other problems. If God's grace is freely given, not earned by human merit (since it is only God's grace which has made that merit possible), why does God, apparently arbitrarily, give only some people the grace to be good? Is it reasonable to blame those who do not have this grace, or expect them to behave better? *gratia* became a technical term of Christian theology, but its ordinary meaning is 'favour' (hence *gratias ago*, 'I acknowledge favours given', i.e. 'thank you'). Fourth-century Roman society was only too familiar with the conferment of favours by patronage. A. chooses the adjective *gratuitus* for his sin (cf. *gratis malus* in 2.4.9), thus emphasising the arbitrariness of *gratia*. Moreover, his willingness to acknowledge that he could not, without God's help, escape from sin seemed to Pelagius (and many other theologians) to undermine the free will which God gave us, and to suggest that it is impossible for us, flawed as we are, to obey God's commands. So God would be requiring us to do what we are clearly unable to do. On the controversy which started when Pelagius heard 10.29.40 quoted in Rome in 405 (*nemo potest esse continens nisi deus det ... continentiam iubes: da quod iubes et iube quod uis*), see Chadwick (1986) 107–17,

Bonner (1986) 312–93 for a detailed account.   **quid enim non facere potui** 'what could I not have done?'   **donas peccata** 'you remit sins', cf. 1.4.4 *donas debita*.   **languoribus:** not 'languishing', but the extreme weakness of those in the grip of illness.

2.8.16 A. did enjoy something other than doing wrong: the companionship of those who stole with him.   **Quem fructum habui:** *quem ergo fructum habuistis tunc in illis, in quibus nunc erubescitis?*, Romans 6: 21.   **nihil aliud, cum et ipsum esset nihil:** the theft was 'nothing' because evil is nothing, that is, has no independent existence (see on 2.6.12). So when A. reflects that he did love something, namely the company of his friends, in addition to the theft, he can then deny the claim *non ergo nihil aliud quam furtum amaui*, 'so I did not love nothing but the theft', in two ways. *immo uero nihil aliud, quia et illud nihil est* can mean 'no indeed, there was nothing else (that I loved), because that too (i.e. the companionship) was also nothing', and simultaneously 'yes indeed, I did love nothing else: it was another nothing that I loved'.   **solus id non fecissem:** the repeated claim is made again, more confidently, in the next paragraph.   **quid est re uera?** 'what is it really?' O'D. takes this as referring to the companionship in wrongdoing: the question is picked up by the repeated *quid erat?* of 2.9.17, which explains that the companionship was a distorted imitation of friendship. But *quid est re uera?* might in more general terms mean 'what is really going on here?', i.e. 'what really motivated the theft?', to which the answer is that A. would not have done it, unless he had actually wanted the pears, without the stimulus of companions. If so, *quid est re uera?* is picked up by *quid est quod mihi uenit in mentem quaerere et discutere et considerare?* The following *quia* means 'that' (see on 1.1.1): A. reflects that, if he had wanted the pears, he could have acted alone *si satis esset*, that is, if he could on his own have achieved the pleasure he wanted.   **confricatione consciorum animorum accenderem pruritum:** for the itch of desire, see on 2.2.2; here it is stimulated by contact of souls, not bodies. The image recurs at 3.1.1 and 3.2.4.

2.9.17 A. would not have done it alone: what then was the state of mind which made him steal together with others? Perhaps it was to share the joke; but people can laugh when alone.   **delicta quis intelligit?:** Psalm 18: 13; cf. 1.6.6.   **risus:** here mocking or

unkind laughter; see on 1.6.7.   **solus non facerem:** A. is now
sure that he has a living memory of his state of mind, *uiua recordatio
animae meae* (compare 2.8.16 *sic recordor*), and is certain that he would
not have done it alone. Why does he insist on this? Not, evidently, to
minimise his guilt: he does not suggest (on the lines of 2.6.13) that
the theft can be understood as a distorted imitation of loyalty or co-
operation. On the contrary, he finds the theft even more baffling
when he has identified the effect of company: *o nimis inimica amicitia,
seductio mentis inuestigabilis!* None of the other motives for sin were
present, but when someone says *eamus, faciamus*, 'let's go, let's do it',
there is shame in not being shameless, *pudet non esse impudentem* (cf.
2.3.7). There is a parallel, which A. does not make explicit, with the
sin of Adam, whose motive for eating the apple is unexplained in
Genesis, but who, when questioned by God, says 'The woman you
gave me as a companion gave me (fruit) from the tree, and I ate'
(Genesis 3: 12).

2.10.18 A. turns from the tangle of his sin to reflect on God and
how in adolescence he went away from God.   **nodositatem**
'knottiness' as in a knotty question.   **insatiabili satietate:** cf.
the paradoxes of 1.4.4; this paradox might describe either God or
A.'s desire for God. The sentence as a whole could mean 'I want
you, righteousness and innocence, (you who are) lovely and splendid
to honest eyes, with an insatiable satiety' or possibly 'I want you,
righteousness and innocence, (you who are) lovely and splendid to
honest eyes, and of an insatiable satiety'.   **intrat in gaudium
domini:** Matthew 25: 21, the reward for those who have made
good use of their talents.   **defluxi:** cf. 2.2.2 *diffluebam*; book 2
begins and ends with images of dispersal and deviation.   **factus
sum mihi regio egestatis:** the Prodigal Son travelled to a far
country, *in regionem longinquam*, and after he had used up all his supplies, there was a famine and he began to feel want: *facta est fames
ualida in regione illa et ipse coepit egere* (Luke 15: 13–14). Here A. himself
becomes a *regio egestatis*: cf. 2.4.9 on *egestas* and *inopia*. In his preaching on the story (see O'D. here and on 1.18.28) he interpreted the
famine as lack of God's truth. Book 2 used the image of fruit which
is not good to eat; books 3–5 continue the metaphor of food
that fails to sustain. In 7.10.16 the reading of the 'Platonic books'
(Introd. §3*b*) makes A. realise that he is in a *regio dissimilitudinis*,

that is, a region of unlikeness to God; this unlikeness is another way
of expressing deprivation and distance from God. He hears a voice
saying 'I am food for adults: grow up and you shall eat me.'

Book III

A.'s 'Carthage book', like Virgil's (book 4 of the *Aeneid*), begins with
erotic love. But A. is at Carthage as a student of rhetoric, and book
3 is concerned with the impact of literature. A. watches plays and
reflects on the emotion, and desire for emotion, which they arouse.
Then Cicero's *Hortensius* inspires him to desire wisdom as passion-
ately as he desired love. Because of his Christian upbringing, he
begins to read the Bible in search of wisdom, but finds its style
and content unrewarding. So he is receptive to the teaching of the
Manichaeans, who offered what seemed to be a more profound
understanding of Christianity. Only his mother's prayers offer a
hope that he will eventually be free.

3.1.1   A. reaches Carthage and is willingly entangled in love-
affairs.   **Veni Carthaginem:** a new starting-point, A.'s first en-
counter with the big city. Carthage in the late fourth century was
the second city of the western empire, with a population of at least
100,000: see further Charles-Picard (1965); Lepelley (1981) 11–53.
A. thought of himself as *urbanus*, 'civilised' or sophisticated. But
Carthage was also, like A. at the end of book 2, a *regio egestatis*,
and A. goes on to explain his spiritual malnutrition.   **sartago**
rhymed with *Carthago* (the distinction of sound between *t* and *th* was
probably not noticed): a *sartago* seems to have been the kind of
cooking-pot which can be used for frying and then simmering. So
A. is now in a different kind of seething water, after the rushing
river of human custom (1.16.26) and the swirling streams of puberty
(2.2.2). In 6.7.11 Carthaginian customs are a whirlpool, *gurges*, which
suck in his friend Alypius.   **secretiore indigentia oderam
me minus indigentem:** the obvious *indigentia* is the lack of someone to love; the *secretior indigentia* might be a need to feel this lack, so
that A. disliked himself (*oderam me*) for being less needy (*minus indigentem*) than he thought he should be. But if the *secretior indigentia* is
the *fames ... intus ab interiore cibo* of the next sentence, that is, lack of

the spiritual food which would be supplied by the love of God, perhaps it was really his spiritual hunger which made him dissatisfied:
'I disliked myself for needing someone to love, though this need
was in fact less (than my need for spiritual food)'. Another interpretation depends on *quo inanior, fastidiosior* (see below): A. felt distaste
(*fastidium*) for the spiritual food which would have made him less
needy, and therefore disliked (the idea of) himself being less needy.
oderam securitatem et uiam sine muscipulis: *securitas* is
freedom from cares (*curae*); *muscipula* seems to have been the standard word for a snare in the version of the Psalms used by A. (see
O'D. for instances), but must have been a disconcertingly live
metaphor for readers who were used to *laqueus* (cf. 3.6.10 for the
laquei of the Manichaeans). In ordinary Latin it meant a mousetrap.
fames ... ab interiore cibo: here *ab* must mean 'for want of'.
quo inanior, [sc. *eo*] **fastidiosior:** cf. 2.4.9 *penuria et fastidio
iustitiae*. Malnutrition (or long illness) can cause revulsion from the
food which is most needed; malnutrition also causes sores, which
provide A.'s next image.   **anima ... ulcerosa proiciebat se
foras:** O'D. notes the parallel with Lazarus (Luke 16: 20), the
hungry beggar covered with sores which the dogs came and licked,
to whom A. refers (*On the Psalms* 145.7) as *pauper ulcerosus ad ianuam
iacens diuitis*. The soul eager to scratch its sores, *scalpi auida*, evokes
Job (2: 8), who sat in the ashes and scraped his sores with a potsherd.
A.'s soul wanted to scratch its sores on things of which his senses
were aware, *contactu sensibilium*: this would make matters worse, because he needed to concentrate on God, not to be distracted by the
outside world, *foras* (literally 'out of doors': see on 3.6.11).   **sed
si non haberent animam, non utique amarentur** 'but they
would not be objects of love if they did not have a soul'. *utique* may
emphasise the logical point that only animate things can be objects
of love (*OLD* s.v. *utique* 3), or may mean 'at any rate' (*ibid.* 5), that is,
A. was at least seeking a relationship with other animate beings (so
G–M and O'D.). C. takes it differently: 'Yet physical things had no
soul. Love lay outside their range.' That is, interest in the outside
world was not enough. This makes an easier connection with the
next point, 'it was sweet to me to love and to be loved, more so if I
could enjoy the body of the lover, so I contaminated the stream of
friendship ... ' A. uses *anima* both for the human soul and for the

'animating soul' of non-human living beings: see further O'Daly (1987) 7–8 and s.v. *anima* in the *Augustinus-Lexikon*, and cf. 4.4.7. **coinquinabam … obnubilabam:** cf. 2.2.2 for the metaphor of overclouding the clear light of friendship; the contaminated stream reappears in 3.2.3.   **de tartaro libidinis:** cf. *o flumen tartareum* 1.16.26.   **misericordia mea:** i.e. God who has mercy on me. **quanto felle:** cf. 1.14.23 for gall in the midst of sweetness. **uinculum fruendi:** the 'bond' of a physical relationship is a chain (*conligabar … aerumnosis nexibus*) securing the willing victim. The 'torments of love', a literary cliché which was no doubt used in the Carthage theatre (see 3.2.2), are described in terms of tortures which were available under late Roman law (*ut caederer uirgis ferreis ardentibus*). This relationship was not necessarily with the woman (see on 4.2.2) who became A.'s long-term partner, but their son Adeodatus, who was 'about fifteen' in 387 (9.6.14), must have been conceived in 370–1, in A.'s first year at Carthage.

3.2.2 Performances of plays intensified his feelings; he reflects on the puzzle that people enjoy being distressed by the fictional suffering they see on stage. After the intense language of the first sentence, A. moves into philosophical speculation on the pleasure people find in watching *spectacula theatrica*: the problem (considered both by Plato in the *Republic* and by Aristotle in the *Poetics*) might be updated in terms of horror films. Why do people look at things which they know they will find disturbing? 'Theatrical spectacles' were not only plays (A. mentions, in *Sermon* 241.5, stage adaptations of the *Aeneid*). Criminals were executed by burning or were torn by wild beasts; the wild beasts were themselves hunted and slaughtered, and gladiator fights, which were banned by the emperor Constantine in 325, are attested in the fourth and fifth centuries (cf. 6.8.13). There were also sexually explicit mimes supposedly commemorating love-affairs of the gods: A. describes in *City of God* 2.4 the rites in honour of the goddess Cybele and her lover Attis which he watched as a young man. Cf. 1.10.16 for interest in *spectacula* as a manifestation of *curiositas*; and see further Markus (1990) 107–23 for the hardening of A.'s attitude to *spectacula*. His disapproval is manifest especially in sermons he preached at Carthage.   **quid est, quod ibi homo uult dolere?** 'why is it that a man wants to be distressed there', i.e. in the theatre, but nowhere else? A. plays on the double meaning of *dolor*, physical or mental pain, in what follows.   **dolor ipse est uolup-tas eius:** for once, a philosophical puzzle (if it is pleasure, can it be pain?) which A. does not explore (cf. 4.5.10). Instead, he labels the condition *insania*, mental ill-health or madness, in accordance with the Platonic and Stoic teaching that strong emotion, because it overcomes reason, is a form of insanity.   **a talibus affectibus sanus** 'in good (mental) health from, i.e. unaffected by, such emotions'. *affectus*, 'emotion', is the mildest possible Latin translation of Greek *pathos*, which means literally something experienced or suffered, and is used of diseases. A. notes in *City of God* 9.4 that Cicero translates it *perturbatio (animi)* and Apuleius (more accurately, he thinks) *passio*. He argues there, and in *ibid.* 14.6–9, that emotions are not bad as such: the important question is whether they express a love which is rightly directed or wrongly directed. Thus a Christian may sorrow for the sin of another. (See further O'Daly (1987) 46–54.) By that test, A.'s imagined spectator clearly has bad emotions, and the less (mentally) healthy the spectator, the more he will be moved by them. C.'s translation reverses *quo* and *eo*, so that the argument – equally true – is that the man who is more moved by plays will be less healthy in resisting such onslaughts of emotion. **cum ipse patitur, miseria, cum aliis compatitur, miseri-cordia:** see on 1.5.5 for the double meaning of *miseria*, 'wretched-ness' either as an emotional state or as a condition which deserves pity. One who feels compassion – literally 'suffers with', *compatitur* – experiences *misericordia*, a heart (*cor*) which takes pity on wretched-ness (*miseria*). *misericordia* in the *C.* is usually the mercy of God, as in 3.1.1 *deus meus, misericordia mea*, 'my God who has mercy on me'. **qualis tandem misericordia in rebus fictis et scenicis?:** the spectator of a suffering which is only pretence is not being called on to show active compassion and to relieve suffering. Instead, the experience of a 'wretched heart' is itself enjoyable. A.'s analysis here is in the tradition of Stoic philosophy, which argued that the wise person will relieve suffering because all rational beings are kin, but that allowing oneself to feel distressed at suffering is a mistake: the feeling of distress implies a wrong judgement that something terrible has happened (whereas nothing is terrible except vice), and disrupts the ability of reason to make the right choices.   **manet intentus et gaudens lacrimat:** V. and O.'D. prefer this reading;

several MSS support the reading preferred by Knöll and Skutella (see Introd. §4*a* for these editions) and translated by C., *manet intentus et gaudens. lacrimae ergo amantur et dolores*. The strongest reason for beginning 3.2.3 *ergo amantur et dolores* is that the phrase is picked up twice in the paragraph, *hac una causa amantur dolores?* and *ergo amentur dolores aliquando*, without mention of *lacrimae*.

3.2.3 Pity involves some pain, and pity is good; but the truly merciful person wants pain to stop, and there is a danger that pity will turn into enjoyment of pain. A. raises the problem of misjudged *miseria* at 1.13.20–1, where he contrasts his weeping for the death of Dido (apparent *miseria*) with his failure to weep for his own dying away from God (real *miseria*).   **et hoc de illa uena amicitiae est:** that is, pleasure in being *misericors* comes from *amicitia*, which A. uses (cf. 2.2.2) as a general term for affectionate human relationships. *uena* means a vein, or things which resemble veins, including a stream of water; metaphorically, it is used for the nature of someone or something (*OLD* s.v. 5, 7).   **ut quid decurrit:** the transformation of the *uena*, when by its own inclination (*per nutum proprium*) it turns away from *caelesti serenitate* (cf. 2.2.2), is described in a violent outburst of language: 'a torrent of boiling pitch' which, like the *tartarus libidinis* of 3.1.1, evokes the horrors of the underworld, in this case the burning river Phlegethon; and *aestus immanes*, which could mean either 'monstrous surges' or 'monstrous heats' (cf. 2.2.2), perhaps both as the pitch seethes (cf. *ebulliebam* 2.2.2 and the *sartago* of 3.1.1). But why does A. speak so violently, even so theatrically, of the corruption of *amicitia* by misdirected pity? Perhaps the vehemence of the language reflects the intensity of his own remembered feeling, and the speed with which sympathy for lovers – illicit and fictitious lovers – became enjoyment of his own sensations.   **repudietur ergo misericordia? nequaquam. ergo amentur dolores aliquando:** a brief return to philosophical debate. Pity is not to be rejected, so pain should sometimes be loved, because pity cannot occur without it. (This is an argument sometimes used to explain why God permits suffering.)   **sed caue immunditiam:** A. uses *immunditia*, 'impurity', also of his extreme grief for the death of his friend, 4.6.11 (q.v.).   **deo patrum nostrorum et laudabili et superexaltato in omnia saecula:** the words used by Shadrach, Meshach and Abednego when they blessed God in the fiery furnace

(Daniel 3: 52): as at 2.3.6, an unspoken context makes a further point about A.'s spiritual state.   **neque enim nunc non misereor ... nunc uero magis misereor gaudentem in flagitio:** A. briefly, as at 2.7.15, contrasts his past with his present spiritual state. He still feels pity, but (see on 3.2.2) it is for those who rejoice in their wrongdoing. At 10.35.54–6, considering the temptations to which he is still vulnerable, he sets the experience of watching plays in the context of *curiositas*, the desire to see or to know what one should not or need not, and uses Plato's example (*Republic* 439e) of looking at mutilated corpses. It is this disease of greediness, he says, which causes amazing things to be shown in *spectacula*: *ex hoc morbo cupiditatis in spectaculis exhibentur quaeque miracula* (10.35.55). By God's grace, although he is not entirely free from *curiositas*, this particular manifestation is over: *sane me iam theatra non rapiunt.* Contrast 3.2.2 *rapiebant me spectacula theatrica*; and for *rapere* compare the effect of Cicero's *Hortensius* in 3.4.8 *non me totum rapiebat.*   **qui germanitus misericors est:** as befits a *germanus*, a brother, contrasted with *quasi misericors* above (A.'s feelings for stage lovers), and with the paradox which A. goes on to reject, *maliuola beniuolentia* which wants someone to suffer so that it may (genuinely and wholeheartedly) pity them.   **nullo dolore sauciaris:** God is *misericors* without experiencing *dolor* (compare, among the paradoxes deployed in praise of God at 1.1.4, *paenitet te et non doles*). A.'s phrasing suggests Plato's argument (*Republic* 380d–81c) that God is not vulnerable; but the emphasis here is that God does show compassion, which (unlike human compassion) is not contaminated by emotional involvement in the pain of another. *animas amas* perhaps makes a further contrast with human concern for the body.   **et ad haec quis idoneus?:** A. quotes 2 Corinthians 2: 16, apparently without reference to the context.

3.2.4 A. wanted the itch for physical contact (cf. 3.1.1) to be scratched by simulated pain which provoked tears.   **aerumna ... saltatoria:** acting often involved dance (*saltatio*). Cf. *Letter* 91.5 *agitur, cantatur, saltatur Iuppiter adulteria tanta committens.*   **infelix pecus aberrans a grege tuo:** both Virgil and the Bible are evoked (cf. 1.17.27 on the vine-shoot). The good shepherd searches for the one lost sheep (Luke 15: 4); Virgil's *infelix pecus* (*Eclogue* 3.3) was being exploited by a hireling shepherd. A., the lost sheep, has *scabies*, 'the itch', which is blistering and suppurating (*feruidus tumor et tabes et sanies horrida*) from being scratched on the surface by the distressing things he watched; he loved these *dolores*, but not any which went deeper than the surface, *quibus altius penetrarer*. The carefully structured sentence which expresses this is followed by a deliberately simple outcry: *talis uita mea numquid uita erat, deus meus?*

3.3.5 A. went further from God, but God's mercy watched over him and punished him.   **circumuolabat ... a longe miseri-cordia tua:** *a longe* is used in the Latin Bible to translate Greek *ek makrou*.   **in quantas iniquitates distabui, et sacrilegam curiositatem secutus sum:** for *distabui* cf. 2.1.1 *contabuit species mea*, and Job 42: 6 (see on 1.6.7). Most MSS have *sacrilega curiositate*, an 'ablative of manner' explaining how A. followed iniquity (so O'D.), but the sentence runs more easily with the accusative (so V.): 'I followed sacrilegious curiosity so that it led me, deserting you, into ... '   **ima infida:** cf. 2.5.10 for the 'lowest' things, furthest from God and therefore faithless in a double sense, both treacherous and lacking faith in God.   **circumuentoria obsequia daemonio-rum:** *obsequium* is respectful attention to the wishes of an important person (hence English 'obsequious', now a pejorative); *circumuentoria* is a (very rare) adjective from *circumuenire*, 'circumvent' or 'cheat'. For demons, see on 1.17.27, where A. also uses the image of sacrific-ing to powers which are hostile to God. A.'s bad actions were in themselves an offering to demons; perhaps he also implies that *curio-sitas* led him to investigate the magic rites which sought to win the (deceptive) favour of demons (cf. 4.2.3).   **flagellabas me** (cf. below *uerberasti grauibus poenis*): cf. 3.1.1 for torments caused by love, and 2.2.4 for the *flagella* of God *misericorditer saeuiens* ('mercifully' because the torment prevents the sinner from being satisfied with inferior loves).   **in celebritate sollemnitatum tuarum:** at the celebration of a feast of the Church. According to Jerome (*Letter* 107.9), such feasts were a danger for Christian girls, precisely because someone might try to pick them up.   **agere negotium procurandi fructus mortis:** the 'business of acquiring the fruit of death' evokes Romans 7: 5 'while we were in the flesh, the pas-sions of our sins, which happened through the law, worked in our limbs so that they would bear fruit for death'. A. is reluctant to say in so many words that he started an affair with a woman he saw

in church.   **refugium meum a terribilibus nocentibus ...
uagatus sum praefidenti collo ... amans uias meas et non
tuas:** the rhythms and language sound biblical, but (as at 2.4.9,
q.v.) there is no obvious model.   **fugitiuam libertatem:** see on
2.6.14.

3.3.6 A.'s studies aimed at successful dishonesty. He was con-
ceited, but at least he did not join the Wreckers, a disruptive student
society; but he stayed friends with them.   **studia, quae honesta
uocabantur:** *honestus* means 'respectable', with strong social overtones (as in 'respectable people'): someone ranked as *honestior* was (in
principle) safeguarded from interrogation under torture, physical
punishment and execution with 'aggravated penalties'. *studia honesta*
were suited to respectable people (just as *artes liberales* were to free
men): they were training for a respected profession, or a suitable education for a landowner. But, A. says, they are not honest.
habebant ... ductum suum intuentem fora litigiosa: the
honesta studia were preparation for a career in the law, either as an
advocate or as legal advisor to a government official (this was the
career followed by A.'s student Alypius, 6.10.16). But *fora litigiosa*
(borrowed from Ovid, *Fasti* 4.188) suggests law as public conflict and
competition.   **tumebam typho:** Greek *typhos*, 'vanity', literally
being swollen or puffed up (cf. 1 Corinthians 13: 4-5 'love is not
puffed up'). A. liked this word, which occurs several times in the *C.*
(instances in O'D. 11 421) to describe conceit. It was a man *immanissimo typho turgidus* who gave A. some Platonic books (7.9.13,
see Introd. §3*b*). But, although A. was intellectually puffed up, he
was *sedatior* in relation to the riotous students.   **euersores:** the
Wreckers raise the same problem of gratuitous wrongdoing as A.'s
friends at Thagaste (2.7.15), but here, A. does not participate, and is
much more explicit in his condemnation of students who disrupt
classes and make life difficult for newcomers. The difference may be
because he himself suffered from riotous students when teaching in
Carthage: he says (5.8.14) that their behaviour motivated his move
to Rome, where, he was told, there was no problem with *euersiones*.
(Instead, 5.12.22, students left before paying their fees at the end of
a course.)   **uelut insigne urbanitatis:** cf. 3.1.1 for A.'s imagined *urbanitas*.   **scaeuum et diabolicum ... nihil est illo
actu similius actibus daemoniorum:** the Wreckers are literally

diabolical, devilish, in what they do and in their motives for doing
it. They seek to destroy, and they assault the modesty (*uerecundiam*)
of their victims by deceiving and mocking them; they do so *gratis*,
gratuitously (cf. 2.4.9), in order to feed their *maliuolas laetitias*, happiness which intends harm. So they are themselves the victims of
demons, who operate by misrepresentation to achieve harm. A.
uses both the non-Christian word *daemonia* (see on 1.17.27) and the
Christian word *diabolicus*, from Greek *diabolos*, 'the slanderer' which
translates Hebrew *satan*, 'the deceiver'.   **pudore impudenti:** A.
presumably regards his *pudor* as 'shameless' in that he stayed friends
with the Wreckers and even enjoyed their company (compare 2.9.17
pudet non esse impudentem); or because he was unaware how bad his
own behaviour was.

   3.4.7 Cicero's *Hortensius* inspired A. with the love of wisdom.
   Cicero wrote the *Hortensius* as 'protreptic', encouragement to the
study of philosophy: it was the introduction to the important series
of philosophical works which he wrote in 46–45 B.C., when his political career seemed to have ended. It was probably on the Carthage
rhetoric syllabus (*usitato … discendi ordine*) as an example of exhortation and a repertory of arguments for renouncing the empty glory
of the world – something which often had to be suggested to dis-
appointed politicians. But A., at eighteen, was deeply impressed by
its content; most of the fragments of *Hortensius* are quotations by A.
For his use of Cicero, see further O'D. II 162–6; for the *Hortensius*,
Hagendahl (1967) 79–94 and 486–97; for philosophy, Introd. §3.
cuiusdam Ciceronis 'one Cicero', cf. 1.13.20 *Aeneae nescio cuius*.
A. may be suggesting that Cicero, as a pagan writer, is of no real
importance; but he refers to Paul as *quidam seruus tuus* (12.15.20), so
perhaps the point is that no human being is important.   **cuius
linguam fere omnes mirantur, pectus non ita:** *pectus*, literally
'chest' and metaphorically 'heart', is the location of thought and
feeling which is expressed (or disguised) by the words which the
tongue speaks. So A. probably means that Cicero's splendid language was not supported by commitment: Cicero was (and is) often
accused of inconsistency and lack of courage.   **mutauit affectum meum:** the *Hortensius* brought about an emotional, rather than
an intellectual, shift (see on 3.2.2 for *affectus*). The vocabulary which
describes it, *concupiscebam aestu cordis incredibili*, suggests excessive

emotion, but A.'s point is that the *Hortensius* gave him different, but equally strong, desires. So far (3.1.1) he had only been aware of an inward hunger.   **ad te ipsum ... mutauit preces meas:** the word order is designed to emphasise *te ipsum*. A. means that the *Hortensius* transformed the content of his prayers to God, not that he now began to pray to God instead of to some other power; instead of thinking about himself (as in his childish prayers not to be beaten, 1.9.14), he was thinking about God.   **surgere coeperam ut ad te redirem** makes it clear that A. is beginning to do the right thing: once again the reference is to the Prodigal Son, saying to himself 'I will arise and go to my father' (see on 1.18.28).   **quod uidebar emere ... ante biennium:** a very odd parenthesis. Perhaps the mention of A.'s heavenly father prompts a mention of his earthly father, who is doubly displaced, by his widow as provider and by God as father (see on 2.3.5), and whose death occurred two years before, when A. left for Carthage. But it is not clear why A. disrupts his sentence (which he has to resume with *non ergo*) to supply this information; or why he makes no mention of Romanianus, who (*Against the Academics* 2.2.3) helped him with friendship and funds when he lost his father.

3.4.8 The *Hortensius* rightly explained that philosophy is the love of wisdom, not the pursuit of misleading teachings; but it did not mention Christ.   **reuolare a terrenis ad te:** the return of the Prodigal is here expressed as the philosophical ascent of reason (Introd. §3*b*) from earthly things to God (cf. 1.18.28).   **amor autem sapientiae nomen Graecum habet philosophiam:** a point made in the *Hortensius* (Hagendahl (1967) 92).   **per seruum tuum bonum et pium:** Paul; the quotation which follows (*uidete ... corporaliter*) is from Colossians 2: 8–9. As in 3.2.3, A. comments on his reactions from the perspective of his later awareness: he did not yet know it, but non-Christian philosopher and Christian scripture are in agreement on what philosophy is – except that Cicero does not mention Christ. Cf. 5.14.24, and 7.9.13–15 where A. describes at length how Platonist philosophy freed him from error – but it makes no mention of Christ.   **diligerem et quaererem et assequerer et tenerem atque amplexarer:** a spectacular run of verbs joined by 'and' (cf. Introd. §2*a*); marked as a quotation from the lost *Hortensius* in C., but characteristic of A. rather than of

Cicero.   **in tanta flagrantia refrangebat:** *flagrantia* as in a blaze of enthusiasm; *refrangebat*, 'resisted', is more commonly spelled *refringebat*, but that loses the pattern of vowel-sounds.   **quamuis litteratum et expolitum et ueridicum:** Cicero has an elegant style and is truthful, but is lacking in that he does not name Christ; but A. is about to find that Scripture, which does name Christ, is lacking in style.

3.5.9 Because he wanted to find wisdom combined with the name of Christ, A. started to read the Bible, but found that it did not bear comparison with Cicero.   **animum intendere in scripturas sanctas:** A. had of course heard the Bible read in church, but it is quite possible that his mother did not have her own copy of the Bible and that he had never read it himself.   **non compertam superbis neque nudatam pueris:** an echo of A.'s favourite text *deus superbis resistit, humilibus autem dat gratiam* (see on 1.1.1), but making the different point that Scripture does not reveal its full meaning to children (*pueri*) who have just begun to study it. Cf. 1.9.14 for A.'s childish awareness of God: he does not suggest that it had developed before he read the *Hortensius*. He needed to accept that he was a *paruulus*, a little child (see below) in Christian experience.   **incessu humilem, successu excelsam** '[a thing] low as one goes in, high as one goes on'. Cf. 6.5.8, 12.14.17 for the modesty and profundity of the Bible.   **uelatam mysteriis:** veils (cf. 1.13.22) are a sign of important secrets; here, the veils cover those parts of the Bible which do not immediately reveal their deeper meaning. cf. *Sermon* 51.4.5 *uela faciunt honorem secreti*.   **indigna quam Tullianae dignitati compararem:** an understandable reaction to the style of the Old Latin Bible (see further Introd. §2a), expressed in very Ciceronian phrasing. As he does for *spectacula* (see above, 3.2.3), A. makes an explicit contrast with his reaction at the time of writing the *C*. The content may also have seemed inferior, especially if A. began at the beginning and encountered some of the more disquieting stories in Genesis. It took Ambrose's skilled rhetorical technique to deal with the more difficult sections of the Old Testament (5.14.24). In *On Catechising the Untrained* 13 A. says that educated converts must be taught to 'hear' the Bible, so that they are not repelled by its style, and will need allegorical explanations of some passages.   **dedignabar esse paruulus:** Jesus said to his followers: 'unless you receive the kingdom of Heaven like a child [*sicut puer* in the Vulgate], you shall not enter it' (Luke 18: 17).

3.6.10 The Manichaeans claimed to offer truth, and spoke the name of Christ, but the spiritual food they offered was unsatisfying.

A. was working on a detailed refutation of Manichaeism, *Against Faustus*, in the years when he was writing the *C.* He also argued against the Manichaeans in his various exegeses of Genesis, a book which they rejected as a false account of creation. Here he is concerned chiefly to show his own response to Manichaean teaching and how it alienated him from the true God. He takes for granted that his readers know, or think they know, something about Manichaeism. See further Introd. §3*a*; Brown (1967) 46–60, Lane Fox (1986) 561–71 for sympathetic treatments of the appeal of Manichaeism; Bonner (1986) 157–236 for a detailed discussion of Manichaeism and of A.'s critique; Lieu (1985) for a full account of the surviving texts and the spread of Manichaeism. **homines superbe delirantes, carnales nimis et loquaces:** A. does not use the word Manichaean until 3.10.18. This description shows why the Manichaeans appealed to A. as he has described himself in book 3: an intellectually confident young man, who wanted to achieve wisdom but also wanted success and a sexual partner. *superbe* as usual connotes over-confidence in human intellect (see on 1.1.1); *delirantes* establishes the theme of hallucination which A. continues below. For *loquaces* see on 1.4.4: the Manichaeans used a lot of words, and used them impressively, but said nothing. *carnales* may mean that they were preoccupied with the life of the body, in that they had strict dietary rules and tried to avoid procreating children. It may also mean that they thought in terms of physical substances: see on 3.7.12, and cf. 5.10.19–20, where A. says he was unable to think of God, or of evil, except as a physical substance. A. does not here make the further point that, although the Manichaeans thought in physical terms, they regarded matter (including human bodies) as evil and so denied the Incarnation: A.'s friend Verecundus was taught *ut ueritatis filii tui carnem phantasma crederet*, 9.3.6. **laquei diaboli et uiscum:** *laquei* are snares, *uiscum* is bird-lime, both used by fowlers. (A. went bird-hunting when he was a boy: *On the Quantity of the Soul* 21.36.) **commixtione syllabarum nominis tui:** the Manichaeans spoke the syllables which make up the names of the

Christian trinity, Father, Son and Spirit, but the names were only sounds, *tenus sono*, because the Manichaeans spoke without truth. Mani interpreted Jesus Christ as a wholly divine being who did not experience birth or death: see further Introd. §3*a*.   **paracleti:** Jesus told his followers that 'the Advocate [Greek *paraklētos*], the Holy Spirit, whom the Father will send in my name, will teach you everything and remind you of all I have said to you' (John 14: 26). Mani claimed the Paraclete as his 'twin self' (5.5.8).   **nomina non recedebant de ore eorum:** an allusion to Joshua 1: 8 *non recedat uolumen legis huius ab ore tuo*, which refers to the Mosaic Law. The Manichaeans refused to recognise the Old Testament as an expression of truth (see on 3.7.13).   **ueritas et ueritas:** the Manichaean claim was to offer truth established by reason, not dependent on the authority of the Church and the Christian scriptures, which, they said, had been heavily interpolated and also misunderstood. **transgredi debui:** A. ought to have passed over even the true teaching of philosophers about the basic components (*elementa*) of the world, because it is inadequate in comparison to the love of God (*prae amore tuo*); but he accepted false teaching (despite the warning in the *Hortensius*, 3.4.8). Later, true teaching by philosophers about the universe helped him to doubt Manichaeism (5.3.3–4).   **medullae animi mei:** literally the 'marrow' of the soul, a well-established metaphor (*OLD* s.v. *medulla* 2b).   **libris multis et ingentibus:** Manichaean texts included the teachings of Mani (in seven volumes) and books of psalms and liturgy. Some of the surviving texts are impressively written and decorated; A. comments on the elaborate manuscripts and bindings in *Against Faustus* 13.18.   **fercula, in quibus mihi esurienti te inferebatur pro te sol et luna:** the image of A.'s hunger for spiritual food (cf. 3.1.1) would remind his readers that Manichaeans were notorious for strict fasting – a pale face led to suspicions of Manichaeism; and the language of 'eating the divine' might also remind them of the Manichaean teaching that particles of light, fragments of the power of good which was dispersed through the universe, could be released when a member of the Manichaean Elect ate food which contained them. *fercula*, here used for carrying food, are used in *City of God* 2.4 to carry the images of the gods.   **sol et luna:** in Manichaean teaching, the sun and moon were made from the Light which had not been damaged by the invasion of Darkness. In *Against Faustus* 20.2, Faustus (as reported by A.) says that Manichaeans believe the Father inhabits 'light inaccessible' and the Son inhabits the highest visible light. They interpret Paul (1 Corinthians 1: 24), who speaks of Christ as the power of God and the wisdom of God, as referring to two aspects of Christ: they think the power inhabits the sun and the wisdom inhabits the moon, so the sun and moon are worthy of worship. A. replies that this is polytheism. In *On Heresies* (written much later, in 428) A. says that the Manichaeans regarded the sun and moon as ships, made from the pure substance of God, which carried back to the kingdom of God all the light which had been freed from darkness.   **priora enim spiritalia opera tua:** A. here assumes that a non-physical creation preceded the creation of the visible world; in his *Unfinished Book on the Literal Interpretation of Genesis* 3.7 he identifies this prior creation with the angels. In *C.* book 12 A. seeks to interpret the reference to the 'heaven of heaven' in Psalm 113: 16, and to explain why 'in the beginning God created heaven and earth' (Genesis 1: 1) is followed by the creation of the firmament which is called heaven (*ibid.* 7–8) on the second day and of the dry land which is called earth (*ibid.* 9–10) on the third. He suggests that the 'heaven of heaven' is a non-physical, timeless creation which does not fall away from God (12.9.9); a second heaven and a visible ordered earth were created in time (12.12.15). **in qua non est commutatio nec momenti obumbratio:** James 1: 17. Like Joshua 1: 8 (above), the verse is used against the Manichaeans: it calls God the 'father of lights', but affirms that God (unlike the Manichaean power of good) is never for a moment obscured by darkness.   **esuriebam et sitiebam:** Matthew 5: 6 'blessed are they who hunger and thirst after righteousness, for they shall be fed'.   **phantasmata splendida:** strictly, images of things which do not exist, whereas *phantasia* is an image of something which does exist, even though one has not seen it or does not now see it, but A.'s use of the two words is not consistent. See further O'Daly (1987) 106–11.   **melius erat amare** 'it would have been better to love'.   **animo decepto per oculos:** the soul is deceived by Manichaean interpretations of physical seeing. **sicut nunc mihi locuta es:** A. is still addressing *ueritas*.   **corporalia phantasmata** 'bodily phantasms' imagined as material, a

conscious paradox which is echoed through the rest of the paragraph. The Manichaean sun and moon were *falsa corpora*, less certain
than the *uera corpora* which can be seen by animals and birds as well
as humans. A. emphasises the perceptions we share with animals
as a challenge to the Manichaean claim of spiritual perception (cf.
3.6.11, below). Imagining such *uera corpora* is less reliable than seeing
them, but imagining is more reliable than conjecturing *alia grandiora
et infinita* which do not exist. But God is not the heavenly *corpora*.
God made them, *condidit*, and they are not even the greatest of
God's creation, *nec in summis tuis conditionibus habes*: A. must mean
that the angels, the *priora spiritalia*, are greater.   **in quem deficio ut fortis sim:** Psalm 118: 81 *defecit in salutare tuum anima mea*,
'my soul has fainted (waiting for) your salvation'. O'D. cites A.'s
interpretation of this verse (*On the Psalms* 70, *Sermon* 1.14): people
faint when they acknowledge their sins and realise they have no
strength of their own; then they can say, like Paul (2 Corinthians
12: 10), 'when I am made weak, then I am powerful'.   **nec ista
corpora es:** A. retraces the steps of his argument. God is remote
from *phantasmata* of non-existent bodies, which are less reliable than
imaginings (*phantasiae*, memory-images as distinct from fantasy) of
bodies which do exist, and the imaginings are less reliable than the
bodies – and God is not the bodies we see in the heaven, nor the
creation we do not see (*ea quae non uidemus ibi*, i.e. the *priora spiritalia*),
nor the soul which gives life to the bodies, but the life of the soul.

   3.6.11 Even the literature which A. studied, and knew to be fiction, was more sustaining than Manichaean mythology, which he
believed to be true.   **longe peregrinabar:** a further reference
to the Prodigal Son. The 'husks which the swine did eat' (Luke 15:
16, AV) were standardly interpreted as unprofitable pagan literature
and philosophy; here, as the next sentence shows, they are the *poetarum fabellae*. This was poor food, but it could provide some suste-
nance (*uera pulmenta*) because A. knew it for what it was, i.e. fiction,
not truth. The reference to the pigs whom A. fed on husks suggests
that he had started teaching (see on 4.2.2); but O'D. notes Ambrose,
On Luke 7.218 'some people take the pigs to be herds of demons'
(because of the demons who took possession of the Gadarene swine,
Luke 8: 32–3), and cites three passages in which A. accepts this
identification.   **Medea uolans:** in a chariot drawn by winged

serpents, according to the Latin dramatist Pacuvius; A. took the example from Cicero (*On Invention* 1.27). Medea is an image of evil, but
A. knows the image is not true.　　**quinque elementa uarie fucata propter quinque antra tenebrarum:** the Five Elements of
Manichaean teaching were smoke, darkness, fire, water and wind, all
belonging to the power of darkness and inhabiting gulfs of darkness,
to which, apparently, their colours correspond. *fucatum* inspires suspi-
cion, cf. the warning in 3.4.7 against false philosophers *fucantes errores
suos.* Different kinds of creatures were born from them (humans and
other bipeds from smoke). This is an image of evil which A. mis-
takenly believed to be true.　　**in profunda inferi:** see on 1.2.2,
and cf. below on Proverbs 9. A.'s remoteness from God is expressed
in his favourite image of destitution, *inopia,* which makes him ill
and feverish, *laborans et aestuans.*　　**non secundum intellectum
mentis ... sed secundum sensum carnis quaererem:** A.
thought that non-human animals (*beluae,* 'beasts') have to rely on
sense-perception of the material world, but humans can reflect on
the activity of the mind and can thus understand that God is a
spirit, not matter (Introd. §3*b*). Because he had failed to understand
this, he was defeated by Manichaean attacks on Christian teaching
(see on 3.7.12).　　**interior intimo meo:** God is within A. (cf.
1.2.2), and introspection would have helped A. to return to God: see
7.10.16 *et inde* [i.e. from the Platonic books, Introd. §3*b*] *admonitus
redire ad memet ipsum intraui ad intima mea duce te ... et uidi qualicum-
que oculo animae meae supra eundem oculum animae meae, supra mentem meam
lucem incommutabilem.* The 'ascent of reason' is described in more detail in 7.17.23. For A. on introspection, see further Rist (1994) 85–
90.　　**illam mulierem audacem:** Proverbs 9: 13–17, part para-
phrased and part quoted from memory. The woman is an *aenigma
Salomonis,* a 'riddle of Solomon', because the Proverbs were ascribed
to the wise king Solomon, and A. interprets the passage as an *aenigma* with a hidden meaning, an allegory. Proverbs chapter 9 contrasts personified Wisdom with personified Folly. Wisdom prepares
a feast, and sends out her maidservants to declare *si quis est paruulus
ueniat ad me* (cf. 3.5.9 for *paruulus*). Folly sits (immodestly) at her
door, calling *si quis est paruulus declinet ad me,* and inviting passers
by to enjoy stolen water and bread eaten in secret. The fool accepts, but does not realise that her guests are in hell: *in profundis*

inferni conuiuae eius.   **inuenit foris:** A. uses *intus* and *foris* for concerns within and outside the soul; cf. 7.7.11 'the light of my eyes was not with me, for it was inside and I was outside'.   **habitantem in oculo carnis meae:** another of A.'s remarkable physical metaphors, odd enough for some scholars to emend the text – but the MSS are in agreement and the image is characteristic of A. He is 'living in the eye of my flesh' because he cannot see anything which is not physical (cf. 3.7.12 *cuius uidere usque ad corpus erat oculis*); and two strongly physical words, *ruminantem* and *uorassem*, describe how he devours, from what he can see, (inadequate) nourishment for the soul, and ruminates upon it.

3.7.12 A. failed to realise that God is a spirit, not a body, and that evil is only the absence of good.

The Manichaeans confronted A. with three challenges. First, *unde malum*: what is the origin of evil? Plato had argued (*Republic* 379–80) that God, being good, cannot be the source of evil; the Manichaeans, according to A. *On the Two Souls* 8.10, pressed the question: 'If it is from human beings, where do they come from? If from an angel, where does the angel come from?' (cf. 7.3.4–5.7). The expected answer was that God created human beings and angels, so God would still be responsible for evil. Their solution was that evil is an independent power in constant conflict with good. Second, *utrum forma corporea deus finiretur*: is God limited by bodily form? The Old Testament appeared to present an anthropomorphic God, in whose image human beings are made (Genesis 1: 26–7). Ambrose's preaching (6.3.4) finally made it clear to A. that this is not Christian teaching: God is spirit, not body, and the image of God in humans is the soul (see below on *ad imaginem dei*). Third, what kind of example was offered by the supposedly 'righteous men', the patriarchs of the Old Testament, who had several wives, killed, and practised animal sacrifice? The Manichaeans rejected the Old Testament; again, Ambrose's preaching showed A. that it could be interpreted allegorically.   **Nesciebam enim aliud, uere quod est:** that is, A. did not know that there is a reality which is not material.   **quasi acutule mouebar** 'I was rather cleverly influenced'. A. is not prepared to concede that the Manichaeans did have good arguments.   **non noueram malum non esse nisi priuationem boni:** cf. 2.8.16 for the argument that evil is, literally, nothing. A.

develops the question of the origin of evil at 7.5.7 and this response at 7.12.18. See further Evans (1982). **cuius uidere usque ad corpus erat oculis et animo usque ad phantasma:** the infinitive *uidere* is used as a noun (cf. *cui esse* below). C. 'for me "to see" meant a physical act of looking with the eyes and of forming an image in the mind', which perhaps underestimates the limitation A. wants to convey: with his eyes he could see only corporeal things, with his mind he could see only (Manichaean) phantasms. **non noueram deum esse spiritum:** John 4: 24 'God is spirit, and those who worship Him must worship in spirit and in truth.' A. was still thinking of God as substance, with extension (*cui membra essent per longum et latum*) and mass (*cui esse moles esset* 'for whom existence was existence as a mass'); thus he could not think of God as omnipresent, because (see on 1.3.3) a substance, even if it is infinite in extension, has less mass in a part or a defined area than it does in the whole. This laid him open to the Manichaean argument that the divine substance does not occupy all the universe, but is dispersed and constrained by the power of evil (cf. 13.30.45). **recte in scriptura diceremur ad imaginem dei:** 'God said, Let us make man in our image and likeness' (Genesis 1: 26–7). A., failing to realise that God is spirit, could not understand that it is the human soul, not the human body, which is in the image of God (cf. 13.22.32). The construction of the sentence is *ignorabam quid in nobis esset* 'I did not know what it was in us', *secundum quod essemus et recte diceremur* 'in accordance with which we exist and are rightly said ...' Cf. the last sentence of 3.6.10 for the soul which is the life of the body and God who is the life of the soul.

3.7.13 A. moves on to the third Manichaean challenge. Here, he did not realise the difference between the unchanging moral law and its expression in rules adapted to time and place.

A. had worked through Manichaean arguments against the Old Testament in his *On the Usefulness of Believing*, which he wrote soon after his ordination in 391 to persuade his friend Honoratus to follow him out of Manichaeism (as Honoratus had once followed him into it). He also discusses them in *Against Faustus*. In this paragraph, A. uses a calm expository style of argument with examples from everyday experience. **iustitiam ueram interiorem:** the Manichaean claim was that the *iusti*, the 'righteous men', of the Old

Testament, failed to show *iustitia*. A. argues that *iustitia* is conformity with the law of God, not with the expectations of a particular time and place. *interior* perhaps suggests a contrast with outward conformity; cf. also *tu autem eras interior intimo meo* in 3.6.11.   **ex humano die:** by human standards of judgement. The phrase comes from 1 Corinthians 4: 3, and is formed by analogy with 'the day of the Lord', i.e. the day of God's judgement (e.g. Isaiah 13: 6).   **calciari** literally 'to be shod'.   **iustitio** 'cessation of business' (including *ius*, the settlement of disputes).   **numquid iustitia uaria est et mutabilis?:** a reminiscence of probably the most quoted words of the *Aeneid* (4.569–70), *uarium et mutabile semper femina.*   **hic seruiunt** 'in this they are slaves [to convention]'.

3.7.14 A. should have realised the principle from his own experience: in poetry, a particular rhythm must go in different places for different metres and even different lines of a poem, but the art of poetry includes all these different patterns. In this paragraph his style becomes more intense, with repeated use of *et* to join clauses and sentences (Introd. §2a).   **futura praenuntiantes:** the Manichaeans refused to acknowledge that the Old Testament included prophecies of the coming of Christ. A. probably also refers (as he does in *Against Faustus*) to the allegorical interpretation of some Old Testament stories, which suggested that what the patriarchs did, as well as what the prophets said, prefigured Christ. In *Against Faustus* 22.25 he compares people who criticise the conduct of the prophets with schoolboys who think Virgil has committed a solecism (see on 1.18.28) by writing *pars in frusta secant* instead of *secat.*

3.8.15 Some moral principles are universal and some sins are against nature. Other acts offend against human custom in a particular context, but custom may be changed on the orders of a ruler, and God is the ruler of all.   **diligere deum ... diligere proximum tamquam te ipsum:** Jesus' summary of the law of God (Matthew 22: 37, 39).   **itaque flagitia:** it is always right to love God and one's neighbour; God made nature; a sin against nature is a failure to love God and one's neighbour whom God made, and therefore is always wrong.   **Sodomitarum:** all the men of Sodom (Genesis 19: 4–5) demanded that Lot should hand over for male rape the two men (really angels) who were staying with him; hence 'sodomy'. Sodom and Gomorrah, the Cities of the Plain, were already notorious for sin and were soon afterwards destroyed by fire from heaven. A. argues that sodomy is not a local custom but a sin (*flagitium*, a sin arising from desire) against nature, 'because God's law did not make people [*homines* here refers to male human beings] in such a way that they should make use of each other like this'. Thus sodomy would be a crime against divine law even if all peoples (not just all male Sodomites) practised it, because our bond (*societas*) with God is damaged when the nature that God made is 'contaminated by perverse lust'. In affirming both that sodomy is forbidden by God's law and that it is against nature, A. assumes (see on 2.2.3, and cf. 3.8.16) that there is a natural and God-given use of sex, namely the procreation of children; so an act which is possible in terms of human biology is classed as unnatural.   **turpis enim omnis pars uniuerso suo non congruens:** human agreement (*pactum*) is supported by an appeal to the ordered and therefore beautiful whole, the *kosmos* of Greek political theory. If the whole is well ordered, a part that does not fit with the whole is *turpis*, both aesthetically and morally repellent (cf. 4.11.16 for the relationship of part and whole, and 4.13.20 for A.'s theories when he wrote *On the Beautiful and Fitting*). In the late 390s A. was moving away from this model of politics as good order, and was beginning to think of social order as a necessary device for restraining human desires. For the development of his thought see Markus (1988) 72–104.   **si enim regi licet:** A. uses the analogy of a human ruler who gives an unprecedented order. If it is obeyed (*obtemperatur*, an impersonal passive), the *societas* of his city is strengthened, because the *pactum* of human society requires obedience to rulers. A. does not mention the problem of obedience to unrighteous rulers, which he discusses in *Against Faustus* 22.75. An order from the ruler of the universe is obviously to be followed. Again, A. does not comment on the difficulty of telling whether an order comes from God (cf. 3.9.17 *beati qui te imperasse sciunt*), and therefore cannot be contrary to the universal moral law.

3.8.16 A. discusses the motivation of crimes (*facinora*) which injure fellow-humans, and argues that, although sin does not harm God, it does harm the sinner.   **item in facinoribus** 'similarly with crimes', that is, like *flagitia*, they always deserve punishment. *flagitia* are primarily sexual sins, which corrupt, and *facinora* are primarily sins which do harm to others, but the words are often paired. See on 2.5.11.   **sola uoluptate alieni mali:** here taken as a manifestation of the desire to dominate, without questioning why anyone should take pleasure in another's pain (cf. 2.5.11, 3.2.3 for relevant analysis).   **principandi et spectandi et sentiendi libidine:** in reverse order, the three temptations of 1 John 2: 16, 'the lust of the flesh, and the lust of the eyes, and the pride of life' (cf. 1.10.16).   **tria et septem:** the first three of the Ten Commandments (the Decalogue) are concerned with love of God, the remaining seven with love of neighbour. The 'ten-stringed harp', interpreted by A. as the ten commandments, comes from Psalm 32: 2 *confitemini domino in cithara, in psalterio decem chordarum psallite ei.* This paragraph, by contrast with the philosophical analysis which surrounds it, makes frequent use of biblical quotation, especially from the Psalms.   **hoc uindicas quod in se homines perpetrant** 'your punishment [sc. of the guilty] is that which human beings do to their own injury' (C.); the words could also mean 'you punish what human beings do to hurt each other', but A.'s point is that when people sin they damage the image of God in themselves, namely their souls.   **mentitur iniquitas sibi:** Psalm 26: 12, also used at 1.5.6. Wickedness deceives itself about what it is doing, that is, corrupting or perverting the nature made by God. **immoderate utendo concessis rebus:** the obvious example (see on 2.2.3) is sexual intercourse within marriage but not for procreation.   **flagrando in eum usum qui est contra naturam** refers to sodomy, which, according to A. *On the Good of Marriage* 11.12, is deplorable if practised on a prostitute but much worse if practised on a wife.   **aduersus stimulum calcitrantes** 'kicking against the pricks' of the goad which drives on an animal. The phrase is used in Paul's vision on the Damascus road: 'Saul, Saul, why persecutest thou me? it is hard for thee to kick against the pricks' (Acts 26: 14).   **tu derelinqueris, fons uitae:** the unstated context evokes one of A.'s favourite images. *fons uitae* is a phrase often used by A.; it occurs with *derelinquere* in Jeremiah 2: 13 'my people have left me, the spring of living water, to dig themselves cisterns, leaky cisterns which cannot hold water'.   **priuata superbia diligitur in parte unum falsum:** people turn away from the *unus et uerus creator* who is the good of all, and with isolated

(C. 'self-concerned') pride love *unum falsum*. This compressed phrase implies both that the 'one' they love is false and that it is not truly one, because it is only one thing among many and is loved *in parte*, that is, in the part but not the whole. The point becomes clearer at the end of the paragraph, *amplius amando proprium nostrum quam te, omnium bonum*. A.'s language here is close to Plotinus, who considers the possibility that things fall away from their original union with the One because of *tolma*, self-assertion (*Ennead* 6.9; see further Introd. §3*b*).   **propitius es peccatis:** Psalm 78: 9.   **exaudis gemitus compeditorum:** Psalm 101: 21. A. extends the image of shackled prisoners with a reference to chains which we make for ourselves (cf. 3.1.1).   **erigamus aduersum te cornua falsae libertatis:** Psalm 74: 5 'do not lift up your horn' (asserting strength as a horned animal does). Cf. 2.6.14 for *falsa libertas*.

3.9.17 Acts which are apparently sinful may not have sinful motives and may be ordered by God for a specific but hidden purpose.   **peccata proficientium:** thus it is (for instance) often argued that 'an eye for an eye' is progress by comparison with un-limited vendetta.   **similia uel flagitio uel facinori:** A. does not give examples, but there is a long list in *Against Faustus* 22.5, end-ing with Moses, who committed murder, robbed the Egyptians, and engaged in wars and other cruelties. A. does not attempt to defend every action recorded in the Old Testament: some, he says, are re-corded for us to judge or to see God's judgement. But he argues (*ibid.* 69–74) that Moses killed a cruel overseer from the same eager-ness to help his people which made him a great leader (*peccata pro-ficientium*), and that God, for whatever reason, told him to rob the Egyptians (an example of an order *contra morem aut pactum*, cf. 3.8.15). God also told Moses to fight wars, but in just retaliation, not from desire to harm. A.'s final defence, as here, is that actions ordered by God may be prophetic (cf. 3.7.14).   **facientis animus:** A.'s em-phasis on the state of soul, as distinct from the thing done, allows him also to absolve soldiers who kill, or judges who order executions, provided that they do so in obedience to lawful authority and with-out desire to harm.   **atque articulus occulti temporis** 'the moment of hidden time'. This may be simply the immediate circum-stances, but may also be 'sacred history', the record of what God is doing to redeem the world. See further Markus (1988) 1–21.   **beati**

qui te imperasse sciunt: see on 3.8.15 for the problem of knowing whether an order comes from God.

3.10.18 A. ridiculed the Old Testament, but was himself ridiculous in his beliefs.   **Haec ego nesciens:** cf. *nesciebam* 3.7.12, *non noueram* 3.7.13, *haec ego tunc nesciebam* 3.7.14, beginning successive paragraphs.   **ut crederem ficum plorare:** A. explains in more detail, in *On the Psalms* 140.12, that the Manichaeans thought there were bodily parts (*membra*) of the divine throughout the universe. Because these parts were also in plants, farming and harvesting hurts God. The milky sap of the fig-tree could thus be interpreted as tears shed for the loss of a fruit.   **nisi electi sancti dente ac uentre soluerentur:** the Manichaean Elect (Introd. §3*a*) led austere and celibate lives. They did not prepare their own food (so as not to injure God) but rewarded with their prayers the Hearers who incurred the sin of picking fruit or grain; and their pure bodies were believed to be capable of releasing fragments of the divine which were trapped in plants. A. uses sharply physical vocabulary for this supposedly spiritual process (cf. 4.1.1 *in officina aqualiculi sui*).   **qui manichaeus non esset:** for the first time A. names the sect. **quasi capitali supplicio damnanda buccella uideretur:** the 'mouthful' eaten by a non-Manichaean would be trapped in that person's impure body, losing (perhaps for ever) its chance to be freed by an Elect.

3.11.19 A.'s mother wept constantly for him, and was comforted by a dream.

A. asked 'where were you?' (3.6.11) before embarking on the sequence of things he did not know. God now reaches out to rescue him because of Monnica's appeal. (The mother of the Prodigal Son is not mentioned in Jesus' story: see on 1.18.28.) Her real tears, prompted by the faith which allowed her to see A.'s danger, contrast with the milky tears of the mother fig-tree in which A. believed (3.10.18).   **eruisti animam meam:** from Psalm 85: 13, but, as often, the unspoken context is important: *confitebor tibi, domine deus meus, in toto corde meo, et glorificabo nomen tuum in aeternum, quoniam misericordia tua magna est super me, et eruisti animam meam ex inferno inferiore.* God's mercy hovers over A. in 3.3.5, but still *a longe*.   **lacrimas eius:** tears which 'wet the ground below her eyes in every place where she prayed' reappear in 5.8.15, where A. says they would be dried when he was rescued from the water of the sea and washed in the saving water of baptism. Monnica's tears may seem excessive, but ascetic Christians valued the gift of tears to weep for sin; tears were the only bodily discharge which did not demonstrate the weakness of the flesh.   **illud somnium:** Monnica said (6.13.23) that by a kind of flavour which she could not explain in words, she could tell the difference between a revelation from God and her own soul dreaming. She had then prayed for a vision about A.'s marriage, but had experienced only *uana et phantastica* which resulted from the activity of her mind. The *somnium* described in this paragraph was a response to prayer (see below, *erant aures tuae ad cor eius*), but not necessarily prayer for a vision.   **ut uiuere mecum cederet:** A. does not explain whether he had left Carthage and returned to Thagaste to teach (see 4.1.2), or whether his widowed mother had come to join him in Carthage (just as she followed him to Italy, 6.1.1).   **stantem in quadam regula lignea:** a wooden ruler (for ruling lines on paper) may well have been a familiar household object, but the vision evokes the *regula fidei*, the 'rule of faith', i.e. the creed, and probably also the wood of the Cross (cf. 1.16.25). A.'s account of his conversion ends (8.12.30) with a reference to Monnica's vision and to her joy that he was now standing upon the *regula fidei*. For A., though not for Monnica, *regula* would also evoke a philosophical tradition: Cicero uses the word to translate Greek *kanōn*, the standard by which our judgements are assessed. Cf. *On Free Choice* 2.12.34, and see further Rist (1994) 70.   **iuuenem splendidum hilarem atque adridentem sibi:** compare with this cheerful smile the mockery exercised and evoked by A. in the previous paragraph (*inridebam ... inriderer*); for human laughter, see on 1.6.7. **docendi, ut adsolet, non discendi gratia:** compare the repeated question to Mary Magdalen at the tomb of Jesus, 'Woman, why do you weep?' (John 20: 13 and 15), asked first by angels and then by Jesus.

3.11.20 A. was impressed by Monnica's interpretation of her dream.   **confiteor tibi, domine, recordationem meam:** A. acknowledges his remembrance of what God did to rescue him. Even at the time he was moved (*commotus*) by Monnica's confident rejection of his misleading interpretation; and the consoling vision showed what would happen nine years on (in 381/2).   **in illo limo profundi:** Psalm 68: 3 *infixus sum in limo profundi et non est substantia.* cf. 2.2.2 for *limosa concupiscentia*, and also *caligo*, which occurs later in this paragraph. Intellectual pride has the same effect as physical desires in keeping A. away from God (cf. 4.15.25).   **uidua casta, pia et sobria, quales amas:** as desiderated in 1 Timothy 5: 3–16. There is a fuller description of Monnica's virtuous widowhood at 5.9.17.

3.12.21 Monnica asked for the help of a bishop who had once been a Manichaean, but was told that A. would find his own way.   **alterum responsum:** the first response to Monnica's appeal was the saying in her vision: *ubi tu, ibi et ille.* The second was the bishop's final words, *fieri non potest ut filius istarum lacrimarum pereat*, which came to her, in the final words of book 3, *ac si de caelo sonuisset.*   **multa praetereo** (as in 9.8.17): A. is aware that he cannot give a full account of all that God did for him.   **episcopum nutritum in ecclesia:** like A., and like A. an ex-Manichaean bishop, who was right in saying that A. would find his own way out of Manichaeism by his reading.   **substomachans taedio:** perhaps a reminiscence of Jesus' story of the unjust judge worn out by the widow's persistence (Luke 18: 1–5), perhaps to show that God works through human failings.

Book IV

Book 4 surveys the nine years in which A. was a Manichaean. His delusive beliefs about God affected both his profession and his human relationships. He taught rhetoric, the art of convincing people, as a route to worldly success. He worked on astrology, which suggested that people are not responsible for their own wrongdoing. He was faithful to his partner, but the bond between them was not a commitment to marriage and child-rearing. Returning to his home town as a teacher, he became deeply attached to a friend, forgetting that the friend was a created and mortal being: when the friend died, his religious beliefs gave him no comfort, and his own anguish was both intolerable and incomprehensible. He was still 'in a far country', remote from God, and his grief drove him away from his

home town. A. reflects at length on the love of God contrasted with
the love of created things; then he returns to his life at Carthage as
an ambitious teacher of rhetoric with delusive beliefs about God.

4.1.1 A.'s brilliantly constructed opening paragraph presents
him as a practitioner of the 'liberal arts' and of Manichaeism.
annorum nouem: A. read the *Hortensius* before he was nineteen
(3.4.7), was inspired by it to read the Bible, and explains (3.6.10)
that he turned to the Manichaeans because he found the Bible
unsatisfactory. At 5.6.10–7.13 he says it was the visit of Faustus the
Manichaean to Carthage, probably early in 383, which made him
decide not to seek advancement within the sect. So the nine years
probably run approximately from his nineteenth birthday in November 373 to his twenty-eighth in November 382. When he went to
Rome in 383 his closest associates were Manichaeans, and he stayed
in the house of a Hearer when he was ill, but he says (5.10.18–19)
that he was losing enthusiasm for the sect and tried to moderate his
host's beliefs. In Milan, influenced both by Ambrose's preaching
and by philosophical arguments on suspending judgement (Introd.
§3*b*), he decided to leave the Manichaeans and become once more
a Catholic catechumen (5.14.24).   **doctrinas, quas liberales
uocant:** the 'liberal arts', literally the arts suited to a free man (cf.
libero studio opposed to *necessitate rei familiaris*, 4.3.5). These were literature, rhetoric and dialectic (techniques of argument and analysis), followed by the more abstract analyses of arithmetic, geometry,
astronomy and the theory of music. They could be interpreted, as
they were by Cicero in the *Hortensius*, as a training in philosophy,
liberating the mind from concern with immediate surroundings and
impressions and encouraging it to focus on underlying principles
(Introd. §3*b*; see further O'D. II 269–78). But A.'s phrasing undercuts the description (cf 3.3.6 *studia quae honesta uocabantur*), and one
of the themes of book 4 is the failure of the *artes liberales* to lead him
to God. Instead, they reinforce his concern for the external world,
for his own cleverness, and for worldly success.   **occulte autem
falso nomine religionis:** there was some danger in being openly
Manichaean. The emperor Valentinian issued an edict against the
sect in 372, and even if this was not enforced, there might be
charges of sorcery (a capital offence) because of Manichaean secret

rites and interest in astrology (see below on 4.3.4). In 381–3 the emperor Theodosius issued three successive edicts against Manichaeans: the second, in 382, encouraged informers. This may have been a factor in A.'s distancing himself from the sect when he reached the imperial capital in 384. **theatricos plausus:** see on 4.2.3. A. is now himself a *spectaculum*. **coronarum faenearum:** literally 'crowns of hay'; compare Isaiah 40: 6 'all flesh is grass, and it perisheth as a flower of the field'. **purgari nos ab istis sordibus:** the prayers of the Manichaean Elect were supposed to purify their followers from sin, especially the sin incurred by harvesting food (see on 3.10.18). **in officina aqualiculi sui:** *aqualiculus*, literally a small water-jug, is the stomach, which can almost be heard gurgling. For the process of manufacturing angels and gods, see 3.10.18 and note. **inrideant me ... ego tamen confitear:** A. reaches this point again (with slight variations) in the last sentence of the paragraph, after his prayer *circumire praesenti memoria ... circuitus erroris mei*. He surrounds his errors with biblical phrases. On a larger scale, he returns in 4.16.30 to the *liberales artes*, after a long journey around his errors. **salubriter prostrati et elisi a te:** cf. Psalm 50: 19, cited in 4.3.4 *cor contritum et humiliatum non spernis*, 'a broken and a contrite heart, O Lord, thou wilt not despise.' **circumire ... et immolare tibi hostiam iubilationis:** adapted from Psalm 26: 6, where *circumiui* refers to the procession round the altar. In his exposition of the psalm, *On the Psalms* 26.2.12, A. interprets *hostia iubilationis* as *abundantissimum et inenarrabile gaudium*. Book 4 scarcely expresses joy, but its exhortations to A.'s soul, and to others who have gone astray, promise joy and security to those who return to God. **sugens lac tuum aut fruens te cibo, qui non corrumpitur:** a double reminiscence of Paul's saying 'As you were little children in Christ I gave you milk to drink, not food, for you could not yet manage it' (1 Corinthians 3: 2) and Jesus' discourse on the bread of life (John 6: 26–59). For A. as a little child (*paruulus*) cf. 3.5.9; Christians as *paruuli* recur in 4.15.26 and 4.16.31. **quis homo est quilibet homo, cum sit homo?:** elegant but unclear. A. presumably means that a human being – any human being (*quilibet homo*) – has weaknesses because of being human (*cum sit homo*) and cannot be fully human without the childlike dependence on God which A. has just described.

inrideant nos fortes et potentes: cf. I Corinthians 4: 10 'we are weak, you are strong; you are famous, we are without honour'.

4.2.2 A. taught the deceptive art of rhetoric, and had a partner instead of a lawful wife, but in some respects he showed integrity.   **Docebam in illis annis artem rhetoricam:** his biographer Possidius says that he taught *grammatica* (see on 1.13.20) at Thagaste (4.4.7), then rhetoric at Carthage, but A. is concerned with the general condition of his life, not with the precise sequence of events. (In 4.15.27 he remarks that he was twenty-seven or twenty-eight when he wrote the book he has been discussing, but 4.16.28 is concerned with Aristotle's *Categories* which he read when he was 20.) A. does not explain why he taught rhetoric instead of himself becoming an advocate (cf. 3.3.6), but it may have been because he wanted to pursue wisdom and saw the liberal arts as a way of doing so while also earning a living (as Vindicianus pointed out to him, 4.3.5).   **uictoriosam loquacitatem:** see on 1.4.4 for *loquacitas*, here combined with the desire to win a case. **malebam ... bonos habere discipulos:** A. undercuts both the goodness of the students (*sicut appellantur boni*, cf. *doctrinas quas liberales uocant* in 4.1.1), and his own teaching (*sine dolo docebam dolos*), but at least gives himself credit for training lawyers so that they might try to save the guilty from death or exile (loss of *caput*), but would not try to cause the death or exile of the innocent. Cicero makes this point in *On Duties* 2.51.   **in multo fumo scintillantem fidem:** *fides* here means 'integrity', because A. is still far from faith in God. But the *fides* too is undercut, because A. shows it to the students whose *socius* he is in the pursuit of fame and falsehood (*diligentibus uanitatem et quaerentibus mendacium*, adapted from Psalm 4: 3). Cf. 3.11.20 for the mud (*lapsantem in lubrico*) and darkness in which A. lives as a Manichaean. The Kingdom of Darkness, according to Manichaean mythology, was full of toxic smoke. There is a reminiscence of Isaiah 42: 3 (quoted in Matthew 12: 20) on the Messiah, 'the bruised reed he will not break, and the smouldering flax he will not put out'.   **in illis annis unam habebam:** the repeated *in illis annis* softens an abrupt transition, but the topics of A.'s profession and his concubine are linked. In both cases A. was behaving well by conventional standards and manifesting *fides*, but he now wants to condemn both the profession and the relationship. The profession traded in lies and served those who wanted worldly success; the relationship was not marriage for the procreation of children. **non eo quod legitimum uocatur coniugio:** perhaps *uocatur* implies a contrast between the legal requirements for marriage and the Christian ideal of commitment (cf. *sicut appellantur boni* above). A.'s concubine probably could not make a legal marriage because of her social class: she might, for instance, have been an actress or the daughter of an actress. But even if she could, he would have been most unwise (as his mother no doubt realised, see on 2.2.4) to marry someone who could not offer property or connections. **quam indagauerat uagus ardor inops prudentiae:** a reminder of A.'s search for an object of love when he came to Carthage (3.1.1); *inops prudentiae* is said of personified Folly (3.6.11), who behaves like a prostitute by sitting outside her door inviting guests. **coniugalis placiti modum ... pactum libidinosi amoris:** for marriage as a *modus* see on 2.2.3. Cf. 1.13.22 for the pair *pactum et placitum*: both mean human convention or agreement, but *placitum* has the overtone 'pleasing, acceptable'. **proles etiam contra uotum nascitur:** A.'s son Adeodatus, who undoubtedly made his father love him (*proles ... nata cogat se diligi*: see 9.6.14 for A.'s paternal pride), was conceived in the first year of this relationship, before A. became a Manichaean. There were no other children. Manichaeans were taught to avoid conception because it entrapped divine souls in matter; A. remarks in *Manichaean Morals* 2.18.65 that they used a 'rhythm method', abstaining at what was thought to be the time of peak fertility.

4.2.3 A. refused to allow animal sacrifice for his success, but himself sacrificed to demons by his false beliefs. **theatrici carminis:** a poem to be recited in the theatre (cf. 4.14.22 for A.'s feelings about actors). **haruspicem:** a *haruspex* was originally a diviner who inspected the entrails of sacrificial victims for omens; in A.'s time *haruspices* offered not only to predict future events but to influence them by sacrifice. **foeda illa sacramenta:** *sacramentum*, which became a technical Christian term ('the outward and visible sign of an inward and spiritual grace', e.g. baptism), is in classical Latin an oath or solemn commitment. Apuleius apparently uses it to mean an initiation or a rite with a hidden significance, Greek *mystērion*: *in sui dico daemonis cultum, qui cultus non aliud quam* *philosophiae sacramentum est* (*On the Daimon of Socrates* 22). In 6.5.8 A. uses *altitudo sacramentorum* of the hidden meaning of Scripture. **necaturus ... animantia:** Manichaeans, according to A. in *Manichaean Morals* 2.17.54, thought it murder (*homicidium*, a word which literally means 'human-killing') to kill a plant or an animal. Both plants and animals have an *anima* in the sense 'animating soul'. **suffragatura daemonia:** the *haruspex* claimed that the demons would exercise the support, *suffragium*, which influences the choice of a candidate. **fulgores corporeos:** light which is material, i.e. the Manichaean deity, cf. 3.10.6. **fornicatur abs te:** see on 1.13.21. The image is reinforced by *non ex tua castitate* (i.e. chastity with regard to God, cf. 2 Corinthians 11: 2–3) and *non enim amare te noueram*. **fidit in falsis et pascit uentos:** Proverbs 10: 4. A. interprets 'feeding the winds' as feeding demons because human folly and confusion nourishes them, cf. 3.3.6, and 1.17.27 on sacrifice to demons.

4.3.4 A. consulted astrologers, but now rejects their attempt to make the stars responsible for human actions. **illos planos, quos mathematicos uocant:** *plani* are those who lead astray; the word may be chosen to evoke the planets, the 'wandering stars', as well as for the word-play with *plane*. *mathematici* are those who have scientific knowledge (*mathēmata*, things learned), specifically mathematicians and astronomers. As in 4.2.1 (*artes liberales*) and 4.2.2 (*legitimum coniugium*), the phrase *quos uocant* undercuts any pretensions to knowledge in the *mathematici*, although its overt purpose is to give the popular name for those properly called *genethliaci* (see on 4.3.5). A. thought at the time that astrology, which was not sharply distinguished from astronomy, was a precise scientific discipline of observation and calculation. Traditional belief that the heavenly bodies were visible gods was strengthened by Platonist teaching that they belong to a higher and more ordered level of being: see further Scott (1991). Manichaean teaching (see on 3.6.10) must at first have appeared to give a more profound meaning to astrology, but A. became dissatisfied with Manichaeism partly because Mani's account of celestial phenomena was incompatible with the work of serious astronomers (5.3.6, 7.12), and he was still expected to believe it on Mani's authority even though the Manichaeans had offered him truth. **plane consulere non desistebam** 'I did not entirely give up consulting'; see on 3.3.5 for possible earlier consultations. Consulting *mathematici* might be a capital offence if there was evidence of treason: for instance, asking when the emperor would die, or whether one's horoscope foretold supreme power. Firmicus Maternus, a senator who wrote an astrological encyclopaedia around 335, advised that consultations should be given in public and that the astrologer should lead a blameless life; he also prudently claimed that it was impossible to consult about the emperor, because he alone is not subject to the stars (*Mathesis* 2.30). The emperor Constantius, in 357, ordered that all *curiositas diuinandi* should stop: this was a general ban (*Theodosian Code* 9.16.8), including *mathematici* and *haruspices*. In practice, and short of suspected treason, it was unlikely that any action would be taken. **bonum est enim ... ne quid tibi deterius contingat:** unusually, A. explicitly quotes Scripture, twice in one sentence (cf. the run of quotations from 1 Corinthians 7 in 2.2.3). *bonum est enim confiteri tibi* is close to Psalm 91: 2 *bonum est confiteri domino*; then *et dicere* introduces direct quotation from Psalm 40: 5 (with *cura* in place of *sana*) *miserere mei, cura animam meam, quoniam peccaui tibi*. The *dominica uox* is from John 5: 14, and was said to the man whom Jesus healed on the Sabbath. These images of healing prepare the way for the doctor Vindicianus in the next paragraph. **Venus hoc fecit aut Saturnus aut Mars:** this evasion of human responsibility is A.'s main theological objection to astrology, which could in principle be simply observations of the stars as signs, rather than causes, of events (cf. the argument of Vindicianus from 'resonances', 4.3.5). For diverse Christian attitudes to astrology, see Chadwick (1976) 191–201. O'D. cites several other instances in A. of Venus being blamed for adultery and Mars for murder. Saturn, according to one theory noted by Servius (on *Aeneid* 6.714), was responsible for laziness. **superba putredo:** cf. 2.6.14. **cor contritum et humiliatum:** Psalm 50: 19. The preceding verse is *sacrificium Deo spiritus contribulatus*, the proper sacrifice in place of the sacrifice which A. refused to make.

4.3.5 A distinguished doctor tried to persuade A. that astrology is worthless. **uir sagax, medicinae artis peritissimus:** named as Vindicianus in 7.6.8, where A. describes how he finally lost faith in astrology. This was because of a familiar argument supported by the personal testimony of his friend Firminius. The father of

Firminius was very interested in astrology, and kept precise records which showed that his son had been born at the same moment as a slave-child on the neighbouring estate, and therefore had the same birth-chart. But Firminius' experience was quite different from the slave's. **pro consule:** Vindicianus (*PLRE* i 967) was apparently himself the proconsul, i.e. the governor of Africa Proconsularis. He had been court physician to Valentinian II and could have been rewarded with an important administrative post. **qui resistis superbis:** see on 1.1.1. **libris genethliacorum:** the *genethliaci* specialised in birth-horoscopes (Greek *genethliakos*, concerned with birth); A. says (*On Christian Teaching* 2.21.32) that they were commonly called *mathematici*. **dicens ita se illa didicisse ... potuisse intellegere:** perhaps the language represents the lively but inelegant speech of Vindicianus. He tells A. that he had in his youth studied astrology to the point of wanting to earn his living by it, and also that, if he could understand medical texts, he could certainly understand astrology. **professionem ... deferre:** a public declaration, not, so far as is known, required by law, but analogous to declaring one's financial status in the census. **si Hippocraten intellexisset:** even in the fourth century, most doctors made extensive use of the Hippocratic Corpus, much of which dates from the fifth and fourth centuries B.C.; in the fifth century many of the more practical treatises were translated into Latin. Vindicianus, according to his pupil Theodorus Priscianus, himself made some translations. Hippocrates, even in Greek, must in fact have been easier reading than manuals of astrology, which were often both complex and obscure, assuming that the serious reader would be guided by a teacher: see further Barton (1994). Vindicianus may have been interested in astrological medicine, which assigned astral causes for illness and used astrology for prognosis and for identifying the time when treatment was most likely to work; some astrologers said that different parts of the body were influenced by different star-signs. In *City of God* 5.2 A. uses Hippocrates (as cited by Cicero) to reject these astrological explanations. Hippocrates recorded a case in which two brothers had the same experience of illness: he deduced that they were twins, conceived together and brought up in the same environment, and therefore liable to the same illness. A. finds this much more plausible than saying they were born under the same configuration of stars. See further Temkin (1991) 131–3.   **uim sortis ... in rerum natura usquequaque diffusam:** Vindicianus' argument appears to be that correct predictions happen not just by random coincidence, but because there are 'sympathies' or resonances (*consonus ... sonaret ... concineret*) linking different parts of the universe. Thus a poet who was writing about something quite different might use words which were relevant to the circumstances of an enquirer who used the *sortes*, the technique of divination by opening an important book (e.g. Virgil) at random. A. used the *sortes*, at a critical moment in his life, with the writings of Paul (8.12.30); but biblical *sortes* are a different matter, because A. would undoubtedly have found meaning and relevance in any text.

4.3.6 A.'s friend Nebridius also rejected astrology, but A. was not convinced.   **Nebridius:** named, whereas Vindicianus is not yet named; perhaps it would be more difficult to give Nebridius a distinctive description? Nebridius came from a prosperous family near Carthage and was one of the group who became Manichaeans (9.3.6): the description there, *castitate perfecta atque continentia*, supports *castus* rather than *cautus* (as in some MSS) here. A. reports (7.2.3) a devastating anti-Manichaean argument which he used to advance at Carthage (see on 4.15.26). He went with A. to Italy, and in Milan was teaching assistant to Verecundus (8.6.13), who needed help, but avoided making important contacts because he wanted time for philosophy. He was baptised soon after A. and returned to Africa to live in chastity on his family estate. A. remembered him as kind and gentle; also (*Letter* 98.8) as very scholarly and very much disliking a brief answer to an important question.   **ipsorum auctorum mouebat auctoritas ... certum quale quaerebam documentum:** these are two themes of A.'s search for truth. He acknowledged the authority of experts, and used this as an argument (e.g. in *On the Usefulness of Believing*) for accepting the authority of Scripture and the Church where it was not possible to give decisive proof (cf. 6.5.8). But, even when he was impressed by Ambrose's interpretation of Scripture, he wanted 'to be as certain about things I could not see as I am certain that seven and three make ten' (6.4.6).

4.4.7 When A. began teaching in his home town, he found a friend who shared his interests.

The death of this unnamed friend is narrated after the general

characterisation of A.'s false beliefs and misguided ambition, and
the episode is a summation of A.'s life so far. His friend is an *alter ego*,
another self, from the same town and of the same age, upbringing
and interests: they were at school together, the friend was a nominal
Christian, and they now share a fervent interest in the liberal arts.
Like A., the friend becomes a Manichaean. He is baptised (as the
boy A. had asked to be, 1.11.17) in a serious illness, and is thereafter
lost to A. both by his baptism and by his death. God has taken him,
inflicting an extreme of salutary bitterness in the sweetest experience
of A.'s life. A.'s real suffering, like the distress for fictitious suffering
which he analysed in 3.2.2–3, traps him in constant awareness, and
even enjoyment, of his own unhappiness. He cannot escape into real
concern for his friend: unhappy as he is, he does not love the friend
enough to feel that he does not want to live without him, or that he
would rather have died for him. He cannot hope in God, because his
God is a phantasm, offering no concern for human suffering. None
of the other satisfactions of life provides any consolation, and he is
left with the burden of his own anguished soul. He is a divided being, a great and puzzling problem (*magna quaestio*) to himself.   **In
illis annis:** cf. 4.2.2; but A. now refers to the beginning of his
teaching career, in Thagaste (*in municipio quo natus sum*). It is not clear
why he does not name his friend: perhaps he prefers not to give
names when he has gone into detail about emotions.   **nimis carum:** because A.'s love should have been for God, and for his friend
as a fellow-Christian.   **caritate diffusa:** Romans 5: 5 *quia caritas dei diffusa est in cordibus nostris per spiritum sanctum qui datus est nobis.*
The unstated context is 'we can boast in our sufferings, because suffering brings patience, and patience brings hope; and hope is not
discredited, because the love of God is poured out in our hearts'.
Contrast A.'s reaction to the suffering caused by his friend's
death.   **cocta feruore parilium studiorum:** *cocta* means
'ripened', like a ripe (and therefore sweet) fruit.   **propter quas
me plangebat mater:** the only mention of Monnica in book 4,
perhaps as a reminder that her constant weeping, unlike A.'s at his
friend's death, was for real *miseria*, her son's self-exile from God (see
on 1.5.5); perhaps also, like Penelope's weeping for Odysseus in
Homer's *Odyssey*, a reminder that the storm-tossed hero does have a
home.   **non poterat anima mea sine illo:** the absolute sense

of *poterat*, 'could not manage'. The distinction between *animo* (*mecum iam errabat in animo*) and *anima* is that *animus* is the intellectual and rational soul, *anima* the soul which animates and which experiences emotion; but in 4.4.8 it is the *anima* which accepts baptism in place of Manichaean doctrine. Cf. 3.1.1 and note. **tu imminens dorso:** cf. 2.2.4 and 3.3.5 for God's punishment as a mercy.

4.4.8 A.'s friend was baptised while unconscious in a serious illness, and accepted the baptism; he died before A. could persuade him to disregard it. **quam inuestigabilis abyssus iudiciorum tuorum:** Romans 11: 33; cf. 2.9.17 for *inuestigabilis*. The context (verses 30–2) is about mercy and about failure to believe in God. **baptizatus est nesciens:** A.'s judgement as a bishop was that baptism could be given to a person in danger of death and incapable of responding, provided there was some indication (for instance, the testimony of the family) that they had wished for baptism. His friend's Christian upbringing might have been taken as evidence. As a Manichaean, A. thought baptism was a meaningless ritual. **recreatus est et saluus factus:** cf. 1.11.17 *nisi statim recreatus essem* – but A. was not baptised in his fever, and the friend was *saluus* in spiritual as well as physical health.

4.4.9 A. found the loss of his friend unbearable; he could not understand his own state of mind, and his Manichaean beliefs brought him no consolation. **paterna domus mira infelicitas:** this return to his father's house is merely literal; the Prodigal Son has not yet returned to his spiritual home (see on 4.16.31). **factus eram ipse mihi magna quaestio:** cf. 2.10.18 *factus sum mihi regio egestatis*. A. is still a *quaestio* to himself in 10.33.50, when his problem is whether the pleasure of listening to music is a help to worship, or a distraction from what the hymn says in praise of God. This may seem unimportant, but the point is that even in the act of worshipping God he can still be distracted by enjoyment of his sensations, so the underlying question is still the same: why do I love this rather than God? Here, the *quaestio* is into his unbearable sadness. He expresses the question in words from Psalm 41: 6 *quare tristis es, anima mea, et quare conturbas me?* This psalm, which begins 'Like as the hart desireth the waterbrooks, so thirsteth my soul after thee, O God' is particularly important in the *C.*, but probably did not mean so much to A. at the time of his friend's death. Here, verse 4 is especially relevant: 'tears have been my bread day and night, while they say to me every day, Where is thy God?' The answer to *quare tristis es*, which cannot at this time be given by A.'s soul, is *spera in Deo, quoniam adhuc confitebor illi*: the question 'why are you sad?' implies 'you need not be' (cf. 3.11.19 *docendi, non discendi gratia*).   **uerior erat et melior homo:** cf. 3.6.10 for physical beings contrasted with the *phantasma* he counted as God.   **fletus erat dulcis:** in his exposition of Psalm 41: 4 (*On the Psalms* 41.6), A. emphasises that the tears were bread – sustaining and pleasant.

4.5.10 A. asks why weeping is pleasant in grief.

A. first distances himself in time from the grief he has evoked; cf. 10.14.21 for remembering emotion without experiencing it, or remembering it but feeling differently about it. He then engages in a general *quaestio* about grief, just as he did in 3.2.2–3 about the enjoyment of fictitious suffering: why exactly is weeping pleasant? He has often remarked on the bitterness which mars the sweetness of pleasure, but here the reverse is happening, *suauis fructus de amaritudine uitae*.   **an tu ... longe abiecisti:** the first of three questions introduced by *an* could (so C.) be taken in relation to *possumne audire abs te ...* : 'may I hear from you ... why weeping is sweet for the wretched, or are you remote from human *miseria*?', i.e. and therefore will not answer the question. A. then refuses to believe that God does not hear our cries, and resumes his question with *unde igitur*. Alternatively, *an tu ... longe abiecisti* could be a first tentative explanation: we are wallowing in our trials (*in experimentis uoluimur*) and God is unaffected by them (cf. the paradoxes of 1.4.4). If so, A. does not make explicit what the sweetness of weeping would be: perhaps that it is a satisfying expression of profound unhappiness. But, if God were remote from human suffering, there would be no hope.   **fructus ... carpitur gemere et flere:** the infinitives are in apposition to *fructus* (cf. in 4.8.13 *alia erant quae ... capiebant animam, conloqui et conridere*).   **an hoc ibi dulce:** the second question introduced by *an* follows from the belief that there must be hope. But the hope that God hears us is expressed in prayers for something, not in grief for the loss of something, and A. had no hope, but only grief for his loss (*miser ... amiseram*).   **an et fletus res amara:** the third question introduced by *an*. Perhaps weeping is not sweet at all, but bitter, and the bitterness is welcome in our revulsion (*fas-*

tidium, cf. 3.1.1) from what we once enjoyed. A. does not pursue the question; for instance, by making the obvious point that bitterness, if it delights, must be sweet.

4.6.11 A.'s attachment to his own grief was stronger than his concern for his lost friend. A. stops his *quaestio* on the grounds that this is a time for confession, not for investigation, but the confession of his misery is in effect a *quaestio* into its nature. It differs from his analysis of pleasurable *dolor* in 3.2.2–3 in that he sets out to convey the depth of his unhappiness, and in that he remains a puzzle, *magna quaestio*, to himself. He can remember why the loss of his friend made him more afraid of death, but he does not know why his unhappy life was dearer to him than his friend was.   **miser eram:** once again A. contrasts a condition which deserves pity – being bound by the love of mortal things – with the feeling of misery (see on 1.5.5).   **requiescebam in amaritudine:** cf. 4.7.12 for A.'s failure to find *requies*, 4.10.15 and 4.12.18 for discussion of where *requies* is to be found.   **sicut de Oreste et Pylade traditur:** an example borrowed from Cicero, who uses it both in *On Ends* 5.22.63 and in *On Friendship* 7.24. In a play of Pacuvius, Orestes is sentenced to death; Pylades claims that he is Orestes, Orestes insists that he himself is Orestes.   **spes mea, qui me mundas a talium affectionum immunditia:** cf. the warning against *immunditia* in 3.2.3. A. was afraid there that enjoyment of one's own feelings would taint compassion; here enjoyment of his grief, and fear of losing his grief-stricken life, displace any wish to die with or for his friend. **bene quidam dixit:** Horace, about Virgil (*Odes* 1.3.8).   **ideo forte mori metuebam, ne totus ille moreretur:** when A. re-read all his books, thirty years later, the only comment he makes on *C.* 1–9 is on this phrase (*Retractations* 2.6.2). It was, he says, a silly piece of rhetoric (*declamatio leuis*), though *forte* softens it.

4.7.12 Nothing except weeping brought any comfort; A. could not escape himself, but fled from Thagaste.   **O dementiam ... humana patientem:** a standard philosophical comment on failure to realise that mortals do die.   **portabam ... animam meam:** A. does not try to analyse who 'I' might be, as distinct from the *anima*, the animating soul which is responsive to emotion (cf. 3.1.1, 4.4.7); instead, he conveys the experience of a divided self with the image of a burden which does not want to be carried but cannot be

laid down. (Contrast 4.16.31, where God carries the 'little ones'.)
non in amoenis nemoribus . . . adquiescebat: since there is a
tendency to overrate the closeness of A.'s relationship with his concubine, it is worth noting that at this time of grief he had a partner
and a three-year-old son. But in his list of consolations which failed,
the climax is not the love of his concubine (described as *uoluptas cubilis et lecti*) but books and poems; and it is the friend who shared his
studies, not the concubine who shared his bed, who provided his
deepest emotional relationship. No wonder A. concludes, in his *Literal Interpretation of Genesis* (9.5.9), that Eve can only have been made
for purposes of procreation, because if Adam had been lonely and
wanted company, another man would have been more use. Nevertheless, A. suffered (6.15.25) when parted from his concubine. He
says far less about the pain when she was 'torn from his side' than
about his grief for his friend, but does use one comparable expression: *cor, ubi adhaerebat, concisum et uulneratum mihi erat et trahebat sangui-
nem*, cf. *portabam enim concisam et cruentam animam* here.   **ad te,
domine, leuanda erat:** Psalm 24: 1 *ad te, domine, leuaui animam
meam*. As in 4.4.9, A. uses the words of a psalm which was probably
not important to him at the time; *sciebam* means that he knew,
in general terms, that he should cast his burden upon the Lord.
non enim tu eras, sed uanum phantasma: see on 3.6.10
for the Manichaean God as *phantasma. uanum*, 'empty', is echoed
by *inane* in the next sentence, and recurs in 4.11.16 and 4.14.23.
per inane labebatur would evoke in readers of Lucretius an
image of atoms falling endlessly through infinite space (and of no
concern to the Epicurean gods). For A.'s knowledge of Lucretius,
see Hagendahl (1967) 211–12, 382–3. But this burden crashes back
onto A., and the image changes from A. as bearer of the burden to
A. as place where the burden lies.   **ego mihi remanseram infelix locus:** cf. *factus sum mihi regio egestatis*, 2.10.18. A. probably uses
infelix, rather than *miser*, because of its connotations in Roman
religious tradition: an *arbor infelix*, on which a criminal had been
executed, was consecrated to the gods of the underworld.   **quo
a me ipso fugerem?:** a commonplace given greater depth by A.'s
account of his divided self. There may again be a reminiscence of
Lucretius on the fear of death, *hoc se quisque modo fugit, at quem scilicet,
ut fit, | effugere haud potis est*: see Kenney (1984) on 3. 1068–9; or of

Horace, *Odes* 2.16.19–20 *patriae quis exsul se quoque fugit?*, which makes a link with *fugi de patria*.   **fugi de patria:** literally from Thagaste, metaphorically from God.   **ueni Carthaginem:** as in 3.1.1, but A. is in a worse state now than in his adolescent emotional turmoil.

4.8.13 Time brought back A.'s former pleasure in friendship; but his love of mortal beings was the cause of further sufferings. **Non uacant tempora:** the familiar thought that time softens distress, briefly mentioned in 4.5.10 (*tempore lenitum est uulnus meum*), here emphasises the effect of time on the mind; cf. A.'s discussion of action in time as a 'distension', a stretching of the mind between expectation and memory, 11.25.32–30.40.   **praeteribant de die in diem:** the phrase *de die in diem* is biblical (e.g. Psalm 60: 9); the slow, repetitive movement of the sentence conveys the gradual effect of time passing, until the pain yields (*cedebat dolor meus ille*). But the word-play *cedebat ... succedebant* immediately reactivates A.'s pain.   **fuderam in harenam animam meam:** mortal friendships, like sand, swallowed up devotion, but could not hold it securely. 'Pouring [something] on to the sand' may have been a proverbial phrase for effort doomed to be wasted.   **ac si non moriturum:** *ac si* (*OLD* s.v. *atque* 14) is here equivalent to *quasi*. **ingens fabula:** Manichaean beliefs, which A. shared with his friends.   **adulterina ... pruriens in auribus:** see on 1.10.16 and 3.2.4. A. combines the images of the itch that must be scratched (cf. 2.8.16 *nec confricatione consciorum animorum accenderem pruritum cupiditatis meae*), and unfaithfulness to God, *adulterina confricatione*, with the help of 2 Timothy 4: 3–4 (quoted on 1.10.16) on people who turn from the truth, *prurientes auribus*, to listen to the stories of false teachers.   **alia erant:** a change of tone. So far, friendship has been doubly misleading, both because A. loves mortals when he should love God, and because friendship encourages him in intellectual wrongdoing (as it had encouraged him to theft in book 2): *cum quibus amabam quod pro te amabam, et hoc erat ingens fabula*. But the rest of the paragraph lists (with a series of infinitives used as nouns) the *alia* which, A. says, *amplius capiebant animum*: that is, these characteristics of friendship mattered more to him than the *fabula* of Manichaeism. These friendships at Carthage, like the friendship at Thagaste, are intensified *feruore parilium studiorum* (4.4.7). The last sentence borrows from Cicero *On Friendship* both the verb *redamare* (*ibid.* 14.49) and *ut unus quasi animus fiat ex pluribus* (*ibid.* 25.92), and adds an image of fusing metal, *quasi fomitibus conflare animos*.

4.9.14 Friends are not lost if they are loved in God, who cannot be lost.   **ut rea sibi sit humana conscientia:** for *conscientia* see on 1.18.29.   **nihil quaerens ex eius corpore:** see on 2.2.2. **hinc ille luctus:** a brief description, in which the incomprehensible grief of 4.4.9–7.12 is evoked with intense language, but becomes an understandable response to the loss of a friend.   **cor madidum et ex amissa uita morientium mors uiuentium:** at first sight, two more standard expressions for deep grief following the darkness of sorrow and sweetness turned to bitterness. The heart is 'sodden' with tears, life is not worth living. But for A. the heart is the place where a human being is aware of God, and a life which is turned away from God is death (see on 1.5.5).   **beatus qui amat te et amicum in te et inimicum propter te:** a very neat summary of the commandments to love God and one's neighbour and the further requirement to love one's enemies (Matthew 5: 44).   **nullum carum amittit:** cf. 2.6.13 on *tristitia*, which wants to lose nothing. **implendo ea fecit ea:** see on 1.2.2.   **quo it aut quo fugit:** cf. 1.2.2, and Psalm 138: 7 *quo ibo a spiritu tuo? et quo a facie tua fugiam?*   **et lex tua ueritas:** Psalm 118: 142 (the next line is *tribulatio et angustia inuenerunt me*).

4.10.15 Created things, however beautiful, are transient.   **Deus uirtutum ... salui erimus:** Psalm 79: 8. A. has been describing attempted flight from God; there is safety (salvation) if we turn to face God, and A. reinforces *conuerte* with *quoquouersum se uerterit* in the next sentence. *deus uirtutum* translates the Hebrew *Yahweh Sabaoth*, 'Lord God of Hosts': *uirtus* has the double meaning 'strength' and 'virtue', and A. several times interprets *uirtutes* as 'angels', e.g. *On the Psalms* 45: 11.   **ad dolores figitur** 'stuck' (cf. below *in eis figatur glutine amore*) rather than 'firmly based' (as in 4.11.16 *ibi fige mansionem tuam*).   **tametsi figitur in pulchris** 'even if the things to which it is stuck are beautiful'.   **quae tamen nulla essent:** cf. 1.2.2 *sine te non esset quidquid est.*   **quae oriuntur ... intereunt** 'those things which rise and set, and in rising begin, as it were, to be, and grow so as to reach perfection, when they are perfected grow old and die; not everything grows old, but everything dies'. The string of verbs joined by *et*, evoking the endless sequence of growth and decay, expands a terse phrase from Sallust, *omniaque orta occidunt et aucta senescunt* (*Jugurthan War* 2.3).   **quasi esse incipiunt:** only *quasi*, 'as it were', because their existence depends on God, not on their rising.   **tendunt esse** 'tend toward being' or 'strive to be'. **sic est modus eorum:** see 2.2.2 for *modus*, the defining limit which makes things what they are, and cf. below *ipse est modus eius*.   **tantum dedisti eis ... uniuersum, cuius partes sunt:** God has given transient things this much (*tantum*), that (*quia*) they are parts of a whole (*uniuersum*). Thus the whole continues even though parts of it die and others come into being.   **sic peragitur et sermo noster:** in fact, as the shift from *uniuersum* (a whole) to *totus sermo* (complete speech) suggests, human speech is an example of something which would not be possible unless part succeeded part, not of something which continues as a whole even though part succeeds part. A. returns to this point when discussing time (11.27.35): he says that we cannot measure a sound until it is over, and uses as an example the hymn by Ambrose which he briefly quotes in this passage (see below). For *peragitur* cf. 1.6.10 and note.   **deus, creator omnium:** the opening line of Ambrose, *Hymn* 1.2, which A. quotes in 9.12.32.   **conscindunt eam** [sc. *animam*] **desideriis pestilentiosis:** cf. 4.7.12 *portabam enim concisam et cruentam animam meam.*   **ipsa esse uult:** the soul wants to exist, but its existence depends on God; A. does not make explicit the contrast with dissipation of the soul among transient things (Introd. §3*b*, and 4.11.16).   **non est ubi, quia non stant:** i.e. there is nowhere for the soul to rest, because transient things do not stand firm; cf. 4.6.11 for *requies*.   **ipse est modus eius:** the *sensus ˋcarnis* is bodily sense, so the body (*caro*) defines and limits what it is.   **hinc et huc usque** 'from here to here': God's word establishes the *modus* for transient things. C. suggests an allusion to Job 38: 11, in which God says to the sea 'You shall come as far as here, and shall go no further'; the entire chapter is about God as creator.

4.11.16 A. exhorts his soul to be fixed on God.   **Noli ... obsurdescere in aure cordis tumultu uanitatis tuae** 'do not be deafened in the ear of your heart by the tumult of your emptiness'. The echoing confusion of A.'s soul is contrasted with the loud proclamation of God's word. There is a reminiscence of John 1: 23

uox clamantis in deserto 'dirigite uiam Domini'.   **ibi est locus:** i.e. with
the word of God.   **ecce illa discedunt ... infima uniuer-
sitas:** A. summarises what he says in 4.10.15 about parts and the
whole; *uniuersitas* is the whole (*uniuersum*) which is everything, i.e. the
universe, which is *infima* because such created things are remote from
God (cf. 1.6.7 *haec ima*).   **ibi fige mansionem tuam:** *mansio*
is a place to stay, and *fige* here means 'set firm' (compare 4.10.15,
where *figere* means 'to be stuck'). Perhaps there is a reminiscence of
Matthew 7: 24–7 'everyone who hears my words and acts on them is
like the wise man who built his house on rock', whereas the fool
builds his house on sand (cf. 4.8.13 *fuderam in harenam animam meam*).
saltem fatigata fallaciis 'at least now that you are wearied of
deceptions' (C.); the contrast seems to be that the soul, though not
yet fully aware of the truth, is at least abandoning error.   **reflorescent ... constringentur:** a roll-call of A.'s favourite
metaphors for the soul's dispersal among created things and its reformation. *putria tua* cf. 4.3.4, 2.1.1 for *putredo. languores* cf. 2.7.15.
fluxa cf. 2.2.4; G–M cite *Sermon* 119.3 *noli sequi flumen carnis. caro quippe
ista fluuius est; non enim manet.*   **non te deponent quo descendunt:** the decaying or sickly or labile parts of the soul (as well as the
body) are descending into non-existence (Introd. §3b), but, because
they are renewed by the truth, they will not cause the descent of the
soul into non-existence; instead, they will stand firm in the presence
of (*ad*) God who stands firm.

4.11.17 A. explains to his soul that the parts of a whole must suc-
ceed one another.

   This paragraph is closely related to 4.10.15 in subject-matter and
vocabulary, but whereas 4.10.15 is prayer to God, 4.11.17 is simple
exposition to the soul which can now understand. A. repeats two
points made in 4.10.15: human awareness is partial and of transient
things, because bodily sense can see only the part, not the whole;
but the whole is made possible by the transience of the parts, as in
the case of human speech.   **ipsa te sequatur conuersam** 'let
it (i.e. the flesh) follow you (i.e. the soul) when you have turned round'.
pro tua poena: because human beings separated themselves from
God by disobedience, they cannot now understand the whole, and
are punished by the limitations of the body.   **ita semper omnia
... si possint sentiri omnia** 'Thus all the things which are made

up of elements – and the elements of which they are made up do not all exist at once – always give more delight by all their parts together (*omnia*) than part by part (*singula*), if they could be perceived all together (*omnia*)'.

4.12.18 A. continues to exhort his soul to love God rather than God's creation; then he tells his soul what to say to those who have wandered away from the love of God.   **deum ex illis lauda:** not 'for them', but taking them as a starting-point for praise of God, cf. 4.10.15 *laudet te ex illis anima mea*.   **in deo amentur** 'let them be loved in God' (C.'s translation, here and below *in illo ergo amentur*, assumes *amantur*, 'they are loved').   **in illo fixae stabiliuntur:** cf. 4.11.16 for this use of *fixae*.   **rape ad eum tecum quas potes et dic eis** 'carry off what [souls] you can to God with you and say to them' (cf. 3.2.3 for *rapere*). What the soul says to other souls continues to the last sentence of 4.12.19, where A. repeats *dic eis ista ... sic eos rape tecum ad deum*.   **ecce ubi est, ubi sapit ueritas** 'look where he is, where there is a taste of truth' (C.); for the taste of truth cf. 3.6.10 *nec sapiebas in ore meo sicuti es*. A. likes the double sense of *sapere*, 'to taste' and 'to have good taste', i.e. discernment or wisdom (*sapientia*).   **intimus cordi est:** cf. 3.6.11 *interior intimo meo*.   **redite, praeuaricatores, ad cor:** Isaiah 46: 8. A. interprets this as an instruction to return to the 'law which is written in our hearts' (*On the Psalms* 57.1), that is, to our knowledge of God who is within us. He continues to use the second person plural, representing his soul as addressing the *praeuaricatores* who 'walk crookedly' (transgress).   **requiescite in eo et quieti eritis:** cf. 1.1.1 *inquietum est cor nostrum, donec requiescat in te*.   **quantum est ad illum** 'so far as it is referred to Him' (G–M).   **quo uobis adhuc et adhuc ambulare:** *quo* here means 'to what purpose (is it) for you'.   **beatam uitam:** a phrase used by Cicero for 'the happy life', that is, a life which is to be judged as blessed. A. wrote his own philosophical dialogue *On the Happy Life* soon after his conversion at Milan. He discusses in 10.20.29 how we know what the happy life is, or recognise it when we have found it, and says *cum enim te, deum meum, quaero, uitam beatam quaero*.   **beatam uitam quaeritis in regione mortis:** the *regio mortis* is the world of mortality, where people die for ever if they turn away from God: see on 1.5.5. There is a reminiscence of Matthew 4: 16 (quoting Isaiah 9: 2) 'they that dwell in the land of the shadow of death, upon them hath the light shined'.   **ubi nec uita** 'where there is not even life' (*nec* here = *ne ... quidem*).

4.12.19 Christ has destroyed death, and calls us to return to him. A. offers a brief account of the Incarnation, which reunited divine and human and thereby overcame mortality; the defeat of death was shown in the resurrection of Christ.   **descendit huc ipsa uita nostra:** i.e. Christ, who is the life of human beings (cf. 3.6.10 for God as the life of souls), came down; *descendit* may imply the usual metaphor 'came down from heaven' or may refer to Christ's taking on a lower level of being, namely humanity (cf. 1.11.17 *per humilitatem domini dei nostri descendentis ad superbiam nostram*). Ascent and descent (*ascendit ... descendit*), going out and returning (*discessit, abscessit, processit, recessit*), echo through this paragraph, together with a sequence of paradoxes, as in 1.4.4, which express the absence and presence of Christ.   **occidit eam:** the resurrection of Christ destroyed death by showing that death is not the end.   **in illud secretum unde processit ad nos:** the place where divine and human are brought together, that is, the heart (cf. below *redeamus ad cor*) where Christ is present; he 'came forth', *processit*, in the Incarnation.   **uirginalem uterum, ubi ei nupsit humana creatura:** the womb of the virgin Mary is thought of as a marriage-chamber in which divine and human are united. Thus mortal flesh, united to immortality, will not always be mortal.   **uelut sponsus ... ad currendam uiam:** Psalm 18: 6.   **fili hominum, quo usque graues corde?:** Psalm 4: 3, which continues *ut quid diligitis uanitatem et quaeritis mendacium?*. The Hebrew idiom translated as *fili hominum* means simply 'men'.   **posuistis in caelo os uestrum:** Psalm 72: 9; A. interpreted this (*On the Psalms ad loc.*) as pride, *superbia*. **cecidistis enim ascendendo contra deum:** the 'ascent against God' was caused by pride.   **dic eis ista:** A. repeats what he said to his soul in 4.12.18.   **in conualle plorationis:** the 'valley of lamentation', Psalm 83: 7 (the preceding verses, in the Vulgate, are *beatus uir cuius est auxilium abs te: ascensiones in corde suo disposuit*).   **ardens igne caritatis:** cf. 3.4.8 for A. on fire with love of wisdom; and 10.29.40 *o amor, qui semper ardes et numquam extingueris, caritas, deus meus, accende me!*

4.13.20 A. did not know that created things must be loved for the sake of God who made them. He wrote a philosophical treatise on beauty.   **Haec tunc non noueram:** A. returns from exhortation to his state of ignorance at an earlier time; cf. 3.10.18 for *nesciebam* and variants at the beginning of paragraphs about his Manichaean beliefs.   **ibam in profundum:** because, in loving *pulchra inferiora*, and in thinking that beauty was in them, he was sinking further away from God. Cf. 3.6.10, where God is addressed as *mi pater summe bone, pulchritudo pulchrorum omnium*, in contrast with Manichaean, and even with true philosophical, teaching about the universe; and 10.27.38 *sero te amaui, pulchritudo tam antiqua et tam noua, sero te amaui!*   **quid est quod nos allicit:** A.'s questions to his friends continued to preoccupy him in later life; under the influence of the 'Platonic books', especially Plotinus, *Ennead* 1.6, he began to think about how he knew that some things were beautiful (7.17.23), and the beauty of physical objects became the first step in the ascent of reason to the beauty of God (Introd. §3*b*; for love inspired by beauty, see further Rist (1994) 152–9).   **uidebam in ipsis corporibus:** A. was still preoccupied with physical objects (cf. 3.7.12), and thought that *decus et species* was in them.   **aliud esse quasi totum:** A. distinguished between the beauty of a whole and the fitness of a part to the whole; cf. 3.8.15 *turpis enim omnis pars uniuerso suo non congruens*, and 4.11.17 on parts which delight when seen all together.   **scaturriuit in animo meo ex intimo corde meo** 'welled up in my soul from my inmost heart', i.e. this is what A. seriously believed about beauty.   **scripsi libros de pulchro et apto:** probably in 380. See further Harrison (1992) for A.'s thoughts about beauty.

4.14.21 A dedicated his *On the Beautiful and Fitting* to the orator Hierius, whom he had never met, but admired.

A. uses this episode to show the misdirection of his life at Carthage. The content of *On the Beautiful and Fitting* illustrates his intellectual failure to go beyond the beauty of physical objects; the dedication to Hierius shows his unworthy aims in life; and his admiration for Hierius shows (as in the episode of the pear-tree) his readiness to be influenced by his friends.   **ad Hierium, Romanae urbis oratorem:** A. admired Hierius both for his oratory in a language which was not his first, and for his philosophical abilities; he was also impressed by an orator who practised in the capital city. Cf.

8.2.3–5 for Marius Victorinus, *rhetor urbis Romae*, who was also a philosopher, and was recognised by the entire congregation when he
made his profession of faith as a Christian. A. speaks only of his admiration for Hierius, but a dedication was a well-known tactic for
bringing oneself to the attention of a great man (cf. 4.14.23 *magnum
quiddam mihi erat*). No response from Hierius is mentioned; he does
not appear again in the *C.* and is otherwise almost unknown.
sed magis: sc. *placebat mihi.* A. was impressed by the admiration
of others.   **utrumnam ab ore laudantis intrat in cor audientis amor ille?:** it is not clear why A. responds so strongly *absit*:
perhaps because he thinks that love must be a response from the
heart, even though *ex amante alio accenditur alius.*

4.14.22 A. would have liked to be praised for the same qualities
as Hierius, but would not have wanted to be praised for other abilities, such as acting, which he admired in other people.   **cur non
sicut auriga nobilis, sicut uenator ... diffamatus:** understand e.g. *amabatur et laudabatur* (*Hierius*) *a me.* The charioteer and the
uenator, who fought wild beasts, were heroes of the games (for which
see on 3.2.2). *diffamatus* in post-classical Latin means 'widely famed'
rather than 'defamed', but A. no doubt chose the word to suggest
the wrong kind of fame.   **eligens latere quam ita notus esse**
'choosing (rather) to be obscure than to be known in that way': that
is, A. would have chosen obscurity rather than the fame of an actor,
had the choice arisen.   **quod rursus nisi odissem:** the problem A. sees is that he loves (for instance) the qualities of an actor;
but he must also hate those qualities, because he does not want to
have them himself. But he and the actor are both human beings:
does he, or does he not, love (and therefore think good) the qualities
in a human being which make him an actor?   **non enim sicut
equus bonus:** a horse may be loved as a good horse, though the
human being who loves it would not want to be a horse even if he
could. But this does not solve A.'s problem. An actor may be loved
as a good actor, though the human being who loves him would
not want to be an actor; but the lover of acting is a fellow human
being who could be an actor (and if he is an orator, he is half way
there: cf. 4.2.3 on the *theatricum carmen* for which A. won a crown).
grande profundum est ipse homo: A. became *magna quaestio* to
himself because of his misplaced love (4.4.9); now his ambition pro-

duces more confusion about what he loves and why.   **capillos tu, domine, numeratos habes:** Matthew 10: 30; both a reassurance and a warning that God knows everything about us (see on 1.12.19). A. adds *et non minuuntur in te*, in effect 'not a hair of our head shall be lost', and comments that hairs are, nevertheless, more countable than human emotions. This might suggest that not even God can follow all the *motus cordis*, but A. believed that God knew every strand of his thought.

4.14.23 A.'s admiration for Hierius depended not on the facts, but on what his friends said.   **errabam typho:** for *typhos* see on 3.3.6.   **et circumferebar omni uento:** 'so that we should no longer be little children [*nēpioi*], storm-tossed and carried about by every wind of teaching', Ephesians 4: 14.   **nimis occulte gubernabar:** A. makes two points at once. He was blown about by the winds, but God was steering; but the steering was too hidden for him to see.   **alius affectus narrantium:** A.'s friends could have given him just the same information about Hierius (a Syrian who spoke Greek and Latin, an orator who knew philosophy) but, if they had felt contempt rather than admiration, so would he have done, and no love would have been kindled.   **anima ... nondum haerens soliditati ueritatis:** *soliditas* is contrasted with emptiness (cf. below *cor uanum et inane*); the heart which is empty of truth can be blown about by every wind.   **et ecce est ante nos:** i.e. *ueritas*.   **ob os contemplationis meae** 'before the face of my contemplation', a phrase which sounds biblical; A. emphasises that contemplation is looking at something, in this instance beauty.   **nullo conlaudatore mirabar:** although A. minded about Hierius' reaction to his book, and although his own opinion of Hierius depended on the praise of his friends, he contemplated beauty without the need of any support for his admiration. C. sees a reference to A.'s feeling for his book: 'although no one else admired the book, I thought very well of it myself'.

4.15.24 A.'s thinking was still restricted by his belief that everything which exists is material. He thought, wrongly, that evil is a substance, and that the human mind is the supreme good.

This paragraph is difficult because A. juxtaposes different stages of his thought, and does not fully expound either what he thought when he wrote *On the Beautiful and Fitting*, or what he thought later.

He declares his errors without explaining exactly what damage each did and what he should have thought instead. It may be helpful to set out first his position in *On the Beautiful and Fitting*, so far as it can be reconstructed, then his later critique.

In *On the Beautiful and Fitting* A. defined the beautiful (*pulchrum*) as that which *decet* of itself, and the fitting (*aptum*) as that which *decet* by being suited (*accommodatum*) to something else. Latin *decet*, 'it is proper', and the noun *decus*, like Greek *to kalon* and English 'fineness', can refer both to beauty and to goodness (because goodness is morally proper). A. suggested that goodness is unity or harmony (like the *pulchrum* which *decet* by itself and the *aptum* which *decet* by fitting well), and evil is discord. He used the technical terms 'monad' (unity) and 'dyad' (duality), suggesting that goodness, the monad, is *animus*, mind or soul (which is sexless, i.e. undivided, like the Manichaean power of light), and evil, the dyad, is anger and lust (conflict and tension, like the disruptive Manichaean power of darkness).

A. later saw several errors in what he had thought. He did not think of God as creator, so he did not realise that everything beautiful is so not in itself, but because God made it. Consequently, he did not use the beauty of the world around him as the first step towards awareness of God. He thought that everything which exists is material (corporeal), so he could not think of mind as a spiritual (incorporeal) substance. Consequently, he was restricted to physical seeing, and did not look into his own mind to discover why he judged some things to be beautiful and right. Because he thought of God as a substance, he could not understand how God is present throughout the creation (see on 3.7.12), and he thought that evil too must be a substance. Consequently, he thought of evil as an agent, not as the privation of good, i.e. nothing (see on 2.8.16). He thought that the human mind is the ultimate good (*summum bonum*), because (though he does not here say so explicitly) he thought of it, in Manichaean terms, as a fragment of the divine Light; he did not think of it as created by God. Consequently, he failed to understand the greatness of God and the need for human beings to abandon their pride.   **in arte tua:** A. imagines God as creative artist.   **qui facis mirabilia solus:** Psalm 71: 8 (and 135: 4).   **ibat animus per formas corporeas:** cf. 10.27.38 *et ecce intus eras et ego foris, et in ista formosa quae fecisti deformis inruebam.* For the soul which is *foris*, preoccupied with externals, cf. 3.6.11.   **definiebam et distinguebam:** technical terms of philosophical debate.   **falsa opinio, quam de spiritalibus habebam:** A. thought everything that exists must be material (corporeal), even if it is, like the soul, very subtle matter (see on 3.7.12).   **inruebat in oculos:** A. thought only in terms of physical seeing (cf. 3.7.12) and therefore could not see the truth that there are incorporeal beings. He did not look into his own soul and find God.   **ad liniamenta et colores et tumentes magnitudines:** we see that which has shape and colour and size; A. thought that we cannot see shape and colour and size in the mind, and therefore cannot see the mind. In *On the Quantity of the Soul* (which he wrote in 387/8), A. inverted this argument: we can see that there are in the mind incorporeal things, for instance, geometrical figures made up of lines, so the mind must itself be incorporeal (see further O'Daly (1987) 23). When he was a Manichaean, A. presumably thought that mind is a substance too subtle to be perceived by the eyes; but what concerns him here is that he turned away from the possibility of looking into his own soul and reflecting on its powers. It is not clear why he gives *magnitudines* the disparaging adjective *tumentes*: C. suggests an allusion to vast Manichaean entities (which, as A. points out in 3.7.12, were *phantasmata* and impossible to see).   **unitatem:** the association of unity with rationality, truth and the supreme good, and of duality (or multiplicity) with irrationality, conflict and falsehood goes back to Plato (Introd. §3*b*). But the further belief that there is a living *summum malum* is not Platonic, but Manichaean.   **quae non solum esset substantia sed omnino uita esset:** probably 'not just a substance but a living thing', but the Latin could mean that A. thought evil was life. This would be possible in terms of Manichaean teaching that the universe came into being only because evil invaded and dispersed the light: living things are part of an immense machine for the release and recovery of light.   **nesciens quid loquerer:** A. means, as the next sentence shows, something stronger than that he was talking pretentious nonsense. He had failed to understand both what evil is (i.e. not a substance) and what the human soul is (i.e. not a fragment of God). For *non enim noueram* cf. 4.13.20 and note.

4.15.25 The rational mind can also be flawed by errors: it is not

itself truth, but needs to be enlightened by God.   **facinora:** A.
had argued that the dyad (duality) was *iram in facinoribus, libidinem in
flagitiis* (4.15.24). He now says that both *facinora* and *flagitia* result from
faults in the soul, which he had equated with the monad (unity) and
with the supreme good. For the difference between *animus*, here implicated in *facinora*, and *anima*, here implicated in *flagitia*, see on 4.4.7;
rationalis mens, which can be contaminated by error, may be the best
part of the soul (*Against the Academics* 1.5) or equated with the soul
(*Sermon* 145.2 *anima humana, hoc est, mens rationalis ad imaginem dei facta*).
See further O'Daly (1987) 7–8 on A.'s terminology, and O'D. on this
passage for further examples. In *On the Trinity* 12.7.10 A. says that the
mind is in the image of God when it directs itself to truth, but not
when it directs itself to lower things.   **alio lumine … particeps ueritatis:** the Manichaeans held that the human soul is a
fragment of light; A. says that it is not itself truth (*non est ipsa natura
ueritatis*) but must be illuminated by God so that (in Platonic language) it may share in the truth. He illustrates this with a series of
biblical texts.   **quoniam tu inluminabis … tenebras meas:**
Psalm 17: 29.   **et de plenitudine tua omnes nos accepimus:**
John 1: 16.   **lumen uerum … in hunc mundum:** John 1: 9.
non est transmutatio … obumbratio: James 1: 17 (see on
3.6.10).

4.15.26 A.'s pride kept him from God: he claimed to be what
God is, he imagined physical entities which had no existence, and he
challenged Christians to explain why the soul goes wrong if God
made it.   **conabar … repellebar:** A. was trying to reach God
by his own efforts and failing to realise that he was in need of
help.   **ut saperem mortem:** see on 1.1.1 for mortality as the
punishment for pride, and for *superbis resistis*.   **me id esse naturaliter, quod tu es:** A. had argued that the human mind was the
same nature as God (*ipsa natura ueritatis*, 4.15.25).   **mutabilis:** A.
had to be capable of change, because he was trying to improve; so,
if he was the same nature as God, God had to be mutable too.
resistebas uentosae ceruici meae: a startling combination of
metaphors. *ceruix* suggests a neck stiff with pride (cf. 3.3.5 *praefidenti
collo*); *uentosa* suggests either something puffed-up or something at
the mercy of the winds (cf. 4.14.23 for both).   **imaginabar formas corporeas:** see on 3.6.10.   **caro carnem accusabam:**

A., a physical being, accused a God whom he believed to be a physical being.   **spiritus ambulans:** Psalm 77: 39 *et recordatus est quia caro sunt, spiritus uadens et non rediens* (see on 1.13.20 for A.'s text). A. modifies 'not returning' to 'not yet returning' (*nondum reuertebar ad te*), so that a reference to the transience of human life becomes an allusion to the Prodigal Son who is still far off, and who is walking in the wrong direction, towards the Manichaean *phantasmata*.   **quae non sunt neque in te ... fingebantur ex corpore:** see on 3.6.10.   **paruulis fidelibus:** for Christians as *paruuli*, see on 3.5.9.   **garrulus et ineptus:** cf. 3.6.10 for loquacious Manichaeans.   **cur ergo errat anima, quam fecit deus?:** see on 3.7.12 for this Manichaean challenge. The answer A. offered, as a Manichaean, is that God is constrained by the power of evil (*tuam substantiam coactam errare* in the last sentence); the soul, which is a fragment of God, is corrupted and changed by these powers (see further 7.2.3, and O'Daly (1987) 31–2 for A.'s argument that Manichaeans actually thought that people have two souls, one corrupted and one capable of return to God).   **cur ergo errat deus?:** A. did not want this challenge to be put to him, because a God who goes wrong under constraint is not a God who is worthy of worship. Perhaps he was already facing the argument of Nebridius (7.2.3): the Manichaeans say that fragments of God's substance are corrupted and changed by the powers of evil and must be purified by God's word. But if God's substance is corruptible and mutable, God's word has no power to purify. On the other hand, if God is incorruptible, the Manichaean story is clearly untrue.   **sponte deuiasse et poena errare:** A.'s answer as a Christian to 'why does the soul go wrong?' is that his soul turned away from God by choice and now goes wrong as a punishment for this turning away (see further on 2.2.3 for human nature disordered by the Fall, and cf. 4.11.17).

4.15.27 A. tried to listen to God, but his false beliefs distracted him.   **uiginti sex aut septem:** if A. is right, he wrote *On the Beautiful and Fitting* at some time between November 380 and November 382.   **obstrepentia cordis mei auribus ... interiorem melodiam tuam:** cf. 4.11.16 for the 'ears of the heart' being deafened, and for the metaphor of 'standing firm'. A. combines these by the use of John 3: 29 *amicus autem sponsi, qui stat et audit* *eum, gaudio gaudet propter uocem sponsi.* The bridegroom is Christ. The *interior melodia*, 'inner melody', is the expression of God-given order and harmony which A., reflecting on the beautiful and fitting, should have heard within himself.   **rapiebar foras:** see on 4.15.24 for things which are 'outside'.   **pondere superbiae meae in ima decidebam:** *ima* are the things furthest from God (cf. 2.3.6). **non enim dabas ... humiliata non erant:** Psalm 50: 10 *auditui meo dabis exsultationem et laetitiam, et exsultabunt ossa humiliata.*

4.16.28 A. had read Aristotle's *Categories* without help, though others found it very difficult.   **quid mihi proderat:** repeated at the beginning of the three remaining paragraphs (cf. the repeated *nesciebam* in book 3, see on 3.10.18); 4.16.29 and 31 also use the contrast *proderat ... oberat.*   **annos natus ferme uiginti:** around 374, not long after A., in his nineteenth year, read the *Hortensius.*   **Aristotelica quaedam quas appellant decem categorias:** the *Categories* discuss ten things which can be said about something (e.g. what it is, what it is like, how big it is, where it is). Greek *katēgorein* means 'say about', hence 'category', which came to mean 'group' or 'class'; the Latin equivalent of *katēgorein* is *praedicare*, hence 'predicate' (*praedicamentum*, cf. 4.16.29) as in 'subject and predicate'. There was a Latin translation of the *Categories*, ascribed by Cassiodorus to Marius Victorinus (see 8.2.3).   **rhetor Carthaginiensis:** unnamed, and mentioned without gratitude; A. acknowledges no debt to any teacher (cf. 4.16.30 *nullo hominum tradente*). **buccis typho crepantibus:** A.'s tutor may have puffed out his cheeks to show how difficult he thought the *Categories*, but A. uses *typhos* for intellectual conceit (see on 3.3.6).   **multa in puluere depingentibus:** i.e. drawing diagrams in the dust to help their students understand.   **loquentes de substantiis ... et quae in illis essent:** the *Categories* speak clearly (as perhaps the teachers did not). *substantia* (Greek *hypokeimenon*) is the (underlying) subject, which may have different predicates (i.e. different things which can be said about it) at different times; these predicates are 'in' the subject because e.g. 'reading' or 'at Carthage' are not independent of the subject. A. paraphrases the list of what can be said about something: substance (what is it?), quality (what is it like?), quantity (how big?), in relation to what, where, when, position (here 'standing or sit-

ting?'), condition (here 'wearing shoes or armour?'), doing something
or having something done to it.

4.16.29 A. thought that the system of classification in the *Categories* also applied to God.

A. was apparently not aware of the philosophical debate on the
Categories. He had not yet read Plotinus, who argued (*Ennead* 6.2.3)
that the Aristotelian categories apply only to this mutable world, or
Porphyry, who argued that the *Categories* is a treatise on logic for be-
ginners.   **mirabiliter simplicem atque incommutabilem:**
God is *simplex* (see on 2.6.13) and cannot be analysed into subject and
predicates; and God is immutable, so God cannot be described as a
subject with varying predicates. (A. used the distinction between
subject and predicate to explain change in the soul. The soul does
not cease to be soul when it changes, as wax, for instance, ceases to
be wax when it is heated; soul continues as the subject, but what is
in the subject, for instance an emotion, may change. See further
O'Daly (1987) 34–8.)   **quasi et tu subiectus esses magnitudini tuae:** a double meaning of *subiectus*. A. had thought of God as
the subject and greatness as the predicate; but that would make God
subject to (defined by) God's greatness (cf. 1.3.3), as if we could say
either that God would still be God even if God were less great, or
that God would not still be God if God were less great. God and
God's greatness are the same; whereas A. was still thinking of God
in physical terms, as if God were a body which would still be a
body if it were less great or greater.   **firmamenta beatitudinis
tuae:** *firmamentum* here probably means 'support' or 'secure base'
rather than the firmament of heaven (Genesis 1: 14); but A. may have
in mind the lights which God set in the firmament of heaven (*ibid.*)
contrasted with the Manichaean *figmenta* (see on 3.6.10).   **ut terra
spinas et tribulos pareret mihi:** 'the earth shall bear thorns and
thistles for you ... in the sweat of your face you shall eat bread', the
punishment of Adam after the Fall (Genesis 3: 18–19). In 2.2.3 A.
uses the thorns as an image of lust; here, as an image of confusion.

4.16.30 A. read, without difficulty, everything he could find; but
he did not realise that his own gifts, and the truth in what he read,
came from God.   **omnes libros artium, quas liberales uocant:** cf. 4.1.1. A. is returning to the starting-point of book 4, and

his prayer in 4.1.1 *da mihi circumire praesenti memoria praeteritos circuitus erroris mei* has been fulfilled at length.   **quoscumque legere potui:** A. means that he could not get all the books he wanted, not that there were some he could not understand. His reading, though much wider than (for instance) that of Faustus the Manichaean (5.6.11), was restricted in comparison with what was available to Ambrose at Milan, especially by his poor knowledge of Greek: see on 1.13.20, and see further Marrou (1938) 3–157.   **dorsum enim habebam ad lumen:** once again A. is looking at things which God has made or inspired (books here, beautiful things in 4.10.15), instead of turning to God. Cf. Jeremiah 2: 27, quoted in the note on 2.3.6, for turning one's back on God.   **dimensionibus figurarum:** geometry. A. gives here a brief version of the 'liberal arts' curriculum (see on 4.1.1): techniques of speaking (*loquendi et disserendi*) followed by mathematical and musical analysis.   **non inde sacrificabam tibi:** i.e. A. did not offer his learning to God. cf. 1.17.27 and 4.2.3 for his sacrifices to false gods, i.e. his devotion to worldly success.   **tam bonam partem substantiae meae sategi habere in potestate:** *substantia*, like Greek *ousia* and as in the English phrase 'a woman of substance', can mean 'property' in the sense 'what one owns', i.e. 'riches'. (The technical philosophical sense 'substance' is used in 4.15.24 and 4.16.28.) A. likes the verb *satagere* for sustained effort: cf. 1.11.7, 2.3.5. He continues with an allusion to the Prodigal Son (see on 1.18.28) who asked his father *da mihi portionem substantiae quae mihi contigit* and went off to a far country, *regionem longinquam* (Luke 15: 12–13).   **fortitudinem:** Psalm 58: 10 *fortitudinem meam ad te custodiam, quia, deus, susceptor meus es.*   **non enim sentiebam:** A. probably means that he did not realise (except from his own attempts to teach) what a remarkable gift God had given him: cf. above *et celeritas intellegendi et dispiciendi acumen donum tuum est.* O.'D. punctuates so that *sed non inde ... meretrices cupiditates* is a parenthesis, in order to make the connection of thought clearer.

4.16.31 A. once more contrasts his misuse of his intelligence with God's nurturing of Christians, and prays for a safe return to the everlasting refuge which he left.   **corpus esses lucidum et immensum et ego frustum de illo corpore:** A.'s clearest statement of Manichaean teaching.   **nimia peruersitas:** *peruersitas* and related words (*auersi, peruersi, reuertamur, auertamur*) echo through this paragraph (cf. 4.10.15 *conuerte, quoquouersum se uerterit anima*).   **confiteri tibi in me misericordias tuas** 'confess to you your mercies towards me'. ⸱   **latrare aduersum te:** A. uses the same image at 9.4.11, looking back on what he had been, *nec inueniebam quid facerem surdis mortuis ex quibus fueram, pestis, latrator amarus et caecus aduersus litteras de melle caeli melleas et de lumine tuo luminosas.* **nodosissimi libri:** cf. 2.10.18 for 'knots'.   **deformiter:** cf. 10.27.38 (quoted on 4.15.24).   **in nido ecclesiae ... nutrirent:** the *paruuli* (cf. 4.15.26, and see on 3.5.9) have now become fledglings in the nest, able to develop in safety. There is a reminiscence of Job 39: 26 *numquid per sapientiam tuam plumescit accipiter, expandens alas suas ad austrum?*, cf. 4.10.15 for chapters 38–9 of Job used as a challenge to human wisdom. Here the wings of the fully-fledged Christian are 'wings of love'; A. then moves to the sheltering wings of God. **in uelamento alarum tuarum:** the phrase is often used in the Psalms (e.g. 60: 5, 62: 8).   **usque ad canos:** in Isaiah 46: 4, God says *usque ad senectam ego ipse, et usque ad canos ego portabo; ego feci et ego feram, et ego portabo et saluabo.*   **quoniam firmitas nostra quando tu es** 'since when you are our firm support, then it is a firm support, but when the firm support is our own, it is in-firmity'.   **uiuit apud te sine ullo defectu bonum nostrum:** cf. 4.15.24 for A.'s former belief that the human mind is the *summum bonum.*   **quod tu ipse es:** probably 'you yourself are our good', but see the note on 1.6.10 for *idipsum* as a name for God.   **non ruit domus nostra, aeternitas tua:** in 1.5.6 the house which is A.'s soul is in ruins and too small for God; here 'our house' is the father's house to which the prodigal son may return, and that house, which is God, is everlasting.

BIBLIOGRAPHY

Books and articles listed here are those referred to by author and date in the Introduction and Commentary. The Bulletin Augustinien in the *Revue des Etudes Augustiniennes* provides an annual update of work on Augustine.

The *Augustinus-Lexikon*, ed. C. Mayer *et al.* (Basle, 1986–) is being published in fascicles.

There is a *Concordance* to the *Confessions*, based on the edition by M. Skutella (rev. edn 1969): R. H. Cooper, L. C. Ferrari, P. M. Ruddock, J. R. Smith (edd.) (1991). *Concordantia Augustiniana pars I: Concordantia in libros XIII confessionum S. Aurelii Augustini*. Hildesheim.

There are also machine-readable texts: *Patrologia Latina Database* for Migne's text (which is the text of the Benedictine edition), and *CETEDOC Library of Christian Latin Texts* (CLCLT) for Verheijen.

Arbesmann, R. (1954). 'The concept of *Christus Medicus* in Saint Augustine', *Traditio* 10: 1–28.

Armstrong, A. M. (ed.) (1967). *Cambridge history of later Greek and early mediaeval philosophy*. Cambridge.

Balmus, C. I. (1930). *Etude sur le style de saint Augustin dans les Confessions et la Cité de Dieu*. Paris.

Barton, T. (1994). *Ancient astrology*. London.

Bennett, C. (1988). 'The conversion of Vergil: the *Aeneid* in Augustine's *Confessions*', *R.E.Aug.* 34: 47–69.

Beuron (1949–). *Die Reste der altlateinischen Bibel*. Edited by the monks of Beuron.

La Bonnardière, A.-M. (ed.) (1960–). *Biblia Augustiniana*. Paris.

Bonner, G. (1963, rev. edn 1986). *St Augustine of Hippo: life and controversies*. Norwich.

Brown, P. R. L. (1967). *Augustine of Hippo: a biography*. London.

(1992). *Power and persuasion in late antiquity: towards a Christian empire*. Wisconsin.

Brunschwig, J. (1986). 'The cradle argument in Epicureanism and Stoicism', in (edd.) M. Schofield and G. Striker, *The Norms of nature: studies in Hellenistic ethics*. Cambridge.

Burnyeat, M. (1987). 'Wittgenstein and Augustine *De magistro*', *Proceedings of the Aristotelian Society* (supplementary volume) 1–24.

Cameron, A. (1991). *Christianity and the rhetoric of empire*. Berkeley.

Campbell, J. M. and McGuire, M. R. P. (edd.) (1931, repr. 1984). *The Confessions of St Augustine: Books I–IX (selections)*. Chicago.

Chadwick, H. (1976). *Priscillian of Avila: the occult and the charismatic in the early church*. Oxford.

(1986) *Augustine*. Oxford.

Charles-Picard, G. (1965). *La Carthage de saint Augustin*. Paris.

Clark, E. A. (1986). *Ascetic piety and women's faith*. New York.

(1992). *The Origenist controversy*. Princeton.

Clark, G. (1993). *Augustine: the Confessions*. Cambridge.

(1994). 'The Fathers and the children', in (ed.) D. Wood, *The Church and childhood*. Oxford.

Coleman, R. (1987). 'Vulgar Latin and the diversity of Christian Latin', in (ed.) J. Herman, *Latin vulgaire – latin tardif*. Tübingen.

Courcelle, P. (1950). *Recherches sur les Confessions de Saint-Augustin*. Paris.

Dionisotti, C. (1982). 'From Ausonius' schooldays?', *J.R.S* 72: 83–125.

Dolbeau, F. (1992). 'Sermons inédits de saint Augustin préchés en 397 (3ème série)', *R.Bén.* 102: 267–82.

Evans, G. (1982). *Augustine on evil*. Cambridge.

Finaert, J. (1939). *L'évolution littéraire de Saint Augustin*. Paris.

Gorman, M. (1983). 'The early manuscript tradition of St Augustine's *Confessiones*', *J.Th.S.* ns 34: 114–45.

Habinek, T. (1985). *The colometry of Latin prose*. Berkeley.

Hagendahl, H. (1967). *Augustine and the Latin classics*. Göteborg.

Harrison, C. (1992). *Beauty and revelation in the thought of Saint Augustine*. Oxford.

Herman, J. (1991). 'Spoken and written Latin in the last centuries of the Roman empire', in (ed.) R. H. P. Wright, *Latin and the Romance languages in the early middle ages*. London.

Hrdlicka, C. L. (1931). *A study of the late Latin vocabulary and of the prepositions and demonstrative pronouns in the Confessions of St Augustine*. Washington DC.

Hunter, D. G. (1993). 'Helvidius, Jovinian and the virginity of Mary in late fourth-century Rome', *Journal of Early Christian Studies* 1: 47–71.

Jones, A. H. M. (1964). *The Later Roman empire*. 2 vols. Oxford.

Kamesar, A. (1993). *Jerome, Greek scholarship and the Hebrew Bible*. Oxford.

Kaster, R. A. (1983). 'Notes on primary and secondary schools in late antiquity', *T.A.Ph.A.* 113: 323–46.

(1988). *Guardians of language: the grammarian and society in late antiquity*. Berkeley.

Kenney, E. J. (1984). *Lucretius de rerum natura III*. Cambridge.

Kirwan, C. (1989). *Augustine*. London.

Lane Fox, R. (1986). *Pagans and Christians*. London.

Lepelley, C. (1979, 1981). *Les cités de l'Afrique romaine au Bas-empire: i, La permanence d'une civilisation municipale; ii, Notices d'histoire municipale*. Paris.

(1992). 'The classical city in late Roman Africa', in (ed.) J. Rich, *The city in late antiquity*. London and New York.

Lieu, S. (1985). *Manichaeism in the later Roman empire and mediaeval China: a historical survey*. Manchester.

Markus, R. A. (1957). 'St Augustine on signs', *Phronesis* 2: 60–83.

(1964). '*Imago* and *similitudo* in Augustine', *R.E.Aug.* 11: 125–43.

(1970, rev. edn 1988). *Saeculum: history and society in the theology of Saint Augustine*. Cambridge.

(1990). *The end of ancient Christianity*. Cambridge.

Marrou, H.-I. (1938). *Saint Augustin et la fin de la culture antique*. Paris; (1949) with vol. II *Retractatio*. Paris.

Meer, F. van der (1961). *Augustine the bishop*, tr. B. Battershaw and G. R. Lamb. London and New York.

Miles, M. (1982). 'Infancy, parenting and nourishment in Augustine's *Confessions*', *Journal of the American Academy of Religion* 50: 349–64.

(1992). *Desire and delight: a new reading of Augustine's Confessions*. New York.

Mohrmann, C. (1958). 'S. Augustin écrivain', *Recherches augustiniennes* 1: 43–66.

(1958–77). *Etudes sur le latin des chrétiens*. 4 vols. Rome.

Oberhelman, S. M. (1988). 'The history and development of the *cursus mixtus* in Latin literature', *C.Q.* 38: 228–42

O'Daly, G. P. D. (1987). *Augustine's philosophy of mind*. London.

O'Meara, D. J. (1993). *Plotinus: an introduction to the Enneads*. Oxford.

Clark recommends (for Plotinus)

Parkes, M. B. (1992). *Pause and effect: an introduction to the history of punctuation in the West*. Aldershot.

Rist, J. (1994). *Augustine*. Cambridge.

Roberts, M. (1989). *The Jeweled Style: poetry and poetics in late antiquity*. Cornell.

Saller, R. P. (1987). 'Men's age at marriage and its consequences for the Roman family', *C.Ph.* 82: 20–35.

Scott, A. (1991). *Origen and the life of the stars*. Oxford.

Scourfield, J. H. D. (1993). *Consoling Heliodorus: a commentary on Jerome, Letter 60*. Oxford.

Shaw, B. D. (1987). 'The family in late antiquity: the experience of Augustine', *Past and Present* 115: 3–51.

Sorabji, R. K. (1983). *Time, creation and the continuum*. London.

Sparks, H. F. D. (1970). 'Jerome as biblical scholar', in (edd.) P. R. Ackroyd and C. F. Evans, *The Cambridge history of the Bible*. 1 *From the beginnings to Jerome*. Cambridge.

Temkin, O. (1991). *Hippocrates in a world of pagans and Christians*. Baltimore.

Verheijen, M. (1949). *Eloquentia pedisequa: observations sur le style des Confessions de saint Augustin*. Nijmegen.

Whittaker, C. R. (1976). '*Agri deserti*', in (ed.) M. I. Finley, *Studies in Roman property*. Cambridge.

INDEXES

References are to lemmata in the Commentary.

1. Latin words

2. General

Psalms, # ref, explained on P. 25
P. 25: Division into books, chapts,
Pars. is explained. Div. into books
is from Aug himself; Into chapts
verses, by later editors
    P 163, on son, Adeodatus